Anonymous

Faith and free thought

A second course of lectures delivered at the request of the Christian Evidence Society

Anonymous

Faith and free thought
A second course of lectures delivered at the request of the Christian Evidence Society

ISBN/EAN: 9783337283889

Printed in Europe, USA, Canada, Australia, Japan

Cover: Foto ©Lupo / pixelio.de

More available books at **www.hansebooks.com**

Faith and Free Thought.

A
SECOND COURSE OF LECTURES

DELIVERED AT THE REQUEST OF THE

CHRISTIAN EVIDENCE SOCIETY.

WITH A PREFACE BY

THE RIGHT REVEREND

SAMUEL WILBERFORCE, D.D.,

LORD BISHOP OF WINCHESTER.

THIRD EDITION.

London:
HODDER AND STOUGHTON,
27, PATERNOSTER ROW.
1876.

PREFACE.

IT is but little that need be said to introduce a Second Series of the Lectures which have been delivered in connection with the Christian Evidence Society. The acceptance of the First Series is proof enough that in many quarters, at least, the existence of the evil they are intended to meet is acknowledged, and that this mode of meeting it has been approved.

It would, indeed, be difficult to deny the existence of the evil.

The literature of the day, which, like the straw borne aloft by the currents of the air, the more ephemeral it is, only the better marks the direction of the flow of common opinion, bears undoubted marks of its presence.

Doubt is everywhere. Sceptical suggestions are wrapped up in narrative; they bristle in short, shallow, self-asserting essays, in which men who really show their ignorance, think they show their depth ; they colour our physical philosophy ; they mingle themselves with our commonplace theology itself.

All this system of doubt has, too, a character specifically its own.

The present assault upon Christianity is altogether different from that of the Deists of the last century, or of the Atheists of the revolutionary æra. There is very little open assault upon the first principles of Theism. The attack is all the more dangerous because its real purpose is so far concealed, because it proceeds by sap and mine, rather than by open assault. For many a soul which would be on its guard if called upon at once to surrender its faith in a God, is led unsuspiciously to parley with the enemy when with fair speeches and professions of respect for that which is most highly prized he proposes only to examine some untenable propositions which have been too long admitted without question, and to clear Faith, not to impair it, by bringing Reason to its aid.

Thus the need man has of religion is admitted ; the existence of some all-pervading spiritual power is not denied. There is an attempt to keep the glow of religion even when the great objective light of which it is an emanation has been withdrawn from the heavens.

Such tendencies are perhaps inseparable from the mental and spiritual constitution of an age like our own. The vast increase of wealth amongst us; the manifold discoveries of science, and through them the subjéction of the material world to the will of man; the greater easiness which these victories of scientific research have imparted to life in almost every rank of society, with the softness and impatience of trouble which this breeds,—all this must have its effect upon the religious tone and upon the tendency to religious belief of a people. Such a temper of mind soon passes into a fretful dislike to all authority. It may not take the trouble to rebel or disbelieve; but neither can it take the trouble to examine and to submit. It is so much easier to be in a quiescent state as to such troublesome claims. And so a state of suspended belief is reached; and in that state doubts spring up and multiply spontaneously.

Then, too, the new discoveries which account for so much that seemed unaccountable; which overturn so many baseless theories; which question so rudely, and often so unanswerably, so many old admitted theories; and which appear to be always advancing, and as they advance promising almost unlimited increase of knowledge;—all this by necessary consequence shakes everywhere the rule of authority; of authority in everything which has been heretofore received. So many false theories have been subverted, so many shams exposed, so many figures of terror before which our fathers shivered resolved into the mere creatures of an utterly ignorant and therefore credulous timidity, that nothing seems left which may not in its turn fall before a bolder assault or a more practised aim.

And for many reasons all this applies especially to authority in matters of religion and faith. Unhappily, there have been so many false defences of the true, that it is hard for the truth not to suffer in the downfall of the falsehoods or errors to which she has been so unrighteously wedded.

Elaborate defences of Theism and of Christianity

have been rested upon what now prove to have been utterly misapprehended scientific facts. In many of these cases there has been no intentional direct falsehood. It has not, for the most part, been that the writers of these evidential works have believed that God could not govern the world without the devil's aid; that truth could be helped by a little falsehood (though, alas, there have been such pious frauds even as these); but it has been, for the most part, the fault of moral cowardice; the not daring to admit that there were apparent contradictions between God's voice in Nature and God's voice in Scripture, which as yet believers knew not how to reconcile; but which they had faith enough to know could be reconciled, and would be reconciled when God saw fit: and so arose the restless, feverish, sad effort to invent a theory of reconciliation, and so a resting the truth of Scripture on the reconciling theory, and therefore a great shock and violence to its true claims when the whole theory came to be swept away like an ancient cobweb by the besom of destruction in the strong hand of advancing science.

Like evils, too, have arisen from the tearing to pieces by the sharp tooth of recent, more severe, and more exact criticism of finely-developed theories as to inspiration, the text of Scripture, and cognate matters.

All of these assaults on old authority have arisen as out of the ground sown with dragons' teeth, and have given forth a harvest of death. It is against such evils as these that the lectures of the first and second series of the Christian Evidence Society have been directed.

We claim for them, that they are calm, sober, earnest, honest dealings with the several subjects they handle. They exhibit the evidence which the order and adaptations in nature around us afford of the existence of a God. They do this from the pen of one who from full acquaintance with all the last discoveries of the branch of science with which he has to deal, and from a manifested readiness to advance wherever true science leads, is an able and ought to be an unsuspected advocate for God.

Metaphysical argument of the highest quality

exhibits in them the true philosophy of human responsibility.

The supposed collision between the Scriptures and Natural Science, is examined with an unfaltering clearness of investigation which can hardly fail to carry conviction with it. The great sore of alleged moral difficulties in the Old Testament is probed to the very quick.

The principle of Causation, as it is opposed to atheistic theories, is examined and exhibited with a metaphysical subtlety and a firm grasp on truth which cannot easily be surpassed; whilst another essay draws out the positive argument for the truth of Christianity which is based on the convergence to a common centre of a number of distinct lines of proof.

Moral arguments in the same direction of the greatest force are drawn from the suitableness of Christianity to all forms of civilization, from its actual existence in them all, and its achievements in every phase of society; a subject drawn out from another point of view in another essay by a masterly contrast between society under Pagan and under Christian influences.

These subjects cover the whole field of sceptical attack. We trust they will be found in the following pages to have been calmly, truthfully, and convincingly handled by men worthy by intellectual might, by knowledge of the times, and by their being thoroughly possessed with the truth of Christ, of dealing with such high arguments.

May God be graciously pleased to give to this effort to maintain His truth His heavenly blessing.

S. WINTON.

WINCHESTER,

September, 1872.

CONTENTS

                                                                                      PAGE

THE PRINCIPLE OF CAUSATION CONSIDERED IN OPPOSITION TO ATHEISTIC THEORIES   . . 1

    BY THE REV. J. B. MOZLEY, D.D., Canon of Christchurch, and Regius Professor of Divinity, University of Oxford.

THE EVIDENCE AFFORDED BY THE ORDER AND ADAPTATIONS IN NATURE TO THE EXISTENCE OF A GOD   49

    BY CHARLES BROOKE, Esq., M.A., F.R.S.

THE PHILOSOPHY OF HUMAN RESPONSIBILITY   . . 87

    BY THE REV. CANON BIRKS, M.A., Professor of Moral Philosophy in the University of Cambridge.

POINTS OF SUPPOSED COLLISION BETWEEN THE SCRIPTURES AND NATURAL SCIENCE   . . . 131

    BY J. H. GLADSTONE, Ph.D., F.R.S.

	PAGE
THE ALLEGED MORAL DIFFICULTIES OF THE OLD TESTAMENT	173

By the Rev. Thomas Pownall Boultbee, LL.D., Principal of the London Divinity College, St. John's Hall, Highbury.

ON THE CORROBORATIVE EVIDENCE OF OLD TESTAMENT HISTORY FROM THE EGYPTIAN AND ASSYRIAN MONUMENTS	213

By W. R. Cooper, Esq., Secretary of the Society of Biblical Archæology.

THE ARGUMENT FOR THE SUPERNATURAL CHARACTER OF CHRISTIANITY, FROM ITS EXISTENCE AND ACHIEVEMENTS	247

By the Rev. Henry Allon, D.D.

CHRISTIANITY SUITED TO ALL FORMS OF CIVILIZATION	291

By Sir Bartle Frere, G.C.S.I., K.C.B., D.C.L.

THE CONTRAST BETWEEN PAGAN AND CHRISTIAN SOCIETY	341

By the Very Rev. Charles Merivale, D.D., Dean of Ely.

	PAGE
THE FORCE IMPARTED TO THE EVIDENCE OF CHRISTIANITY FROM THE MANNER IN WHICH A NUMBER OF DISTINCT LINES OF PROOF CONVERGE IN A COMMON CENTRE	389

BY BENJAMIN SHAW, Esq., M.A., late Fellow of Trinity College, Cambridge.

MAN A WITNESS FOR CHRISTIANITY	437

BY THE REV. JOSEPH ANGUS, M.A., D.D.

THE PRINCIPLE OF CAUSATION

CONSIDERED IN

OPPOSITION TO ATHEISTIC THEORIES.

BY THE REV.

J. B. MOZLEY, D.D.,

CANON OF CHRISTCHURCH,
AND REGIUS PROFESSOR OF DIVINITY, UNIVERSITY OF OXFORD.

THE PRINCIPLE OF CAUSATION

CONSIDERED IN

OPPOSITION TO ATHEISTIC THEORIES.

BEFORE I go to my subject I will make some general remarks on metaphysics, regarded as adapted for popular thought. When people in general regard metaphysics, as they appear to do, as a curious puzzle, in which arguers give reasons for things which have nothing to do with nature or common sense, but entirely belong to an artificial speciality created by an understanding among themselves, they should be reminded sometimes of the fact that everybody is a metaphysician, and cannot help being one. Metaphysics could not possibly have had any existence except there had been some great leading ideas in man's mind upon the foundation of which they had arisen. These elementary metaphysical ideas, then, belong to everybody; nay, and they are evidently so simple a part of our natural reason, that we do not look upon them as metaphysical at all. We are aware of a certain profoundness and grandeur that belong to them, which distinguishes them from other ideas; but they are as perfect realities to us, at the same time, as truths of ordinary common sense. They do not belong to any fictitious world, though they raise us to another type of truths, other modes of existence in this. They are actualities of a most stupendous kind. Thus, take the first idea of this class that occurs to one—the idea of Infinity. This is a metaphysical idea; it arises out of our own minds, it is not a copy from nature, as many images in our minds are. I need not say that we never saw any object or extent that was infinite; it would be a contradiction to say that we had. But there is something in me by which I know antecedently that space is going on all the same as space, however differently it may be occupied, beyond my sight as within it. Having raised in my mind the largest portion of space I can, so that if I try to increase, I simply repeat it, I have still a sense of limitation. There is at the furthest line of the horizon an excess which baffles me; which is not included in the imagined space, or it would not be an excess, and which yet belongs and is attached to it and cannot be removed; an incipient beyond, which must be endless for the very reason that it begins; because this indefinable excess, for the very reason that it exists itself, must be succeeded by the like. Infinity, then, is a metaphysical idea; but is it an idea without reality, without interest, without popular attractions? On the contrary, it is an idea which appeals vividly to our imagination, which is impelled to efforts at the pursuit of it, vain indeed, but which exalt the intelligent spirit in the very act of overpowering it. And so far from being fictitious and illusive, it is an actual attribute of this material world; it belongs to the actual space around us in such a way that we cannot by any mental effort remove it; we cannot prevent this outward material portion of space in which we are from going off into an incomprehensible mystery. Give me a fragment of space, and I can understand it; but carry this fragment itself onward, and by simply extending, simply going on, it becomes as absolute a mystery as has ever been contained in a creed. The idea of infinity has within it, as soon as men enter into it at all, a perfect romance which all the flights of human fancy cannot overtake; the strange and insoluble enigmas of reason which come out of it act as a spell upon the imaginative curiosity of the human mind. It is thus that the ideas of metaphysicians, so far from being unreal, are bound up with this very field of vision in which we are; and so far from being artificial, dry, and technical, belong to the very mystery and romance of nature. Infinity is a fact, and at the same time a mystery. We can no more deny that there is Infinity on all sides of us, wherever we point a finger, than we can deny our eyesight. And yet what is material Infinity, sidereal space? endless everywhere? It is as mysterious as a spectre.

Everybody, then, is a metaphysician, just as everybody is a poet. Just as everybody is endowed with those elementary sentiments and affections, and is influenced by those associations, which, taken up by language, become poetry ; so everybody has the primary ideas and maxims of metaphysics. Even the Bible can no more be understood without the aid of these great metaphysical ideas than it can be without grammar.

So, when we take up the idea of Cause, which is the foundation of so large a branch of metaphysical argument, we go at once to an idea which is one of the most obvious of all our principles of thought, and which appeals to us as most simple and rudimental truth. It is a self-evident maxim that every event must have a cause. After contemplating any event in life or nature, I find myself going in thought beyond it, to consider how it came to pass ; by some instinctive law, some constitutional motion inherent in my mind, I go in the direction of a cause, of that event ; something not merely antecedent to it but which stands in such a relation to it as that, in consequence of it, that event or thing exists. The intellect pushes on to this resting-place, as a satisfaction of its own indegenous want and desire. It is evidently upon this principle that we entirely depend for the slightest real connexion between the present, the past, and the future ; otherwise, and but for this principle, this whole connexion is annihilated. Is it, can we imagine it to be indeed the case, that anything can in a moment begin to exist without there being any cause for it? Then no link whatever exists between one event in the universe and another; the whole concatenation of things falls to pieces, and the whole fabric of the world is dissolved, other than as a mere spectacle to the eye. Everything is perfectly independent, has nothing to do with anything else, begins of itself and ends of itself.

But when we look into the idea of Cause, we find immediately that it involves the most astonishing thoughts and conceptions. We cannot help ourselves having it, we cannot help ourselves being bound by the necessity of it, we cannot release ourselves from its grasp; but it is at the same time such an unfathomable idea that we pause under the impress of it, and feel ourselves under some great solemnizing shadow as soon as we enter into this region of thought. As soon as the gates of the awful kingdom of Causation have unclosed, we are instantly upon, I will not say magic ground, for that is to convey a sense of illusion and unreality, but upon mysterious ground; and we are in company with majestic, inconceivable ideas, which we cannot grasp, and yet cannot do else than accept. For while the movement *towards* a cause is part of my rational nature, I find on reflection that I can form no distinct conception of what a cause is. What is that of which existence is the necessary fruit and result? We can form no idea of what goes on previous to, and with infallible cogency and force for producing existence. All this preliminary agency is entirely hid from us, and our faculties completely stop short of it. The order of nature puts before us an endless succession of antecedents, but in no one instance can we see any necessary connexion between the antecedent and its consequent. But though we cannot raise the distinctive conception of what a cause is, we are not the less absolutely certain that there must be a cause, and that nothing can take place without one.

Again, the very first consequence of this idea of cause, and one which is implied necessarily in the very conception of a cause, is a result which appals us by its tremendous inconceivability: and yet it is a truth of the most absolute and obvious necessity; nay, it is an absolute and certain fact,- which every single rational being, whether he is a believer in religion or not, must accept as simply and unreservedly as he does the evidence of his senses; and that is, that from all eternity something has existed. "This is so evident and undeniable a proposition," says Samuel Clarke, "that no Atheist in any age has ever presumed to assert the contrary. For since something now is, it is manifest that something always was. For whatever now is has a cause, a reason, a ground of its existence —a foundation on which its existence relies, a ground or reason why it doth exist, rather than not exist, and this foundation [of a thing which has come into existence] must have existed before it. That something, therefore, has really existed from all eternity is one of the certainest and most evident truths in the world, acknowledged by all men and disputed by none. Yet as to the manner how it can be, there is nothing in nature more difficult for the mind of man to conceive than this very first plain and self-evident truth. For how anything can have existed eternally, that is, how an eternal duration can be now actually past, is a thing utterly as impossible for our narrow understandings to comprehend as anything that is not an express contradiction can be imagined to be. And yet to deny the truth of the proposition, that an eternal duration is now actually past, would be to assert something far more unintelligible, even an express and real contradiction."

The idea of cause is thus the key to an eternal past, which has contained being of some kind or another. By means of that necessary *regress* which exists in the idea, this mental principle holds the entrance into that interminable and infinite retrospect, which in metaphysical terms is called the *ex parte* ante-eternity. There the vista is ; and so long that it is true that every event must have a cause, it must exist—this unceasing past duration, going back endlessly and for ever. An Atheist and a Materialist has this endless past that he must look back upon, just as much as a believer in a God has. In his view the action of matter goes back in successive steps, each leaning upon one still further back than itself, and the retrospective chain of operations never stops, but goes back for ever. This is indeed an absolutely inconceivable idea—the actual pastness, if I may use the term, of an eternal duration of time: that an eternity is now over. And yet an Atheist must believe this, simply because it is a fact. It is just as much a fact as yesterday. Yesterday existed yesterday: that is certain enough. The day before existed next. And so every portion of time goes back to a prior portion, and in the eye of the Materialist each has its material contents just as solid and actual as those of yesterday: this visible world goes back for ever. This is not a mere idea. A past eternity of material operations is an actual fact to an Atheist, though a past eternity is utterly incomprehensible; but a God, because He is incomprehensible, is not even an object of faith. Such a mistake would it be for the Materialist to assume that because he believed only matter, he had therefore escaped from the yoke of mystery. That ghostly power waits like a giant, ready to pull him back as soon as ever he thinks he is out of his reach, and throws him into the coils of the very enigma which he had run away from. Space and time introduce to consequences which are as inconceivable as articles of faith; and yet these consequences are actual facts; just as much so as the experience of our senses.

We have now got as far as the idea of cause, or the

instinctive maxim of our nature that every event must have a cause. And here I pause to make two observations. One is, that it is most important to distinguish between the philosophical idea of the necessity of a cause and any perception of the necessary character of *physical* causes—those phenomenal causes which precede events in nature ; which precede them uniformly and invariably, and therefore obtain the name of physical causes, but which do not in the slightest degree reveal their own nature as causes, and therefore do not reveal their own necessity. To say in general that a cause is necessary, is not to say that we see causes in such and such phenomena. The one is a maxim of our intellectual nature, the other would be a judgment upon a fact, which we are unable to pronounce. But though the operation of real causes nowhere comes under our cognizance, but only a chain of antecedents, we have not the less still inherent in our minds the idea of cause, and the certainty that every event must have a cause.

The other observation is, that so long as we put the maxim that every event must have a cause in such a way to ourselves as recognizes the necessary character of it, it is not of much importance what special philosophical explanation we adopt of it; whether we regard it as an ultimate and primary law of the reason, or as a derivation from some prior and more general law. Hume denied indeed the necessary character of the maxim that every event must have a cause. "The separation," he says, "of the idea of a cause from that of the beginning of existence is plainly possible for the imagination; and consequently the actual separation of these objects is so far possible that it implies no contradiction or absurdity; and is, therefore, incapable of being refuted by any reasoning from mere ideas, without which it is impossible to demonstrate the necessity of a cause."* Hume accounted for the idea of the necessity of a cause by custom—the impression which the constant sight of uniform antecedence made upon the mind which was the same as if they were necessary, or real causes. To which Sir. W. Hamilton replies, that this could not create in the mind that idea of necessity which we actually find there, and concludes :—" The alternative is plain : either the doctrine of sensualism (*i.e.*, accounting for the idea of cause from mere sensible experience) is false, or our nature is a delusion. . . . It is manifest that the observation of certain phenomena succeeding certain other phenomena. . . could never have engendered not only the strong but irresistible conviction that every event must have its cause."† But though the denial of all reality in the necessity of a cause of events, or the assertion that events can take place without anything really to cause them, must be rejected as a paradox, there is no reason why room may not be allowed for different

---

* "Of the Understanding." Sect. iii.
† Ibid. Appendix I.

philosophical explanations of the origin of the casual judgment. The more ordinary course has been to refer this to a special idea inherent in the human mind, to maintain it as a "primary datum, a positive revelation of intelligence;" and Sir. W. Hamilton reckons Leibnitz, Kant, and Cousin, as holding this position. He himself, however, is opposed, as he expresses it, "to the assumption of a special principle," and maintains that the idea of causation comes under a larger law, and is only one of the operations of that law. "The law of parsimony, which he regards as nature's general rule," he observes, "prohibits the multiplication of entities, powers, principles and causes above all the postulation of an unknown force, where a known impotence can account for the phenomenon. We are, therefore, entitled to apply 'Occam's razor' to this theory of causality, unless it be proved impossible to explain the causal judgment at a cheaper rate, by deriving it from a common, and that a negative, principle." His theory reduces the judgment of causality "into a form of the mental law of the Conditional. . . . The mind is astricted to think in certain forms. . . . we must think under the condition of existence—existence relative—and existence relative in time. But what does *existence relative in time* imply? It implies that we are unable to realize in thought either an absolute commencement or an absolute termination of time. . . . We cannot know or think a thing to exist except as in time; and we cannot know or think a thing to exist in time, and think it absolutely to *commence*. Now this at once imposes on us the condition of causality."* Sir. W. Hamilton's theory, then, seems to be, that as we cannot conceive any real commencement, while at the same time there is phenomenal commencement, the cause is only the shape in which a thing exists, before its present shape —a rationale of causation which is substantially the same as Mr. Baines's, but which the latter extracts not out of metaphysics, like Sir. W. Hamilton, but from physical science. "A great advance," he says, "in the mode of viewing causation is made by the discovery of the law named conservation of force. The great generalization of recent times, variously designated the conservation, correlation, convertibility, equivalence, indestructibility, of force, is the highest expression of cause and effect."† Dean Mansel, however, does not accept Sir. W. Hamilton's explanation of causation. "His statement of the causal judgment, as an inability to think that the complement of existence has been either increased or diminished, is open to various objections. In the first place, I am not conscious of any such inability. . . . I have no difficulty in conceiving that the amount of existence in the universe may at one time be represented by A, and at another by A and B. . . . In the second place, whether we represent the new appearance as a

---

* " Discussions on Philosophy." Appendix I.
† " Logic," iii., iv., 8.

change or as a *creation*, we are equally compelled to suppose a cause of its taking place. To say that B previously existed under the form of A, is not to explain the casual judgment; for we have still to ask why A became B. In the third place, the theory fails to account for the origin of the idea of *power*, which, whether rightly or wrongly, all men instinctively attribute to the supposed cause. To represent it as a delusion is not sufficient; unless it can be shown how, consistently with the limits of thought, such a delusion could have originated."*

But while new explanations have recently been given of the causal judgment, or the maxim that every event must have a cause, our older metaphysicians, Locke and Clarke, were satisfied with the evident necessity which upon common principles of reason attached to the truth, and they treated it virtually as an axiom, the contrary of which was a plain absurdity, and involved an absolute contradiction. They regarded the reasoning that necessarily flowed from this metaphysical axiom as demonstrative reasoning. Nor, indeed, is it easy to see, if we treat this maxim as a necessary one, and consider it possesses self-evident force, how we can avoid the demonstrative nature of the truth. It would be a lame and impotent decision, such as could satisfy no rational person, to say that it was probable that every event had a cause; but if we say

---

* Metaphysics, p. 271.

this maxim is necessary, then we must admit that it is of the nature of metaphysical mathematics. Notwithstanding, then, the modern ingenious rationales of this maxim which have been offered to us, I must confess myself disposed to fall back upon the judgment of our older metaphysicians upon this point.

If we apply this maxim then to actions and determinations of the will, all that every event having a cause can mean is that every action has an agent. The agent is the cause of the action in the sense of doing it, and it depends upon our theory of the will whether he is a necessary or a free cause of it. If he is a necessary cause, this is the doctrine of necessity in human actions; if he is a free cause, this is the doctrine of free-will, or that the will determines its own acts, and is a self-moving substance. But this maxim, as used in the metaphysical argument for the existence of a God, has only an application to events which happen in the sphere of substance which is not self-moving, but the characteristic of which is that it is moved from without. If we except the invisible wills of moral beings, the whole world we are in belongs to this mechanical nature; not only the whole order of physical nature, but the whole of history and the whole course of human action, so far as it is visible and comes under the cognizance of our senses. War, trade, government and administraion, manufacture, art, language or speech, everything that we do, so far as it is visible and tangible, consists of a number of material and mechanical movements which are all caused by prior material and mechanical movements, and these again by others as far as we can trace. Spiritually we are conscious of what we call free-will, or of a nature which determines its own acts, *i.e.*, moves itself; but outwardly and visibly all nature is moved from without, and does not move itself. In every action we perform, all that is seen is the motion of matter, the same in speaking, the same in our looks and expressions. Certain muscles are put in motion, which produce certain effects on the body itself, which in some cases stop there, and in other cases go beyond the body, to surrounding objects. Such is all visible nature : either it is what we call the order of nature. or it is action of man : under either head, it consists of the motions of matter, and of matter alone, which is not self-moving, but is moved from without.

But with this application it is difficult to say that the maxim that an event must have a cause is not mathematical in its nature. We apply it to motions of such things and substances as do not move themselves. But if these motions do not proceed from the substances themselves, whence can they proceed from but from without them ? But in that case, whatever it is without them which makes them move is the *cause* of that motion.

The maxim, then, that every event must have a cause, or that what cannot move itself must be moved from without, differs from mathematical axioms in this, that whereas mathematical axioms stop with themselves, and we do not apply them to actual things, this maxim we apply to the actual material of this world. Did we apply, *e.g.*, the axiom that things which are equal to the same are equal to one another to actual things, we should first have to ascertain the fact that the two things were exactly equal, which we could not demonstratively do. But we do not give the axiom an application to actual facts, but leave it resting upon an assumption or definition of two things as equal; which being the case, it continues a pure mathematical truth. In the same way, if we simply said that what could not move itself must be moved from without, or, which would be the same thing, if we made it enter into our definition of matter, that it could not move itself, and upon this definition asserted that matter must be moved from without, this maxim, that every material movement must have a cause, would be a mathematical one. But we do not let this maxim stay in this mathematical stage; we apply this definition of matter to the whole actual material of this world, and we say that this actual material cannot move itself, but must have been moved from without. Here, then, we no longer rest upon a definition, but we assert a fact; and we cannot prove this fact mathematically, but only take it as a moral certainty, which is evident to common sense. If matter possesses an original power of motion, or has will, all we can say is that we have made a great mistake; but appearances are universally against such a supposition. The maxim, then, that every event must have a cause is the axiom of mathematical metaphysics, that what cannot move itself must be moved from without, operating upon a supposition of *fact*, viz., that all actual matter comes under the head of this category, of what cannot move itself.

We have now got the idea of cause, with the preliminary considerations attaching to it. But now that we have got the idea of cause, or the principle of causation, comes the great distinction in the interpretation of the idea, upon which depends the issue whether we can apply it to constituting the proof of a God or not ; whether we can raise a religious conclusion upon it or not ; whether we can use it as the foundation upon which an Eternal and Supreme Moral Being can be shown to exist, or whether it is reducible to a barren and fruitless succession which ends in nothing. It is upon this question that the whole of the great metaphysical argument for the existence of a God from causation depends. We assert that the whole of this argument is strictly extracted and evolved from the idea of a cause, as it is naturally conceived and entertained in our minds ; that it is simply the contents of that idea brought out, when by an act of the attention we have entered into the idea, and seen how it is constituted and what there is in it. On the other hand, this constitution of the idea is denied by the Atheist; and he claims to hold the idea in such a sense as leads to no such conclusion.

When we speak of a cause then, and of the idea of a cause which we have in our minds, the question to be decided is, does this idea demand finality, or is it satisfied by an infinite chain and series of causes? We assert, then, that this idea demands finality; and adopting the maxim, "*Causa causæ, causa causati*," we say that if a cause goes back to a further cause, then the first of these two causes is not a true and real cause, and does not satisfy the idea of a cause in our minds; and so on through ever so long a chain, until we come to a cause which has no further cause to which it goes back. That is our interpretation of the idea of cause, and we say that any other interpretation of the idea is a false one, and sets up a counterfeit cause instead of a real and true one. Let us examine what we do in our minds, in conceiving the idea of cause. First we go back for a cause; the natural want and ὄρεξις is a retrogressive *motion* of the mind. But just as the first part of the idea of cause is motion, so the last is a rest; and both of these are equally necessary to the idea of cause. And unless both of these are fulfilled in the ultimate position of our minds, we have not the proper idea of causation represented in our minds; but a law of thought is violated, that law which we obey in submitting to the relation of cause at all. In other words, a cause, exactly by the same necessity of thought by which on the one side it causes, on the other side must be uncaused; as it is the cause of its own effect, so it must itself be the effect of nothing. That is what I call the rest, which the idea of a cause demands. There is an end implied in the idea: as things move up to a cause, so at the cause there is an absolute stop; and itself does not move back at all. It is not a whit more necessary to a real cause that it should be the cause of something else, than that it should be uncaused itself: and without both of these elements alike represented in our idea we have not the true idea of a cause in our minds. And the alternative is either to decide upon rejecting the idea of *cause*, and ridding metaphysical nature and the world of mind altogether of it, or taking this idea of cause.

But thus understood, the idea of cause has only to be applied to this universe, and it becomes the proof immediately of the existence of an Eternal Original Self-existent Being. For what are we to call that Cause of the universe, beyond which there is no further cause—the uncaused cause of the world—but this? The attributes of this First Cause of the universe, indeed, must depend upon what the universe is; the Cause must take its character and rank from what it causes. But that there must be an Eternal Self-existent Unchangeable Being is certain.

But while this is the necessary result of the idea of cause understood as we have understood it, let us take the idea of cause as fulfilled and satisfied by another interpretation; and no such conclusion as this will follow. There is such a thing as a proximate or secondary cause, which goes back for its own causal efficiency to a prior cause; and we may make the supposition of this dependence of one cause upon another going on indefinitely. We are familiar indeed with this notion, and we speak of a chain of causes, a series, a succession of causes. But it must be remembered that when we apply the term cause to a chain or succession, *i.e.*, to causes which are caused, we apply the term in a secondary sense, and a sense which does not correspond to the true idea of a cause, as our minds possess that idea. The Atheist then falls back upon this notion of a cause: he hangs the world up upon an infinite chain and succession of causes; and thus he satisfies himself upon the subject of causation, and at the same time avoids the admission of an Eternal Supreme Being. But the answer to such an arrangement is, that it does not satisfy the idea of cause which we have in our minds. *Causa causæ, causa causati:* if from one cause we have to go back to another, that which we go back *from* is *not* the cause, but that which we go back *to* is. The very idea of cause, as I have said, implies a stop; and wherever we stop is the cause. If we stop provisionally at any stage of this backward journey, we have a cause provisionally: but as soon as we go on to another the provisional cause vanishes and surrenders its character as a true cause. And so on until we come to an Universal Cause, *i.e.*, a First Cause. A true cause is a First Cause. When, then, the Atheist throws the universe back upon an infinite series of mechanical causes he must be told that an infinite chain does not represent the idea of cause ; that it is a false conception, and a departure from the genuine principle of reason. An end is included in the very idea—a final rest and repose beyond which there is no advance ; an appetency for a cause precedes in the idea, but rest in a cause concludes it.

Wollaston's illustration, with which we are so familiar, of the chain with an infinite number of links, suspended from the sky, of which he asks the question, what holds it up ? one link holds up the one below it, but what holds up the whole ?—this metaphor of a suspended chain simply illustrates, by a contrast, the actual idea of causation as we have it in our minds. It illustrates the requirements of the rational mind which that idea creates, and its corresponding dissatisfaction and sense of void when those wants are not satisfied. It is in form an *argument* with steps in it, but at the bottom it only states what the idea of causation in man's mind *is*. The Atheist says, " I hold to causation, I believe in cause, but why am I obliged to believe in a *First* Cause ? What greater difficulties are there in an infinite succession of causes than in an original and self-existent one ? I cannot in the least comprehend an infinite chain of causes ; but neither can I comprehend an original unchangeible being, which goes back to all eternity. Both are absolutely beyond my conception, and both raise difficulties which I cannot solve, both issue in dilemmas out of which I cannot find my way. But if both are incomprehensible, why should I be compelled to choose one of them, and adopt the hypothesis of a First Cause instead of an infinite series ?" The answer is— because an infinite series of causes does not make a cause, and your reason demands a cause. It is a false criterion of truth and falsehood, to judge simply by difficulties in the way of conception; there are undeniable difficulties, and insuperable ones, which result from truths which are certain, such as Infinity and Eternity; but we hold those truths because they are ideas which are part of our reason, and which we cannot throw off. And so with respect to causation. The question is, what is the idea of a cause that you have in your rational mind? And to that the answer is, that it is the idea which has been stated: viz., a cause which stops. But this idea of cause is not fulfilled in an infinite series. There is by the supposition no finality here; but a final standing-ground is demanded by the very idea, as my reason presents it to me. An infinite succession of causes rests by the very hypothesis upon no cause; each particular one rests upon the one which follows it, but the whole rests upon nothing.

The Atheistic idea thus does not correspond to the idea of reason. The Atheist appears to acknowledge the necessity of a cause, and appears to provide for it; but when we come to his scheme it fails exactly in that part of the idea which clenches it, and which is essential to its integrity; it fails in providing a step. His scheme represents solely the appetency for a cause, but not the rest in one; it represents only half of reason; it breaks down midway. One might say to him, Why do you give yourself the trouble to supply causation at all? You do it because you consider yourself obliged in reason to do it; but if you supply causation at all, why not furnish *such* a cause as reason has impressed upon you, and which is inherent in your mind—a cause which stands still, an original cause? If you never intended to supply this it must have been because you thought a real cause was not wanted; but if you thought a cause not wanted, why not have said from the first that causes were not wanted, and said from the first that events could take place without causes?

It is this in substance which Clarke does in his celebrated work, "The Demonstration of the Being of a God." He brings out simply at bottom the meaning and signification of an idea in the human mind; that there is implied in the very idea itself of a cause, firstly, that it causes something else; and secondly, that it is uncaused itself. He thus extricates the true and genuine *cause* from all confusion and mixture with secondary causes; and he brings the Atheistic infinite chain to the test of simple juxtaposition, putting it side by side with the true idea. He virtually says to the Atheist, this is the true idea, yours is a false one; and the false one is detected by being put by the side of the true; human reason recognises its own idea. The fault of Clarke is that he clogs his argument with superfluous positions, which he puts forward as different arguments, while they only are one and the same argument differently stated. But it would be the greatest mistake to say, as some do, that Clarke's argument is a mere train of technical subtleties and dry abstractions. This is what those say who acknowledge no reality in metaphysical ideas; all reasonings in this sphere are to them jejune and arid inanities, because the sphere itself is a vacuum to them. How can the evidence of the existence of God, they say, be contained in such hard abstruse forms of abstract logic as these, which it is difficult to endow with any life or force whatever appealing to our nature? But Clarke's chain of reasoning, when we examine it, is the bringing out of a fact of our nature, for an idea of our nature is a fact of our nature; it is the bringing out of the idea of Cause. Is there no reality, nothing vital, nothing solid in that which belongs to our nature, which is part of us, which influences our whole view of things? These ideas of our minds are as much facts as history is, and as our emotions, affections, and feelings are. These dry sticks of formulæ, which they are set down as being, have sap in them, sap which is derived from the trunk of nature. There is a kind of injustice done to arguments of this class, although the term is proper as distinguishing a class, by calling them *antecedent* arguments; an injustice in a popular aspect; for it gives an impression as if they were prior to anything *actual*, belonging to a region of emptiness before fact existed. Whereas this particular argument for a First Cause is as much founded on a fact as any other argument can be; it is founded on a fact of our nature, the sense of and appetency for a cause of things.

The use of such arguments as Clarke's is not, however, all shown by the mere logical aspect of the case. We have, as I have been saying all along, the sense of causation, the want of a cause in our nature; but it is astonishing how idle, how sleepy, how stagnant, and how comparatively dormant this lies in us, until some great appeal is made to it, or until some great argument awakens it. It is astonishing what an indisposition the mind has for thinking of a cause and realizing a cause, even when we know perfectly that there must be a cause. With what effort do we pursue anything that we have, any work of construction—the watch in our pocket, our clothes, our furniture, our books—to their causes. We know, of course, they all go back to their rudimental state and birth, and that they have all very definite retrospects, which end in special arts of workmanship. But it is a decided effort of imagination to us. So it is to go back with any reality to early ages, to remote conditions of the world, to say to ourselves this really took place at such a time—the earth was once in such a geological stage—all this once happened—it only requires a miracle of anachronism and I should have seen it;—all retrospects to be real require imagination. I have been struck often with the thought in Wordsworth's celebrated sonnet, one of those on the River Duddon :—

> " What aspect bore the Man who roved or fled,
> First of his tribe, to this dark dell—who first
> In this pellucid current slaked his thirst ?
> What hopes came with him ? What designs were spread
> Along his path ? His unprotected bed
> What dreams encompassed ? Was the intruder nursed
> In hideous usages and rites accursed,
> That thinned the living, and disturbed the dead ?
> No voice replies ;—both earth and air are mute ;
> And thou, blue streamlet, murmuring, yield'st no more
> Than a soft record, that whatever fruit
> Of Ignorance thou mightest witness heretofore,
> Thy function was to heal and to restore,
> To soothe and cleanse, not madden or pollute."

Here is a call to a remote past. There must have been some man who saw the River Duddon *first*—before any other human eye rested on it. What kind of a man was he ? What was he thinking of at the time ? What was he hoping for ? Of what nature was his faith ? The first seer of the River Duddon had all this attaching to him—he was a real man, with his own past and future, thoughts and hopes. But to go back in this way is an exercise of the imagination. And so even in the logical process of going back to a cause—reasoning here cannot do much without some imagination; it must be stirred and enlivened by it. Metaphysics and other sciences as well summon one to entertain vast periods, remote regions, immeasurable vistas, and the dim contents of time's infancy, before it can be thought of almost as being time at all. Here is the region of cause. Can we enter into it, or is it all delusion to us? The average human mind tends to a deep torpid stagnation in present fact, not wanting more; remoteness is inanity to it; origin or cause fiction; the lethargy of the hour hides distance from it, and the distant realm of reason among the rest. It is all unreal, all false to it. Now, here such a book as Clarke's comes in as a person determined to wake a man out of sleep; it forces him to reason, it says to him — You must, you shall believe that something existed before you; that there were causes of what is now present fact; that these stretch into eternity, and that there was being in that eternity. The hard formulæ are vices into which the torpid reason of man is put till it is constrained to exert itself; the logical apparatus acts really as a stimulus to the imagination, forcing the mind to acts of conception.

The idea of causation applied to this Universe, then, as has been said, takes us up to an Eternal, Original, Self-existing Being. For "how much thought soever," says Clarke, "it may require to demonstrate the other attributes of such a Being, ... yet as to its existence, that there is somewhat eternal, infinite, and self-existing, which must be the cause and original of all other things; this is one of the first and most natural conclusions that any man who thinks at all can form in his mind. . . . . All things cannot possibly have arisen out of nothing, nor can they have depended on one another in an endless succession. . . . . We are certain, therefore, of the being of a Supreme Independent Cause; . . . . that there is something in the Universe, actually existing without, the supposition of whose not-existing plainly implies a contradiction."

Kant agrees with Clarke up to this point in the argument. He coincides with him in the necessity of an ultimate or a First Cause, as distinguished from an infinite chain of causes. "The reason," he says, " is forced to seek somewhere its resting point in the *regressus* of the conditional. . . . . If something, whatever it may be, exists, it must then be admitted that something exists necessarily. For the contingent exists only under the condition of another thing, as its cause, up to a cause which exists not contingently, and, precisely on this account, without condition, necessarily. This is the argument whereon reason founds its progression to the original Being. . . . . I can never complete the regression to the conditions of the existing, without admitting a necessary being. . . . . This argument, though certainly it is transcendental, since it rests upon the internal insufficiency of the contingent, is still so simple and natural, that it is adapted to the commonest intelligence."* Kant differs from Clarke, indeed, in a point which concerns rather the abstract subtlety of metaphysics than the actual strength of the conviction which the reasoning produces; he does not allow absolutely the necessity of a being as an "objective reality," *from any train of reasoning*, except that which is founded upon the *very conception of the being itself*. In this case " the non-being of a thing is absolutely inconceivable ;" but if the existence of a being is founded upon reasoning from a mere *fact*, then, however necessary the existence of the being would be if the fact from which we argued was necessary, if this foundation fact is not necessary, the being—which is the conclusion from the reasoning from it—is not absolutely necessary either. But in the present case, as he observes, " the proof begins properly from experience ;" it begins from the *fact* of this world, and thence by causes it ascends to a necessary being ; but this world, as an object of sensible experience, is not a necessarily existing thing. " The proof *a contingentia mundi*, the proof of a necessary being which begins from experience, and is not deduced wholly *à priori* or ontologically," is therefore not with him a demonstrative proof of a necessarily existing being. But with this distinction Kant and Clarke agree in the

* Kant, Critick of Pure Reason, pp. 406, 407, 428.

proof from causation of an original and self-existing being. The English school of metaphysics was satisfied with the certainty of the existence of this visible world as a ground of reasoning ; and when a train of reasoning was conducted with rigid accuracy from this starting point, it wa sregarded as necessary reasoning.

This is the first stage of the argument for the existence of a God derived from causation. But now we come to the main part of the argument, that, viz., which decides the *attributes* of this Self-existent Being. " This is the question," says Clarke, "between us and the Atheists. For that something must be self-existent, and the original cause of all things, will not bear much dispute." But can this self-existent being be called God ? That must depend upon His characteristics and qualities ; and the characteristics and qualities of the First Cause can only be gathered from the character of that universe which He has caused—its arrangement and disposition, and the order and rank of the existence which has been produced in it. Here then we take leave of demonstrative argument, and we depend on the evidence of fact, and upon the natural conclusion which is to be formed from it.

We see, then, that what has ultimately come from the First Cause and Original Being is not only a material and corporeal world, but that world as connected with moral and spiritual being. Whatever criticism the ordinary and popular distinction between matter and spirit may be subjected to—that there is something which we call spirit, which is different from something that we call matter, is a simple fact of our consciousness, which can no more be got rid of than our very selves can—we are conscious that we are intelligent, moral beings. But if this is the case, this intelligent and moral existence must, like all other existences, be traced back to the original Self-existent Being ; and if it is traced back to that Being, how can it possibly not affect the character and nature of that Being ? The argument of Clarke, Cudworth, and all our religious metaphysicians was the argument of an *adequate* cause — that there must be a proportion between the Cause and the Effect ; and this is no more than a necessary and consistent carrying out of the principle of a cause. For what can be the meaning of acknowledging a cause at all, if anything is able to cause anything—the meanest material existence the highest moral existence? It is evident that we must combine adequacy and sufficiency with our idea of causes, or that the whole doctrine of causation will go to the winds. Can the motion of a stone cause a man, or friction produce mind, or the nebular theory account for the moral sense? There must then be a natural relation between the cause and the effect, and if causation is true at all it must be proportionate. It may be said, how are we judges of proportion and sufficiency in causes ? but reason does not allow its voice to be stifled by mere difficulties which perplex us, but which do not prevent us from seeing the plain and downright wants of reason. If there is such a thing as mind, will, personality, which has had a beginning and come into existence in the world; and if these are thrown back, through secondary and vanishing being upon the original Eternal Being, that Being cannot be matter. What we call matter is obviously insufficient to cause mind. Human personality cannot be accounted for by mechanical causes. The cause of intelligence must be intelligent.

The materialists of the last century then denied the position that the cause of intelligence must be intelligent upon the general ground, which they asserted to be true in physics, that a cause need not be like its effect. And it need not be said that the materialists of this century have wielded the same arguments, with all the advantage of that growth of physical knowledge which has been the special boast of this age. They have multiplied physical rationales of mind, and they have diversified this species of reasoning with the utmost ingenuity and power, and carried it into all those subtler and finer forms, which a profounder acquaintance with material causes has enabled them to discover. Thus it has been announced by a scientific man of this day, that thought is a secretion of the brain. And we have been told that, "Many who hold the evolution hypothesis would probably assent to the position that at the present moment all our philosophy, all our poetry, all our science, all our art—Plato, Shakespeare

Newton, and Raphael—are potential in the fires of the sun."* Undoubtedly then we see as a matter of observation physical causes wholly changing phenomenally in the effect, and the composition and combination of particles producing a totally different substance to the eye, taste, and touch from any or all of the ingredients separately ; nor only do we see the greatest and most entire metamorphoses in chemistry; but even the very doctrine of causation itself requires a difference between causes and effects. Causes do not produce causes— they do not simply repeat themselves ; they produce effects, which effects are different from what produced them. But though a cause need not be similar to its effect, it must be sufficient for its effect. A *sufficient* cause, as has been said, must be combined with *cause;* otherwise if anything can produce anything, the whole doctrine of causation goes to pieces. It is the only mode of carrying out the doctrine. What difference is there in saying that there is no cause of a thing, and that it need not have any ; and giving an *insufficient* cause? If you say human intelligence need have no cause at all—it came into existence of itself : that is, according to the doctrine of causation, absurd and ridiculous ; but if you say it came out of a metal, it issued out of volcanic smoke, it flashed out of an Aurora Borealis—that is just *as* absurd. Our reason does not see the slightest distinction between saying that intelligence has no cause, and giving it an inadequate one.

*Tyndall's Discourse on the Scientific Use of the Imagination.

One is just as much no cause at all as the other. A sufficient cause, then, is only the consistent carrying out of cause ; and if you admit the principle of cause at all, you cannot say that matter was the cause of intellect ; or, therefore, that the Original Self-existent Being need not be intelligent.

It is true that matter has lately been set before us as claiming more vicinity to mind than it has been usual to assign it ; and a scientific man, of the highest genius, has regretted that "mind and matter have ever been presented to us in the rudest contrast—the one as all noble, the other as all vile." I am not aware that people now, or for many centuries, whatever the Gnostics and Manichæans may have done, have spoken more slightingly and depreciatingly of matter, than to say that matter cannot move itself. That is all. It is charged with inertia. Therefore, if Professor Tyndall wants an alteration in the ordinary language of mankind respecting matter, I know of no other alteration that can be made in it, except that matter *can* move itself. This is the only new rationale which is open, because the contrary of this is all that has been said. Hobbes, in the 17th century, anticipated this claim, and laid down "that all matter as matter is endued not only with figure and a capacity of motion, but also with an actual sense and perception, and wants only the organs and memory of animals to express its sensations."*

---

* Quoted in Clarke's Demonstration.

But were such a theory of matter revived, and revived with new gifts and attributes with which to awaken the inert substance, I know not what the whole metamorphose would have to do with the position that matter cannot be the cause of mind. You elevate matter into a higher rank, and you raise its pretensions to be the cause of mind. But then, in proportion as you have done this, matter has ceased to be matter, and become mind. The chasm then is as wide as ever between mind and matter in the ordinary sense; and the obstruction as strong as ever to matter in the ordinary sense producing mind. What ordinary people mean by matter is substance which is without mind, or any element of it. I assume this description of it, this is my definition of it, when I argue about matter; if the definition is wrong, the argument as such is not affected; for the argument assumes the definition, and is right upon that assumption.

What such a view amounts to is that intelligence in the world is a *growth;* and that it began in a very small way as a blind unconscious action of matter, from which it gradually ascended to its present height and greatness. And taking this as the position asserted, we may drop the term matter, which is wholly irrelevant to it, and represent it as being the assertion that the highest intelligent existence may have been caused by the lowest intelligent existence (if we may call blind instinct such) through the medium of a succession of steps. But the lowest intelligence could not cause the highest; it is as obviously insufficient a cause as brute matter. If we suppose an original plan, upon which mind ascends from that of an oyster to that of Plato, there is no intrinsic objection to such a supposition: but in that case it is not the oyster which causes Plato, but the Intelligence to whom the plan is due, upon which the ascent from the oyster to Plato is made.

The attribute of intelligence, then, and the moral nature of the Self-existing Being, are shown by the beings whom He has caused, possessing those qualities. Another great evidence of the intelligence of the Self-existing Being lies in the works of nature; and at this point the argument of causation for the existence of a God joins on to the argument of design; and one argument cannot be separated from the other. The contrivances of nature require a cause, and a sufficient cause; the properties of matter are not a sufficient cause. Another lecturer, however, has handled this subject, and done it with great ability, and I will only make one or two observations in connexion with it.

We have a right, I think, to complain of the attitude of scientific men—a considerable section of them—in one respect; and that is, that they will neither say that the world was formed by chance, nor that it was formed by design; and yet one or the other it must be. What they say is, that it was formed by Law: but this is saying nothing; Law is quite consistent with either of these, either with chance or design. Laws are simply uniformly recurrent facts; if then these lines of facts are in disorder and confusion; if they are unmeaning, if they conspire toward no end, and make up no structure, then these laws are by chance. If they make up, on the other hand, an elaborate and useful apparatus; then, we say, they are by design. But the scientific men I refer to will say neither the one nor other; they stay at law, and rest in law as an intermediate verdict between chance and design, which saves them the absurdity of chance, and the mystery of design. This is not a consistent position. Laws must be just as much either by chance or design, as facts must be; and it is just as untenable that men should stop at laws as an ultimate rationale of the world, as that they should stop at facts.

And yet there is a great deal said now about Mind in Nature, and scientific men talk enthusiastically about Mind; the old notion of chance is obsolete, and in spite of the strength of a materialist school, there is a tendency to a consensus of scientific men that there is Mind in the universe. Would any one in any public meeting of scientific men dare to stand up and *deny* that there was Mind in Nature? It would be thought monstrous. It would be set down as the revival of an old stupidity. It is the only form in which they find they can speak of nature which at all ennobles it or which satisfies their own idea of the sublimity of nature.

But if a Mind is admitted in nature, how can that Mind be excluded from design in nature? The state of the case is this: Nature has all the *look* of design, and is full of contrivance and construction, which force the idea of an intention upon us; and with this aspect of nature, we also, and at the same time, say there is Mind in nature. Why then should not that Mind have something to do with that look of design? If both exist, to make one have nothing to do with the other is indeed an extraordinary arrangement. If there *is* Mind, why should the construction of the world be singled out as the special subject of prohibition to it, from which its exclusion is necessary, and with which no interference on its part can possibly be allowed? There is at first sight a singular appearance of adaptation in the power to the work; if such care is to be taken to shut it out, and resist its intrusion, the reason must be an unusually recondite one. But this is the course taken by the scrupulous physical philosopher. He seems to have a conscience upon the subject. This Mind in nature must do anything but design. You are permitted to contemplate its majesty; but if you hint about intention on its part, it is quite out of order. If you whisper about construction belonging at all to it,—it is, hush! speak reverently about the Universal Mind.

Again, if there is a Mind in nature, and that Mind has anything to do with nature, that Mind must be in harmony with our own personal mind. It provides a frame for it. What is that but a connexion with it, as a scope and object? And it must be a Personal Being, who thus *provides for and understands* a personal being. Creation has evidently man in its view; it shows its comprehension of, its insight into, what man is. That insight must belong to a Personal Mind in nature. The intelligence which is at the bottom of an elaborate contrivance *for* a person declares in that very act something respecting itself, and discloses a secret affecting its own nature. Whether the apparatus might *of itself* reveal the truth or not, its *application* does; the application of it to the support of a personal being, discloses a recognition and cognizance of—if we may say so—a sympathy with, a consultation for personal existence, which is inexplicable, unless there is something in that Mind which, for lack of adequate language, we must call Personality; unless the mystery of that individuality which is *provided for*, resides also, in some sense, in the Universal Mind which *provides for* it. The personality which is at one end is reflected upon the other. The Divine nature is not all cloud, with no light breaking through. Here is a gleam of light. The contrivance in behalf of, with a view to, the life of a personal being, involves in the very act an idea of that personal mode of existing, a knowledge of it, and entering into it. And what mind could enter into personal existence, but one which had in some sense personal existence itself?"*

Professor Tyndall's conclusion then may well be embraced for our own:—"Be careful that your conception of the Builder of the Universe is not an unworthy conception. Invest that conception with your grandest and highest and holiest thoughts; but be careful of pretending to know more than is given you to know." We *are* careful for our conception of the Builder of the Universe, and for that reason we attribute to Him design and personality. In what possible way can we human beings, think of the Builder of the Universe really as such, except in this way? Of course we do not know what design in the Deity is; we do not know what personality in the Deity is—not, *i.e.*, as they

---

* "The Cosmos without us displays an intelligence far reaching as the farthest fixed star, but this infinite power the physicist hesitates to pronounce a personality. That microcosmos, our moral nature, displays undoubted personality: and unless the intelligence which forms and transforms the whole universe is somewhat infinitely less than man, we have found the true God. . . . . Why unsatisfied by long chains of sequency, by a world pendant upon nothing, moving no-whence, no-whither, and for no reason, do we, incredulous as to these airy nothings, seek after a First Cause, an Author, a Creator, and refuse to relinquish our quest? It is because we find the facts of Causation within our minds. Will is the cause, and we are directly conscious of our own will. . . . Thus where the physicist hesitates the psychologist steps in. Our moral nature utters what is voiceless in irrational nature, and pronounces that will sovereign over all it creates is the one known, the only conceivable First ground."—"*Right and Wrong,*" a *Sermon by the Rev. William Jackson.*

are in themselves; but that is granted and allowed for in all our thoughts and reflections and considerations as to the Deity. This ignorance has its own effect proper to it; but this effect cannot be to prevent us from representing the Deity with practical truth relatively to ourselves: this practical truth then must not be undone by harking back again to our ignorance. This has already been taken into the calculation; it must not be taken in again and afresh, after all the proper reduction has once been allowed for it. Therefore His personality stands, His design stands, because this is the only way in which we can conceive a Deity *being* or *causing*.

It is untenable, indeed, to tie us up completely with ignorance, when you give something to do which wants knowledge. Whatever be the speculative defence of this method, it is practically untrue, because it is unfair —first, to make our ignorance an insuperable impediment to conception, and then tell us to conceive. Do not impose this on us, and ignorance is fair; but if it is assumed that we must think, conceive something about God—"if we are to take care that our conception of Him must not be an unworthy one;" then, however we may keep the fact of our ignorance as a truth in the background, we must practically assume some knowledge. God must be to us as God. How can He be without personality and intelligence?

But in the argument from causation for the existence of a God, there is yet a gap, which must be bridged over, before we can arrive at the religious conclusion, viz., the interval between even a moral and intelligent Self-existent Being, and a God. The argument from causation is essentially an argument from fact; we begin from the *fact* that we exist, and that runs up through causes to a Self-existent Being : we see the *fact* of a moral as well as a material world, and that runs up to a *moral* Self-existent Being. But God is an Ideal, an Infinitely Perfect Being, and how do we get an ideal out of facts ? We have only in the world a sphere of actual fact ; in mind, in will, in character, all is limitation ; and we see no perfection. If the attributes of the First Cause then are to be gathered from the qualities of creation, how can we upon simple experience erect the existence of a moral Ideal, an Infinitely Perfect Being, of boundless intelligence and goodness? And yet unless we have argumentatively reached this Ideal, we have not reached the truth of the existence of a God, for God essentially means all this.

The older metaphysicians then made this gap in the argument less of a difficulty than the later school. Clarke extracts the ideal character of the Self-existent Original Being out of the simple pre-eminence and excellence of a cause as compared with an effect. "Since in general," he says, "there are manifestly in things various kinds of powers, and very different excellencies and degrees of perfection, it must needs be that in the order of causes and effects, the cause must always be more excellent than the effect ; and the Self-existent Being, whatever that be supposed to be, must of necessity, being the original of all things, contain in itself the sum and highest degree of all the perfections of all things." With the older metaphysicians the effort of the argument lay in the proof of a Moral Self-existent Being; and that gained, they considered the infinity and perfection to follow as a matter of course; and certainly if one thinks of the mysterious nature of a cause, it leads us unavoidably to such a transcendental estimate of the First Cause of all things, as cannot naturally stop short of an Ideal. But Kant, on the other hand, fixes the great difficulty of the argument after a Moral Self-existent Being has been proved, viz., between a Moral Self-existent Being, and a God: he announces his utter perplexity how upon a simple ground of experience or the basis of causation—he is to erect a proof of the ideal. "For can ever experience be given," he says, "which should be conformable to an *idea*? That which is peculiar to this last consists precisely in this, that an experience can never be congruous to it. The transcendental idea of a necessary, all-sufficient, original Being is so immensely great, so raised above all that is empirical, which is always conditional, that we can never collect matter enough or experience in order to fill such a conception." But when we examine Kant's attitude as a reasoner to the ideal, it does not substantially differ from Clarke's; Clarke gives up "demonstration strictly and properly;" and Kant allows a natural strong ground of conviction. He considers that the chasm which presents itself to the passive and composed intellect between the actual and the ideal is arched over by an intuitive impulse, which springs from the whole view of the Creation, and carries the mind by a quick movement of thought, which it cannot resist, to the transcendental conclusion of an Infinite, Perfect Being. "The present world," he says, "opens to us so immense a theatre of diversity, order, fitness, and beauty, whether we seek after these in the infinity of space, or in its unbounded division; that even according to the knowledge which our weak reason has been enabled to acquire of the same, all language lacks its expression as to so many and undiscernibly great wonders—so that our judgment of the whole must terminate in a speechless, but so much the more eloquent, astonishment. Everywhere we see a chain of effects and causes, of ends and means, regularity in beginning and ending : and since nothing has come of itself into the state in which it is, it always thus indicates further back another thing, as its cause, which renders exactly the same further inquiry necessary; so that the great Whole must sink into the abyss of nothing, if we did not admit something existing of itself originally and independently, external to this Infinite Contingent, and as the cause of its origin. This highest cause, in respect of all things in the world, how great are we to think it? The world we are not acquainted with according to its whole extent: still less do we know how to appreciate its magnitude by comparison with all that is possible. But what prevents us, that, since we require in respect of causality an external and supreme Being, we should not at the same time, in respect of the degree of perfection, place it *above everything else possible?* . . . It would consequently not only be comfortless, but also quite vain, to wish to take away something from the authority of this proof. Reason, which is unceasingly elevated by means of arguments so powerful, and always increasing under its hands, although only empirical ones, cannot, through any doubts of subtly-deduced speculation, be so pressed down that it must not be roused as it were out of a dream, from any meditative irresolution, by a glance which it casts on the wonders and majesty of the Universe; in order to raise itself from greatness to greatness up to the highest of all—from the conditional to the condition—up to the supreme and unconditional Creator."*

I would only add to this argument that it must be considered that an ideal is contained in the moral nature of man; and that we have to account for its being there. It is evident that the peculiar character or construction, as we may call it, of the conscience and the moral sense is such, that the very instrument it works by is a kind of restlessness and discontent with all fact in us, and a desire to be something which we are not. The condition of good-

* "Critique of Pure Reason." Book 2, c. 1., div. iii. s. 6.

ness is not that of attaining a defined sufficient end : it is not that of reaching a resting place. That is counter to the law of our being. St. Paul has given an exposition of conscience, which plainly and vividly describes it as insatiable, swallowing, like some unfathomable abyss, all the duty, sacrifice, and effort that is thrown into it, and still demanding more. And though in the Christian dispensation the sense of a Divine justification is the remedial and appointed relief for the natural insatiableness of conscience, there remains a sense of short-coming which is ineffaceable, and is inherent and rooted in the man. What can this be the effect of but the existence of an ideal in man, the spontaneous erection of his own heart, which dwarfs every act of his, and reduces his whole life to failure and imperfection ? Moral beauty, goodness, rises up before him in his conscience in a form and height which has no embodiment in fact ; he sees there a whole, while all experience only shows what is fragmentary. How has he got in his nature a type, of which he has no representative in actual existence ? The only answer can be, if we acknowledge causation, that whence he has the moral nature which he has, thence he has this *peculiarity and manner* of that nature : viz., from the original Self-existing Being. This ideal is implanted in him ; but if so, how can that Being, who has implanted an ideal, be other than Himself, the fulfilment of it ?

THE EVIDENCE

AFFORDED BY THE

ORDER AND ADAPTATIONS OF NATURE

TO THE

EXISTENCE OF A GOD.

BY

CHARLES BROOKE, Esq., M.A., F.R.S.,
CONSULTING SURGEON OF THE WESTMINSTER HOSPITAL.

The Evidence Afforded by the Order and Adaptations in Nature to the Existence of a God.

THE writer having undertaken the elucidation of this comprehensive and important subject, in consequence of the inability from indisposition of the Rev. Charles Pritchard to fulfil that duty, he cannot but express his regret that the mantle of so distinguished a divine and philosopher should not have fallen on worthier shoulders than his own.

In the consideration of this subject it is not proposed to enter into any metaphysical disquisitions, since the "order and adaptations in nature" are physical questions; and in the metaphysical treatment of such questions the writer has not much confidence. It has been stated* that there are metaphysical difficulties in the summation of infinite series, and in the theories of ultimate ratios, and of impossible quantities: if so, the difficulties must lie, not in the principles themselves

* Transactions of the Victoria Institute.

but in their metaphysical treatment, because on the validity of these principles rests our knowledge of the grandest cosmical phenomena; such for example as the accurate prediction of eclipses, and the approximate determination of the place and magnitude of a large but hitherto unknown planet, from the observed disturbance of the remotest previously known member of the solar system. It is proposed rather to illustrate the subject by a careful observation of facts, and by the obvious inferences that may be drawn from them.

The subject naturally branches off in two directions, first, the order, and secondly, the adaptations in nature, both of which may be pursued far beyond the possible limits of this address. As illustrations of infinite wisdom may be taken, firstly, the gradual and progressive development of the earth, and the adaptation of its successive denizens to the circumstances under which they existed; secondly, the correlation of the materials; and thirdly, the correlation of the powers of nature.

I. When we contemplate a fossil bone or shell, which has lain buried it may be some thousands of feet below the earth's surface, or embedded in the solid rock that may have been by some vast convulsion heaved up to a similar height above it, we are led irresistibly to one of two conclusions: either that there has been (not to speak it disrespectfully) a sportive exercise of creative power, and that these portions of matter, bearing all the physical characters of what they represent, were never really associated with animal life; or otherwise, that they must be received as evidences of animal existence at very remote periods of time; and if the teachings of Geology and Palæontology be admitted, it must likewise be admitted that the Mosaic account of the creation is not susceptible of a literal interpretation.

Let us take a single illustration : on some elevated mountain range we meet with a bed of conglomerate, consisting of water-rolled stones cemented together ; on breaking out one of these, it is found to contain organic remains, the shells of marine mollusca. Now what a vast series of cosmical changes does this represent! This shell must have been deposited in an ocean bed, which after an unknown period of time became consolidated into a rock ; this by some subsequent great convulsion must have been broken up into fragments, and these fragments subsequently rounded by long-continued attrition, probably by tidal action on the sea-shore. These rounded stones, again, must have been cemented together by processes which, so far as can be judged from existing known facts, must have occupied vast periods of time, and the stratum thus formed must have been, by another violent convulsion of nature, upheaved into the position in which we met with it, or left exposed by denudation and the wearing away resulting from long-continued glacial or aqueous action.

It would appear then that the surface of our globe has been adapted to the exigencies of its present inhabitants not by any sudden act of creation, but by a gradual and progressive development, requiring countless ages for its accomplishment; and that as we descend in the order of strata that have successively formed a part of the earth's surface, the type of organization is generally successively lower, and also generally more and more remote from existing or more recent types: from these facts it may not unreasonably be inferred that the beneficence of the Creator has ever been exemplified in adapting the organization of His creatures to the conditions and circumstances under which they existed.

But a new theory of successive development has recently been promulgated, the obvious tendency of which is to supersede the necessity of creative intelligence; although, perhaps, the author of the theory of "Natural Selection," and probably some of his followers, may not be disposed to admit the validity of this inference. The theory of natural selection assumes that advances in development have taken place not by design, but by accident, or the force of circumstances, and that in the struggle for existence the individuals evincing an imperfect development have been annihilated; and thus that advanced development has ever held its own against inferiority, until existing perfection was attained; and as a crowning point, the theory does ot exclude the development of man from the lower animals. If then man has been "developed" from a jelly-fish, or some other equally low type of organization, this theory needs only to be coupled with that of spontaneous generation (which assumes that some of the lowest types of organic life may be spontaneously developed from inorganic matter), and the necessity of an omnipotent Creator is altogether superseded! These theories have, however, one important point in common, namely, that they are alike destitute of any substantial foundation in fact: if only sufficient care be taken to exclude the invisible germs of organization with which the atmosphere is unquestionably loaded, no organisms are developed from the admixture of the most suitable materials; and on the other hand, of the countless missing links of imperfect development not a trace has ever been found. The very term "Natural Selection," by which is meant *selection* without *volition*, is self-contradictory, for the term "Selection" not only "seems to imply" (as Mr. Darwin admits), but actually does imply "conscious choice," and can imply nothing else.

In order to bridge over this admitted preliminary difficulty, Mr. Darwin quotes the intended explanatory remark of Professor Huxley, that "when the wind heaps up sand-dunes, it sifts and *unconsciously selects* from the gravel on the beach grains of sand of equal size."

Now this from so professedly close a reasoner as Mr. Huxley is rather surprising. What is the fact?

Both masses and particles, stones and grains of sand, that the retiring waves chance to have left at the surface, are alike acted upon by gravitation and by windpressure. But the amount of gravitation or weight-pressure depends upon mass, while the amount of wind-pressure depends upon surface; and the amount of surface is increased by subdivision or extension, without any increase of mass, as for example the surface of an apple is increased by slicing, or that of a sovereign by beating it into gold-leaf. But it happens that in the stones vertical gravitation beats horizontal wind-pressure, and they remain behind, while in the grains of sand wind-pressure beats gravitation, and they are carried away, as the gold-leaf would be if scattered amongst a heap of sovereigns; there is, therefore, no more sense in imputing "selection" to the wind, than to gravitation; none in fact in imputing it to either. If, moreover, the scraps of a torn-up love-letter happened to have been scattered on the beach, the wind would have probably made a further "selection," and instead of leaving them exposed on the dune, would most considerately have wafted them to some more secluded spot. Mr. Huxley might with perfect propriety have written, "The wind unconsciously *separates* from the gravel on the beach grains of sand," etc., but that expression would not have answered his purpose.

When Mr. Darwin proceeds to remark, "For brevity's sake I sometimes speak of natural selection as an intelligent power, in the same way as astronomers speak of the attraction of gravity ruling the movements of the planets," he cannot for a moment imagine that any one, astronomer or otherwise, imputes intelligence to gravitation. Mr. Darwin should remember that

> . . . . Brevis esse laboro
> Obscurus fio ;

and if he had written, "for obscuration's sake," he would probably have been much nearer the mark.

The crowning triumph of "natural selection," in which the immeasurable chasm existing between the monkey and the man is assumed to be bridged over by accident and chance-medley, is the only point of that theory that need be further noticed. A belief in the progressive development of man from any inferior animal whatever is absolutely incompatible with a belief of the existence in man of an immortal spirit, for by no conceivable process can that which is essentially not material be developed from any combination of mere material elements. It is nowhere stated of any inferior animal that "God breathed into his nostrils the breath of lives" (not life, as in the authorized version; the revisers will, it is hoped, notice this); and it may not unreasonably be assumed that the plural noun *chayim** stands in the same relation to man's tripartite nature, that *elohim* does to the tripartite existence of the Godhead.

* It might seem pedantic to insert the Hebrew characters.

That the various orders of animal and vegetable existence in an ascending scale of organization might have been formed by a countless succession of almost imperceptible changes, if such had been the will of the Almighty, cannot for a moment be denied; but that any such course of events could have happened *independently of that will*, appears to be inconceivable. Nor is there any satisfactory evidence that such has actually been the course of nature; for admirably adapted as is the organization of the various orders and genera to the conditions and circumstances of their individual existence, no examples have ever been met with intermediate between two genera, and imperfectly adapted to fulfil the conditions of either; and even in the few instances in which individuals have been obtained by cross-breeding which exhibit the mixed characteristics of two species of the same genus, they have invariably been found to be infertile, and incapable of originating a progeny exhibiting their own intermediate character. The only known facts that give the slightest countenance to the theory of natural or unintentioned selection are the results of intentional selection in varying to a certain extent the peculiar characteristics of different varieties of the same species, notably for example in the varieties of the pigeon tribe; but how slender and insecure a foundation is this for the huge superstructure of groundless hypothesis that has been raised upon it!

A valid argument against the supposed progressive

change of organisation may be found in the persistence of some of the lowest types through countless ages of pre-historic time. For example, the white calcareous mud that forms the bed of the greatest ocean-depths is found to consist almost entirely of the shells of minute foraminifera; and little doubt can exist that this mud constitutes, by slow and gradual consolidation, a progressive chalk formation; for if a small portion be taken from any chalk stratum, and carefully brushed asunder under water, it is found to consist of exactly the same organic elements as the ocean mud in question.

II. The extreme simplicity of the ultimate elements which constitute all organized beings, and the endless variety of the proximate elements, arising from different combinations of the former, which serve to build up the animal and vegetable tissues, may well be cited as an illustration of the infinite wisdom by which such arrangements were established. The four elements, oxygen, hydrogen, nitrogen, and carbon, constitute the bulk of organization. The chief constituents of vegetable tissue are oxygen, hydrogen. and carbon, or, it may be said, water and carbon, as the oxygen and hydrogen exist in the same proportion as in water; and various proportions of these constitute the proximate elements of vegetable tissue, such as starch, gum, sugar, glucose, and lignine, or woody-fibre, as may be shown by pouring a little strong sulphuric acid on a small portion of sugar: the acid will, by its stronger affinity, abstract the water, and leave a black spongy mass of carbon behind. Nitrogen enters sparingly into the constitution of the vegetable tissues, but almost universally into that of the animal tissues. The power of vegetable life in combining the inorganic elements, and thus preparing them for a higher state of organization in animal development, may likewise be noticed; but this power is wholly wanting in animals. Thus an important function may perhaps be ascribed to some of the humblest members of the animal economy; the despised earthworm, for example, is employed in continually reclaiming to a higher state of organization the effete vegetable matters on which it feeds, that are fast relapsing to the inorganic world.

One cannot but be struck by the simplicity of the arrangement by which carbon and water, elements of both earth and air, are combined into the various materials of vegetable tissue; and, moreover, that these proximate elements are so readily interchangeable by merely slight variations in the relative proportions of carbon and water, as, for example, the conversion of starch into sugar by the agency of warmth and moisture only, in the process of converting barley into malt, and of acid into sugar in the ripening of fruit. It may also be stated that, while animals are incapable of combining for their own nutrition the inorganic elements, they are capable of assimilating and drawing nutriment from those elements when already combined in the formation of vegetable tissues. And the same simplicity of construction, but variety in design, marks the building up of animal tissues; they are mostly slight modifications of a basis called protein, which is composed of oxygen, hydrogen, nitrogen, and carbon in certain definite proportions.

As remarkable compensatory actions, it may be stated that the combustion of carbon, or, in other words, its conversion into carbonic acid by combination with oxygen, is the chief source of that heat which is essential to the due discharge of the functions of the higher animals; while, on the other hand, the reduction of carbonic acid, and the corresponding evolution of oxygen, is constantly going on in the development of the vegetable kingdom.

III. Recent scientific research has pointed out the harmonious correlation and mutual convertibility of the various powers or energies of nature, such as light, heat, electricity, and magnetism; and likewise the definite convertibility of heat and mechanical work: and these views have rendered much more intelligible the mode in which these several agents become subservient to the exigencies of organic development.

Thus, for example, while the combustion, or, in other words, oxidation of the farinaceous and fatty elements of food continuously supplies the animal economy with the amount of heat which is necessary for the due maintenance of all its varied functions, a portion of this heat is transformed into dynamic energy in the muscles, and a further portion probably into electricity in the nervous system ; for the mutual convertibility of heat and electricity is a well-ascertained fact. Moreover, the proceeds of combustion, the same as in our fire, candle, or gas-burner, namely, water and carbonic acid, are continually eliminated from the system, and restored to the inorganic world by the agency of the skin and lungs, to be again deoxidized in the development of the vegetable economy. It appears to be far from improbable that the energy which reaches the eye as light paints its photographic impression on the retina as chemical action, and then travels to the brain in the form of electricity. Again, the influences of light and heat in promoting, and of their absence in restraining animal development are too notorious to require any specific illustration ; but do not these considerations lead irresistibly any unprejudiced mind to the conclusion that indeed we are fearfully and wonderfully made ? and it is much to be regretted that the great principle of the Conservation of Energy should ever have been held to countenance the views of those who would supersede the necessity of creative intelligence, instead of perceiving in that theory only additional evidence of the infinite wisdom of the Creator.

As one of the leading objects of the Society at

whose instance this address is made is to counteract any apparently irreligious tendency in the teachings of modern science, the writer feels bound to notice some passages in a recent work by Professor Tyndall, entitled "Fragments of Science for Unscientific People," as being eminently likely to mislead some of those for whose edification it is especially designed. A grievous error appears to underlie two of the essays in this work, those on "Matter and Force" and on "Scientific Materialism," in the tacit admission of an identity of causation in the structural development of inorganic formations, and of organised beings. In the former of these essays, the substance of a lecture addressed to the working men of Dundee, during the meeting of the British Association in September, 1867, after showing the quasi-structural arrangement of iron filings scattered on a plate of glass placed over the poles of a magnet, and the laminated leaf-like crystals of silver and lead formed by gradual deposition from solutions of their respective salts, and after pointing out the arborescent forms of crystals formed by the evaporation of their solutions thinly spread on a plate of glass, and of the ice-crystals formed on our window-panes in the winter, the author asks (p. 86), "What is the vegetable world itself, but the result of the complex play of these molecular forces?" But he suggests no reply. Again, after alluding to the formation of vegetable tissues by the decomposition of carbonic acid, the union of the carbon with the elements of water, and the evolution of the oxygen, under the influence of solar radiation, he proceeds to state (p. 87), "Just as the molecular attractions of the silver and the lead found expression in the production of those branching forms seen in our experiments, so do the molecular attractions of liberated carbon and hydrogen find expression in the architecture of grasses, plants, and trees." This is undoubtedly true, but it is not the *whole truth;* and the author surely ought to remember that the "suppressio veri" is sometimes equivalent to the "suggestio falsi."

The error above alluded to consists in ignoring throughout these essays the indispensable influence of a germ derived from a precisely similar organism in determining the organisation of any individual plant or animal. While the atoms of lead or silver, from whatever compound they may be gradually disengaged, will in obedience to their inherent polar forces respectively form laminæ, the edges of which are inclined to each other at invariable angles, the same elements derived from the same earth, air, and water, as for example in a field or garden, will constitute an indefinite number of different vegetable organisms, the formation of each individual kind being determined *solely* by the influence of a preexisting germ derived from the same kind : and thus while mere molecular forces may be considered as alike the immediate cause of the formation of the metallic crystals, and of the proximate elements of vegetable tissue, those forces are not the immediate cause of the formation of any particular organism.

Again, in p. 91, the author writes: "Trees grow, and so do men and horses; and here we have new power incessantly introduced upon the earth. But its source, as I have already stated, is the sun; for he it is who separates the carbon from the oxygen of the carbonic acid, and thus enables them to recombine." Now this is not strictly true; for if a stoppered bottle be filled with carbonic acid, probably no amount of exposure to solar rays would have any effect in producing decomposition; all that the solar rays can do is, to impart to the molecules of carbonic acid such an amount of vibratory motion as enables the vital energy of the leaf-cell more readily to tear the atoms asunder, appropriating the carbon to its own nutrition, and rejecting the oxygen;—here again the influence of vitality is ignored.

No formation of the proximate elements of vegetable tissue is known to take place independently of the influence of previous organisation; while, on the other hand, the development of plant-life, imperfect and abnormal though it may be in some cases, is met with when solar radiation is excluded; it therefore seems to be altogether illogical to put forward solar radiation as the sole, or even the main, antecedent of vital development.

The author subsequently proceeds to observe:

"Some estimable persons very possibly shrink from accepting these statements; they may be frightened by their apparent tendency towards what is called materialism—a word which to many minds expresses something very dreadful. But it ought to be known and avowed that the physical philosopher, as such, must be a pure materialist."

If by materialism is meant the investigation of the laws of matter, as magnetism (as a science) is the investigation of the laws of magnetic force, it may safely be conceded as a truism that the physicist, as such, must be a pure materialist; but if materialism be taken in its ordinary acceptation to mean a denial of the exercise of either creative power or superintending intelligence in the formation and development of the universe, then it is most emphatically denied that "the physical philosopher, as such, must be a pure materialist;" and if the author persists in the use of a common phrase in a very uncommon sense, he must not be surprised if his motive is sometimes misunderstood.

A little further on the author states: "Depend upon it, if a chemist, by bringing the proper materials together, in a retort or crucible, could make a baby, he would do it."—No doubt he would; and if you or I could jump over the moon, we should be proud of showing our agility in so doing; but the fact is, we cannot — the principle of the conservation of energy forbids it: for if all the combustible material in our frame were instantly burnt up, and the heat produced converted into energy, the resulting amount would be wholly insufficient for the purpose;. and the author's hypothetical baby-making is not less antagonistic to the universal law—

"Omne vivum ex ovo."

The germ is as indispensable as the constituent material atoms in the development of a living organism.

To identify as much as possible the forces conducing to the development of organic and of inorganic structures, may be presumed to be an object of "Scientific Materialism;" but the Author has, in p. 116, endeavoured to support this conclusion by an erroneous analogy, namely, that the phenomena observed on transmitting polarized light through starch grains are "similar to those noticed in crystals." In the crystals, undoubtedly, the molecules are "self-posited" in obedience to definite polar forces; and in order that they may influence a beam of polarized light, it is necessary that these forces be unequal in at least two of three perpendicular directions in each molecule, and if the crystal be regularly formed, the disturbance of polarized light is the same in all parts of the same slice ; but in starch grains, as in quill, horn, hoof, and all other organic substances, that disturbance is due to molecular *strain* consequent on desiccation, and not to definite aggregation, just as is in unannealed glass it is due to the molecular strain consequent on sudden cooling; in fact, it is well known that any molecular strain upon a plate of glass, such as that produced by bending or compressing it, or throwing it into a state of sonorous vibration, will confer upon it the power of de-polarization. That the de-polarizing power of a plate of unannealed glass is not due to a polar aggregation of its molecules, as in a crystal, is further evident from this, that if a square plate be ground into a round one, and then the circumference of that into a scolloped outline, the visible influence of the plate on a polarized beam will in the three cases be very different, and not as in the crystal, uniform.

On the slender analogy just alluded to the author, in p. 116, bases this dogma of "Scientific Materialism":—
"But if in the case of crystals you have rejected this notion of our external architect, I think you are bound to reject it now, and to conclude that the molecules of corn are self-posited by the forces with which they act upon each other. It would be poor philosophy to invoke an external agent in the one case and to reject it in the other."

The author's inference is plainly this, that the formation of the crystal and of the starch-granule is solely due to the action of atomic force. But if this be so, how happens it that while crystals of the same substance, from whatever source derived, present the same characteristics of external form and internal structure, the starch-granules of wheat, of tous-les-mois, and of cassava, exhibit marked but invariable differences of structure, as shown by their optical characters, although composed of the same atoms, combined in the same proportions? Just for the same reason that the plants in which they were formed derive their respective characteristics, not from the inorganic forces of the atoms of which they are composed, but from the organic power of the germ derived from a precisely similar organism, which, while it calls into play the inorganic atomic forces, at the same time determines the whole course of subsequent structural development; as the tiny electric spark actuates those atomic attractions by means of which the resistless force of the mine or the torpedo is developed. How mysterious is it that the vital power determining the reproduction of parental characteristics of form and feature should once have been locked up in a vesicle of microscopic dimensions!

But if the influence of a germ be indispensable in the organisation of life, whence came the first germs, or the first germ-producing organism? While materialism will answer, "I cannot tell," it is to be hoped that the unbiassed convictions of reason, and the promptings of our moral sense, will ever point to the infinite power, wisdom, and goodness of the Creator. Thus it appears that "Scientific Materialism" is not more scientific, because not more logical, than other forms of materialism with which we were previously acquainted.

The author may perhaps, with some show of reason, demur to this criticism on the actions of polarized light, on the ground that as he is avowedly addressing his arguments to "unscientific people" it would have been futile to enter into the differences between the black cross as seen in a starch granule and in a slice of calcite : very good, but if analogy of structure be made use of as an argument in favour of identity of causation, then the strength of the argument depends on the strength of the analogy, and in that case we are bound to look into it, and to see how much it is really worth.

Having now cursorily considered some of the more striking indications of infinite wisdom as manifested in the order of nature, it remains to illustrate the same attribute of the Creator by the obvious adaptation of things created to the functions they are designed to fulfil. The careful observer cannot but perceive that throughout the whole range of natural objects the admirable adaptations of means to ends are unlimited alike in their number and variety ; but it has appeared to the writer that some of the more special and recondite examples of adaptation are the farthest removed from the possibility of accidental formation, and therefore afford the most conclusive evidence of beneficent design. And in order to bring the subject within the reasonable limits of an address, it is proposed to confine attention to three points in the economy of man, the mechanism of the absorbent system, and of the organs of sight and hearing.

The Mechanism of the absorbent system.—In order to render this subject intelligible to a general audience it may be observed that whenever any organ of the body exercises its peculiar function, as, for example, a muscle in contracting, or the brain in thinking, a certain portion of the organ itself is used up by a process analogous to combustion, by which the amount of heat is generated that is equivalent to the work done by the muscle, and probably also to the amount of electrical action that takes place in the brain. This used material and all other kinds of effete matter require to be constantly removed from the animal economy, and for this purpose they are collected from every part by a system of vessels called absorbents. Moreover, the waste of the system demands constant renewal, and to effect this, nutriment is collected by absorbents from the inner surface of the alimentary canal. Both the materials for the repair of the system, and those requiring removal, are conveyed by these vessels into a common receptacle, whence the contents are emptied into the veins by a very peculiar mechanism, and carried into the general circulation of the blood. The mechanism of the absorbent vessels themselves is remarkable, and entirely different from that of any other system of vessels. The venous system commences from the union of the smallest or capillary vessels, into which the blood is constantly urged from the arterial system; and it is a noteworthy fact that in all classes of the animal kingdom the capillaries are of such diameter as just to allow the blood-particles to pass through them in single file, the blood-discs themselves varying very greatly in size in different tribes of animals. The smaller veins are formed by the coalition of capillaries, and the larger are continually formed by the coalition of the smaller, but it is only in the large venous trunks that any special valvular arrangement exists to prevent regurgitation of the blood; and as man was designed for the erect posture, as might be expected, the valves occur at shorter intervals in the lower extremities, in which the return of the blood to the heart is opposed, than in the upper portion of the frame, in which that return is assisted, by gravitation.

But the conditions of fluid-movement in the absorbent vessels are totally different; there is no *vis a tergo* to urge onward their contents, and their action, instead of being continuous, is intermittent, depending on the amount of fluid matter to be absorbed. Moreover, the absorbents are mainly dependent on the movements of the body for urging on their contents, and their structure is in complete accordance with their requirements. This structure may be roughly described as consisting of a succession of pear-shaped funnels, the nozzle of each being inserted into the wider end of the next, and these act as a continual succession of valves, by means of which all regurgitation of the fluid contents is prevented. A, in the following figure,

represents a portion of one of these vessels, and B the same laid open to show the valves.

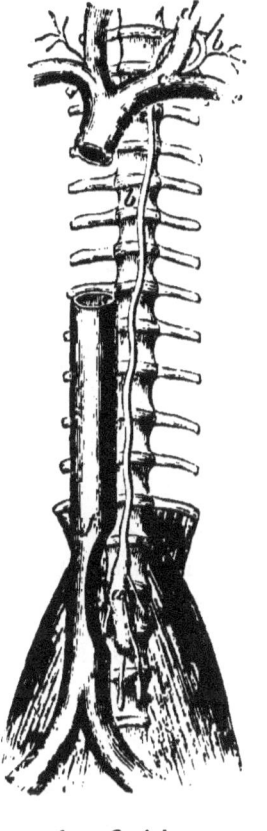

The most signal instance of design is met with in the means by which the main absorbent trunk discharges its contents into the venous system. The absorbents from the greater portion of the frame pour their contents into the common receptacle *a*, and hence the duct, *b b*, mounts upwards towards the neck, and pours its contents into the venous system at *c*, the angle of juncture of two large veins, the jugular, *d*, and subclavian, *e*. Now if the communication between the chyle-receptacle and the adjacent venous trunk *f* had been first formed by any imaginary process of " natural selection," by any conceivable attraction or affinity between the fluid contents of the two vessels, they might have been expected to form their junction at the point of nearest proximity : but no ;—the chyle-duct is found to pursue for some distance a nearly parallel course with the great vein, and then to mount upwards in order to reach the point at which it can empty itself into the venous system at the greatest mechanical advantage.

It was first shown experimentally by Bernouilli, and by the writer demonstrated geometrically,* that if a current of fluid be driven through a diverging tube, into which a smaller branch enters laterally, there is not only no tendency of the current to flow out through the lateral branch, but on the contrary, if its orifice be immersed in another fluid, a portion of the latter will actually be drawn in by the current in the larger tube; this fact may be demonstrated with very simple apparatus. And this effect takes place more energetically at the point of convergence of two tubes, as at *c* in the figure : this may be readily shown by a model in metallic pipes of the arrangement, through which a column of water may be urged with sufficient energy.

The Mechanism of the Eye next comes under our notice, and without attempting to enter into all the details of its wonderful and beautiful mechanism, which time forbids, it is desired specially to draw attention to the means by which the eye is adapted to the distinct vision of objects at different distances. In the interior of the eye a lens, analogous in its properties to an ordinary lens or magnifying glass, is placed between two chambers, the anterior of which is filled with a limpid fluid, the posterior with a somewhat

---

* Elements of Natural Philosophy, Ed. 1867, p. 239.

denser substance, the vitreous body. At the back of this is stretched a nervous membrane of exceedingly complicated structure, the retina, on which the impressions of all luminiferous vibratory motions are made.

It is the ordinary property of a lens that the rays falling upon it from any given point of an object are refracted in passing through the lens, and converge more or less accurately to some point on the opposite side of the lens; and these corresponding points are called conjugate foci: and it is further found, both practically and theoretically, that as the focus of the incident rays approaches the lens, that of the refracted rays recedes from it, and *vice versâ*. The normal condition of the eye is that when parallel rays, *i.e.*, rays proceeding from objects at indefinite distances, enter the eye, they are brought to a focus on the retina, and as the rays from each point of an object are collected on a corresponding point of the retina, it follows that a perfect image or picture of the object is traced upon the retina. If now the eye be directed to a near object, and there be no change in its internal arrangements, it is evident from what has preceded that the focal point of each cone of refracted rays from each point of the object will now fall behind the retina, and the image of each point of the object *on* the retina will no longer be a point, but a patch, and the perpetual overlapping of these patches is the source of all indistinct vision, not depending on any optical imperfection of the organ. How then is the distinct vision of near objects to be accomplished? By some internal change in the eye itself, by which the focus of each pencil of rays incident from a near object is brought forward, so as to fall exactly on the surface of the retina, and so form a distinct image of the object; this is termed the *accommodation* of the eye. But how is this effected? It may be effected either by increased convexity of the lens, arising either from internal action of its fibres, or from equatorial pressure, by which its focal length is shortened; or it may be effected by bringing the lens forward without any change in its focal length.

Now this is clearly not a voluntary action; so far from it, that the most eminent physiological authors are by no means agreed as to how it is accomplished. The writer believes himself to be in the minority in thinking that accommodation is effected by bringing the lens forward; and to explain how this may be effected in the human eye would require a more profound discussion of minute anatomical details than is consistent in a lecture addressed to a general audience; but examples of a much more readily intelligible action may be met with in the lower animals. The figure* represents half of an antero-posterior section of the eye of an eagle-owl, in which a is the transparent cornea, b the lens, $c\ c$ the choroid membrane, d the retina, and i the iris. The lens is pretty firmly attached to the choroid: e is a section of the ring of osseous plates that surrounds the eye;

* Drawn *ad nat.* by Dr. R. J. Lee.

from the anterior edge of this ring of bone arises a funnel-shaped muscle f, which is inserted all round into the choroid at g; and from the same point, g, there passes down to the posterior margin of the ring of bone an elastic ligament, $g\ h$. It must be observed that the parts are here represented somewhat strained out of their natural position, in order that they may be distinctly seen: in the natural position the choroid, $c\ c$, lies close to the ring of bone e, separated from it only by the muscle, its tendon, and the elastic ligament. The function of this annular muscle, f, is clearly to bring forward the choroid, and with it the lens to which it is attached, and it is equally obvious that the function of the elastic ligament is to pull the lens back again into its normal position, when the muscle has ceased to act. The eagle-owl is a nocturnal as well as a carnivorous bird, and in order to fulfil its functions in securing its prey, requires rapid and accurate accommodation of the eye, for accomplishing which the eye is provided with an unusually powerful muscle. Can any one seriously maintain that these perfect adaptations of means to an end formed themselves, or resulted from the blind action of atomic force?

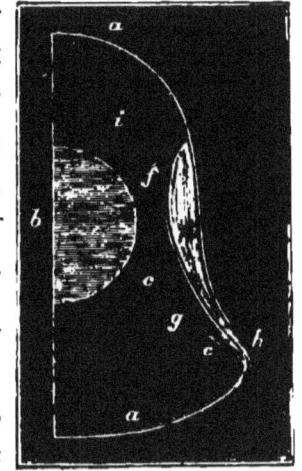

The Mechanism of the Ear.—In order to render intelligible some of the more recondite adaptations of this organ, the accidental formation of which is the most inconceivable, it is necessary briefly to premise the general mechanism. Sonorous vibrations impinge on the tympanum or drum of the ear, hence they are conveyed by a curious chain of minute bones to another membrane which closes a cavity filled with fluid, which constitutes the vestibule (as it is called) leading to two special receptive apparatus abundantly supplied with nerve-filaments, the cochlea and

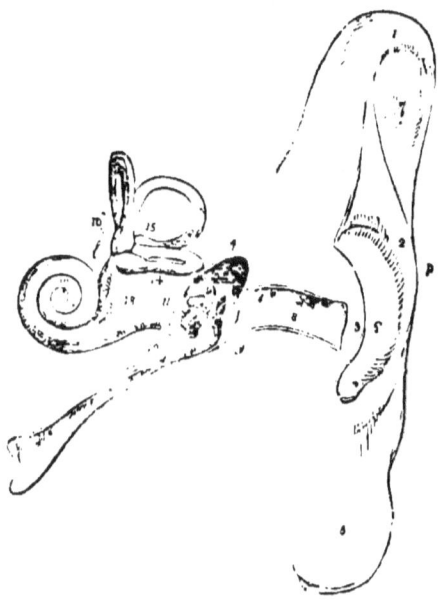

9. The tympanum.
10. The ossicles.
14. The vestibule, leading to
15. The three semicircular canals.
17. The cochlea.

the semicircular canals. These several parts will be seen in the diagram.*

* This figure is from Wilson's "Anatomist's Vade Mecum."

The cochlea in form resembles a snail-shell, the spiral chamber being divided into two parts by a membrane stretched across it, the transverse fibres of which are capable of being rendered more or less tense by a muscle extending throughout the length of the chamber. As the diameter of this spiral chamber decreases gradually from the base to the apex, it is obvious that the transverse fibres of the spiral lamina must also gradually decrease in length. On this membrane rest the free ends of a series of remarkable organs called the rods of Corti, placed parallel to each other like the keys of a manual, and their attached ends are embedded in nerve cells. There is little room for doubt that sounds of a given pitch, or frequency of vibration, specially affect a corresponding fibre of this membrane, (just as the shorter strings of a harp or piano correspond respectively to higher tones,) and that the nerve-tissue adjacent to the rod resting on this fibre *feels* the sonorous vibration, and transmits to the brain its perception of it: and thus that the special function of the cochlea is to appreciate the frequency of the vibrations, that is to say, the *pitch* of musical sounds, and also probably their *timbre* or *quality*. The mechanical means by which vibrations of given period are specially transmitted to the corresponding portion of the spiral lamina, have not yet been explained, but the writer is not without hope of being able to unravel this intricate question.

The three semicircular canals (each of which, how-

EVIDENCE OF DESIGN.

ever, comprises more than a semicircle) are chiefly remarkable for their *invariable* relative position; they are, without exception, found to lie in three planes, each of which is perpendicular to the other two; or in the language of geometry, in three rectangular co-ordinate planes. From the simplest geometrical considerations it follows, that if an impulse travel in the direction D O, the portions of that impulse which are effective in the directions of three co-ordinate planes O A, O B, O C, will be proportional to a O, b O, c O respectively, the cosines of the angles which the direction of the impulse makes with the three planes. Moreover, it is a dynamical law that waves will retain their original direction, unless that direction be changed by reflection or refraction; consequently, if the nervous apparatus of the semicircular canals be capable of appreciating the relative intensities of the impulses communicated to each, which is without doubt the case, it is obvious that, by means of these canals, the ear can appreciate the direction from which sound proceeds.

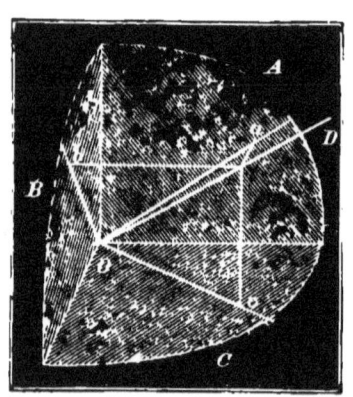

The faculty of perceiving the direction of a sound, and hence the direction whence danger may be apprehended, must obviously be a much more wide-spread necessity in the animal economy than the faculty of discriminating tone and quality of sound ; accordingly, the perfect development of the semicircular canals is met with as low in the scale of organisation as the cartilaginous fishes, while in the cochlea and the ossicles we meet with various stages of progressive development, each obviously adapted to the exigences of the individual organism ; and especially in the fish and reptile tribes that do not emit vocal sounds, the construction of the auditory apparatus, apart from the semicircular canals, is exceedingly simple. Can any one really believe that all these admirable adaptations resulted from blind chance, or from the necessity of the case, unintentioned and undesigned ?

But the evidence of design in the ear does not end here ; and in order to render the sequel intelligible to those who are unacquainted with physiological details, it becomes necessary to briefly indicate the general relations of the nervous system. This consists of two distinct parts ; one, the cerebro-spinal system, comprising all nerves that terminate in the brain and spinal cord, which fulfils all the functions of perception and volition ; this system exists in all vertebrate animals, in an ascending scale of development up to man. The other, the ganglionic system, consisting of fibres terminating in nerve centres, or ganglia, distributed over various parts of the frame, but chiefly in two parallel rows arranged on either side of the central axis, or the vertebral column ; the office of this system is to fulfil the involuntary functions essential to the development and maintenance of animal life; this system is common to men and all kinds of animals, down to the slug, the worm, and the caterpillar.

It is an obvious necessity that the ear should possess some means of adaptation to the intensity of the vibrations reaching it, in order that while the feeblest sounds may be appreciated, its delicate mechanism may not be deranged by the most powerful ones; just as the eye is adapted to the intensity of incident light by the contraction and dilatation of the iris. For this purpose there is a little muscle by which the tympanic membrane can be tightened; a second by which is regulated the tension of the membrane which connects the base of the stapes, the innermost of the ossicles (so called from its stirrup-like shape), with the margin of the oval aperture in the wall of the vestibule; and a third muscle, or rather series of muscles, by which the tension of the spiral lamina of the cochlea is regulated. But how is this exquisite mechanism brought into play? how, in fact, is the ear itself informed of the adjustment required? The foremost member of the chain of ossicles is firmly attached to the tympanum, and is carried to and fro by its vibrations: proceeding laterally from this bone, and in a direction nearly parallel to the plane of the adjacent portion of the tympanum is a slender and taper bony filament, in its relative proportions resembling a lady's riding whip; and immediately behind this slender process lies the tympanic nerve, a branch of the ganglionic system, which pursues a very tortuous course, for no other assignable reason than that of coming into relation with the filament of bone just mentioned. What happens then? The very first sound-wave that strikes on the tympanum makes, by means of this tiny bone, an impression of corresponding intensity on the nerve, which is flashed to an adjacent centre of nerve power, and the mandate to "make taut" or "let go," as the case may be, is returned and acted on, ere a second wave can impinge upon the tympanum.

The train of actions just described is altogether removed from the domain of the will; it is, moreover, so far from being obvious, that it is believed to have escaped the notice of every writer on physiology. If, then, the mere explanation so far taxes the powers of the human mind, what shall be said of the infinite wisdom by which the whole was designed? Well indeed may we be prompted to declare with the sacred Psalmist, " He that planted the ear, shall He not hear? or He that made the eye, shall He not see?" It would be far more unreasoning to believe that that unrivalled mechanism, the human frame, was self-developed, than to believe that if a "fortuitous concourse of atoms" of brass and steel, swept up from a workman's floor, were put into a bag and thoroughly well shaken, they would spontaneously evolve a first-rate chronometer.

If this experiment were made, and, as is highly probable, attended by failure, the advocate of undesigned evolution would probably exclaim, "Aye, but you have not shaken the bag long enough; if you will only shake on for countless æons, no reasonable doubt can be entertained that your efforts will ultimately be crowned with the happiest results. The course of development, you may reasonably anticipate, would probably be something of this kind: the atoms of brass and steel would respectively aggregate themselves into rounded masses, and these, when old enough to cut their teeth, would become wheels and pinions. As time rolls on, you must expect some examples of imperfect development; one, for example, without a main-spring, another without a balance, and a third without face and hands; but, never mind, pitch them back again into the bag, where they will, no doubt, 'perish in the struggle for existence,' and be shaken to pieces again, that their *disjecta membra* may re-form themselves more successfully. Moreover, if you want your chronometer to go on a diamond, and to be jewelled in eight or ten holes, you must put into the bag a little soot and a little pipe-clay."—Soot and pipe-clay, what good can they do?—"All the good in the world; we only want the material atoms, you know, and chance and plenty of time will enable their inherent powers to accomplish all the rest. The diamond, as you are aware, is only carbon, and in due course of time the carbon-atoms will rush into each other's embrace, and constitute little diamonds, which will grow bigger by accretion. I know that these carbon-atoms are very coy ; no one has ever yet induced them to take the final step, but time, my friend,—time will work wonders. Again, the rubies for the holes are nothing more than alumina, with a small quantity of iron, and a trace of lime, which they can easily pick up; and pipe-clay is the handiest source of pure alumina that I can suggest to you."—Is not the unintentioned evolution of organised beings indefinitely more absurd, *à fortiori*, than this?

If any hearer or reader of this address should think that a little banter is out of place in so serious a subject, he may, with all due respect, be reminded of the opinion of a profound thinker of the olden time, that

"Ridiculum acri
Secius ac melius magnas plerumque secat res."

In conclusion, as the adaptation of means to beneficent ends, such as those which have been imperfectly described, are the more special and recondite, it may fairly be assumed that in the same proportion they bear the stronger evidence of the boundless wisdom and goodness of the Creator; well indeed may the devout believer exclaim with heartfelt gratitude,

"When all Thy mercies, O my God,
My raptured soul surveys,
Transported with the view, I'm lost
In wonder, love, and praise."

THE
PHILOSOPHY OF HUMAN RESPONSIBILITY.

BY THE

REV. CANON BIRKS, MA.,
PROFESSOR OF MORAL PHILOSOPHY IN THE UNIVERSITY OF CAMBRIDGE.

THE PHILOSOPHY OF HUMAN RESPONSIBILITY.

IS Man responsible at all for his conduct? On what fact or principle in his nature does this responsibility rest? Why must he make answer for himself, and to whom? Is there any ground in the reason of things to confirm the sayings of Scripture: "It is appointed unto men once to die, but after this the judgment;" "So then every one of us shall give account of himself to God"? These are the questions now before us. They call for a grave examination, and, if possible, a clear reply; for they plainly involve an issue of immense importance to ourselves and to all mankind.

There is in these days, you are aware, a so-called philosophy, which denies that man is a responsible being. He is, in its view, a certain amount of developed protoplasm, or of transformed solar force, which has some strange dreams it mistakes for realities, and thus fancies itself to be an individual being, a responsible agent. But these delusions, with the parcels of matter to which they adhere, were all once potentially in some wide ocean of cosmic vapour. From the forces then at work in that wonderful matrix, a sufficient intelligence, it is thought, could have predicted, among other changes, these day-dreams of the human portion of the earth's Fauna, " with as much certainty as one can say what will happen to the vapour of the breath on a winter's day." If so, all conscience of right and wrong must be a delusion, judgment to come a mere fable, and immortality a dream. In the name of natural science, the common foundations of morality and religion are assailed. It is needful, then, to examine them once more.

The negative philosophy professes to trace three steps in the history of every science, the childish or theological, the youthful or metaphysical, and the positive or perfect stage, in which religion and metaphysics have been completely cast aside. A counter law may be laid down, far nearer to the truth, which distinguishes a low starting point, and three successive stages in the ascent to perfect wisdom. The starting point is simple ignorance, or natural and moral nescience. The first stage is that of Natural Science and Moral Nescience. The second is that of Natural and Moral Science, but Spiritual Nescience. The last and highest is that of Natural, Moral, and Spiritual Science, when the awakened conscience finds rest and peace in a still higher truth, revealed to it from above. It then begins to see all nature, and all the complex varieties of human life, in the light that streams down from His presence, all whose ways are judgment, and whose name is Love!

First, then, we live in a world of perpetual change. Every child of man has his lot cast amidst a sea of countless phenomena, varying every moment. In this first stage of thought he sees them, and watches them with curious, wondering eyes, but looks no farther. Every thing merely *happens*. Countless changes are happening daily. But why they happen, whence they come, and whither they go, he makes no inquiry. The kaleidoscope has been shaken, and another image succeeds the one which fades away. Chance reigns without, and this is merely another name for ignorance within. All is appearance only, and nature is nothing more than a restless phantasmagoria of worthless dreams.

Now Positive Science, as defined by its own promulgator, really answers to this first and infant stage of thought, where ignorance reigns and science is unborn. Theology has been shut out, and with it the Great First Cause, on whom all science depends. Metaphysics are shut out also, and with these all second causes, and those metaphysical ideas, Being, Force, and Substance. Phenomena are to be simply registered, and their laws ascertained. But those laws are laws of force, laws for things and persons, material and spiritual substances. Exclude all force, and we have countless phenomena, perpetually changing, but nothing beside. There is no person to observe and register them, no object whose changes are to be noted and observed. Our beads have no string on which they can hang together. The ears lie scattered on the wide harvest-field, and there is no reaper, and no swathing-band, to bind them into sheaves. Without a person, and without a thing, those metaphysical conceptions; without forces, which are causes of motion, and therefore metaphysical; there can be only a chaos of phenomena, fleeting, momentary, causeless, unconnected, inexplicable, and unexplained. Science is bound hand and foot with the ropes of the theory, like Samson by the Philistines, and cannot stir. For what can be more inconceivable than for a bundle of phenomena, with nothing to bind them, to call itself a person, and singling out a few other phenomena, to use these for bands to tie together a third set of phenomena, and then call them a thing? Thus the logical result of Comte's definition of this perfect stage of science is precisely what he assigns to the theological stage. It is "second childishness and mere oblivion;" a registration office for countless phenomena, with no person to register them, and no materials, no paper on which to record them, not even red tape wherewith to tie them together. Our Samson must burst asunder these new ropes of Positivism, before he can use his mighty strength, or make one step towards dominion over the secrets of the natural world.

The first stage in the ascent of science is the recognition of causes, of persons who think and perceive, and of objects endued with force, the secret cause of their motions and changes. " I think, therefore I am." This maxim of Descartes is no demonstration, but simply the analysis of a compound intuition. I not only think, but I act. I lift a weight. I grasp a ball with my hand. I thrust a door, and it opens. I look on the face, I clasp the hand, of a friend. I am conscious of exerting power, and an effect follows. I repeat the exertion of force, and the effect is repeated. I vary the effort, and the effect is varied. I forbear to lift, and the weight falls to the ground. I cease to grasp the ball, and it descends or rolls away. I pull what I pushed, and a reverse motion follows. Thus I gain the consciousness of force in myself. And I learn, also, the presence of force in things around me. For the weight presses on my hand that raises it, and needs an effort to overcome the pressure. The ball resists the hand that grasps it, and forbids it to close. The eye of the friend returns my own glance of affection, his hand returns my own greeting with a friendly pressure. I am conscious of force and power in myself. But I learn that there are powers and forces around me, everywhere present, and constantly at work. In every phenomenon I act as a sentient being, and I am acted upon in return by persons and by things on every side.

Natural Science deals, then, not with mere phenomena, as Positivism affirms, but with forces, the secret cause on which these shifting appearances depend. This one key serves to unlock the wonders of the natural universe. The chaos of mere phenomena is replaced by a Cosmos of persons, living creatures, and lifeless things, each endued with forces that act by laws, partly discovered, partly unknown, on which those transient appearances depend. And hence one of our ablest physicists, of the school most akin to the Positive Philosophy, exactly reverses the fundamental exclusion of causes and forces on which Positivism is based. " The scientific mind," he says, " can find no repose in the mere registration of sequence in nature. The question intrudes with resistless weight—whence comes the sequence ? What binds the consequent with its antecedent in nature ? The truly scientific intellect never can attain rest, until it reaches the forces by which the observed succession is produced. It was thus with Torricelli ; it was thus with Newton ; it is thus pre-eminently with the real scientific man of the present day."

The conquests of natural science, from the days of Newton onward, have been great and wonderful in its own domain. It has measured the earth, and scaled the heaven. It has swept away the vortices of Descartes and the spheres of Ptolemy, and has determined the orbits of the planets and comets by the law of universal gravitation. It has measured the speed of light, detected the unseen ether spread through all space, and measured the subtle vibrations on which colour and sight depend. It has analyzed the air, decomposed the earth and the water, detected fifty unknown elements, and created whole sciences of chemistry, mineralogy, electricity, galvanism, unknown in former days. It has weighed, not only mountains, but the earth, the sun, and the planets, in its balance. Chance, that shadow of human ignorance, has fled before it. The reign of law has been established to the farthest bound of the visible universe. And it marches on still to fresh conquests, forgets, like the Apostle, the things behind, and seeks to add new and rich provinces to the vast dominions it has already won.

After such successes in their own field, it is not surprising that some natural philosophers, with their strong phalanx of physical laws, should dream of universal empire, and seek to carry their arms into the region of moral and spiritual truth. That force, which the founder of Positivism would proscribe and banish as a youthful dream, his English disciples would exalt into a divinity, and seat on the throne of the universe. The scientific mind, they affirm, knows that the sequence he sees is necessary, and this knowledge is essential to his repose. "Not till then is the law of reason rendered concentric with the law of nature, nor can the philosopher rest in peace." The permanence of Force is the fulcrum with which he can uproot miracles, and move or build the universe. Nothing, he thinks, has occurred to indicate that the operation of law has been for one moment suspended. "Nothing has ever intimated that nature has ever been crossed by spontaneous action, or that a state of things at any time existed which could not be rigorously deduced from the preceding state. Given the distribution of matter, and the forces, in the time of Galileo, the competent mathematician of that day could predict what is now occurring in our own." Our Miltons and Shakspeares, our Newtons and Herschels, all were potentially in some cosmic vapour millions of years ago; so that a competent analyst, by some formula of due complexity, might have worked out accurately the Principia and the Paradise Lost, as singular points in his vast curve of universal being.

These are stupendous assertions of the natural philosopher. We are bound to examine them rigorously, before we sacrifice to them the solemn voices of conscience, the deepest instincts of the human heart, and the hopes and promises of the Gospel of Christ. Is the conclusion contained in the premises, or does it go immensely beyond them? "There is no God but physical force, and natural philosophers are its prophets." Does this new Islam, preached by some almost with the fanatic zeal of the first Saracens, really possess any reasonable claim to the faith of mankind?

What, then, is this Force, this "new god, newly come up," which we Christian believers are summoned to adore? It is a slippery and changeful Proteus, impossible to define. Now it is accelerating force, now acquired momentum; now a potency, and now actual motion. It glows in the stars. It blossoms in the trees. It spreads itself out in a cosmic sea of mist. It condenses itself into suns and planets. It flashes through the universe in sunshine. It forms animals that fancy themselves to be alive, and men that dream themselves immortal, and then scatters them into worms and corruption again. But whence came it, and whither does it go? Its amount, some tell us, is always the same; its increase or decrease is "unthinkable," though its forms are ever changing. Who, then, fixed for it this total amount? and what power or force, higher than itself, impels it to these ceaseless transmutations? It is like the Genie of the Arabian tale. Now it buries itself, as highly condensed sun-force, in the depths of the ocean or of the coal measures. Anon some fisherman or miner drags it forth to light, and unseals its dark prison-house; and, lo! it shoots upward in clouds of steam, or exhales in "thousand wreaths of dangling water-smoke." It shrieks its wild cry of escape and liberty on all our railways from the lips of ten thousand engines, and then vanishes into the depths of space again. It is a mighty slave of the lamp and the ring, well suited for the control and guidance of divine or even of human wisdom; a most useful drudge, that can work marvels at the bidding of a higher reason; but, after all, a sorry and shameful divinity. Set up by philosophy for the true King and Lord of the universe, it explains nothing, and needs itself to be explained. It is the shifting Proteus and eyeless Polyphemus of Homer, both alike stripped of thought and reason, and then rolled together in one;—

> Monstrum horrendum, informe, ingens, cui lumen ademptum.

It has no mind, no heart, no choice, no reason, and no will. Its changes have no purpose. It begins with chaos and darkness, and ends in utter darkness and chaos again.

Let us turn from this abortive philosophy, which sets up physical force for its idol, and catechize the facts once more. We are conscious of power in ourselves. This consciousness, reflected on things around us, which plainly act on us as we act on them, reveals one great law of being, common alike to lifeless and living things. The chaos of phenomena now resolves itself into a Cosmos, or at least becomes its pledge and earnest. We are conscious of our own sentient mind, and perceive and know countless objects, endued with force like ourselves.

But we are conscious of sensations, as well as of power to act. And in things around us we learn soon to distinguish that some have power to resist, or act upon our senses, but nothing higher; while others live, or seem to possess a power of voluntary motion, and sensations of pain and pleasure, like our own. The doctrine, then, that nature "has never been crossed by spontaneous action" sounds very strange on the lips of a philosopher. He must invent an esoteric sense for a familiar term. For spontaneous action, in contrast to mechanical impulse, is the term which, in popular apprehension, from the highest forms of life down to the lowest, severs living things from lifeless matter. Even in the Amœba, almost the lowest type of life, an able microscopist can describe that phenomena in no other way ; and speaks of "that marvellous power which one portion of the living mass possesses, to move in advance of another portion of the same."*

It is needless, and time will not allow, to dwell on the lower forms of life ; or to discuss the Cartesian theory, that instinct is mere mechanical force, and that all animals are simply machines of complex mechanism. The common sense of mankind rebels against it. But here no consciousness can assist our inquiries. The faculties of mere animal life are limited, and the contrast with lifeless matter is less complete. But for ourselves, we are conscious of something beyond mechanical force, and higher than mere sensation, with its aversion from pain, and appulse to pleasure. We can reflect on ourselves, on our sensations, and the objects around us. We can act, and refrain from acting. We can choose and refuse. We can reason on the desirableness of things within our power, and open to our choice. We can compare higher and lower objects of desire, nobler and less worthy motives of action, the more immediate and the more remote, and decide between them.

* Beale, Protoplasm, p. 39.

From a long induction, even in childhood, we can discern powers of sensation and self-motion in animals, determined by no compulsion, but by some form of spontaneous choice, which lifeless matter does not share. And a like experience teaches us that their range of thought, feeling, and choice, has limits which do not apply to ourselves. Their instinct, even in its highest forms, does not rise to the level of our human reason. Their choice seems to have very narrow limits, however perfect within these limits it may seem to be. Ours includes wider and nobler elements, the past and the future, as well as the present,—not sensible objects only, but the thoughts and feelings of reasoning minds like our own, the joys of benevolent desire and action, and real and deep longings, however dim and vague they may be, after things unseen and eternal.

These powers of reason, choice, and will, are revealed to us by our consciousness just as clearly as the power to push and pull, and thus to act on matter around us. The lower consciousness gives birth to Natural Science, and replaces dreamy, transient phenomena by substances endued with force, or permanent subjects and objects of human thought. The higher gives birth to Moral Science, and involves issues no less wide, and still more important. To such a power of internal reasonable choice, the "must" of purely mechanical forces can never apply.

Is man only like a piece of sea-weed, driven and

drifted to and fro blindly, and without choice, by the force of circumstances, by some "environment" of things without and around him? Then reason would be dethroned, and all ideas of right and wrong be an illusive dream. He would be no person, but only a thing. Against such a false view of his nature, the spirit of man within him bears perpetual witness. Various objects of choice, good for food, and pleasant to the mental vision, are spread around him like the trees in Paradise. But another grows continually, closely planted by their side, the tree of knowledge of good and evil. Man's consciousness of reason, and of the power of inward choice, forbids him to believe that he is chained by any physical laws or fatal necessity. But because his powers are nobler and higher than mechanical forces can define, is he therefore wholly lawless? To such a conclusion his own reason is no less opposed. Chance is only the reflection on the outer world of that ignorance, which stifles the instinct that points ever to causes, force and substance, and is content to gaze idly on appearances alone. Fate, with its series of physical and necessary laws that admit no choice, and are blindly obeyed, is the enlarged reflection of that stage of inward thought, wherein men are conscious of power, and trace out its cosmical results, but forget or deny their own higher consciousness of reason and will. Yet this consciousness is just as clear and simple as the other. When once awake, and simply obeyed in its teaching, it reveals a vision higher than all physical law, of Right, Duty, and Goodness, of moral laws which ought to be observed, and still may be perversely disobeyed. Man's internal consciousness then rises to a higher stage, and becomes a conscience. He feels himself to be parted by a wide chasm, which no subtle reasonings of comparative anatomy can bridge over, from the beasts of the field. He recognizes in himself powers and answering obligations of a higher kind,

"God's image, not imparted to the brute."

"Must" and "ought" are like watchwords and inscriptions on the standards of two vast and mighty empires. The first includes under its sway the countless range of material and lifeless things; the second and higher, all the actions and mutual relations of men, or of beings endued, like men, with choice and reason. The two are equal in breadth, for all outward things are objects of human thought, and the higher law extends to all the thoughts as well as actions of men. But the moral empire is nobler than the physical, and contains more complex and more weighty truths. The intuition "I ought," or "I ought not," follows as immediately on the consciousness of our own powers of reflection and choice, as the intuition of persons and of things endued with force on our consciousness of power and muscular action.

The general sense of Duty, as distinct from the clear discernment of *what* is right to be done, is thus a fundamental instinct of human thought. Even those who tell us that we *ought* not to recognize it, recognize it themselves in that denial. No sooner do they strive to displace it, than it reappears. If they resolve morals into a sum of arithmetic, a calculation of pleasures, the accountant may do his work, and add up his imaginary total, but where is the obligation, the mainspring of action? We must fall back on some intuition of right and wrong. Conditions are assigned that "utility may gain the efficacy *it ought to have*." "Those eternal and irresistible sentiments, to seek pleasure and avoid pain, ought to be the great study of the moralist." " We ought not to hold utility responsible for mistakes contrary to its nature." "Every one must judge for himself; such is the fact, and such it ought to be." "A man is bound by the general utility of engagements." (*Bentham's Theory*, etc.) Those who erect the calculation of results, in pleasure and pain, into the sole test of morality, are thus compelled silently to own a fundamental conception of right and wrong, the "ought" and "ought not" of man's conscience. Without this their principle cannot work, and all their calculations are thrown away.

On this grand intuition of the heart and conscience, the doctrine of man's responsibility rests as its sure foundation. But three different causes have sometimes clouded the perception of its unassailable truth.

The first of these is the dispute on Liberty and necessity, the connection between choice or volition, and the motives by which that choice is determined. It is urged by one class of reasoners, that pure indifference, in which some place the freedom of the will, is inconceivable and impossible; that every event must have a sufficient reason, that motives enter into every act of judgment, and some act of judgment must precede and determine every act of the will. They ridicule the idea that a power of acting from pure caprice, with no reason at all, can be the grand privilege of a moral agent, without which he becomes a machine. Such a doctrine, they hold, makes foresight of human actions inconceivable. After chance has been banished from physics by the growth of science, it would set up its throne once more in the higher field of morals, and thus consign the whole world of human action and thought to chaos and darkness.

This reasoning of necessitarians against a liberty of pure caprice and indifference is just and decisive. But when some of them would infer that the will of man is determined wholly by outward circumstances, and thus bind down all human life in a chain of physical constraint and co-action, they enthrone blind Fate instead of Chance, and err equally on the other side. There is a path of truth, in harmony with conscience and experience, which lies evenly between these extremes. The will is determined by motives, it is true. But these motives are not like weights in the market, or coins on the merchant's counter, fixed and constant in their relative force and weight, in all circumstances, and for men and characters of every kind. They decide the acts of the will; but their relative force depends on something deeper than the will, the moral state, the disposition and character, of the agent to whom they appeal. Men are sensual, prudent, honourable, or holy, as the motives which chiefly prevail with them are momentary pleasure, remote prospects of worldly gain, the highest principles of conduct habitually recognized among their fellows, or love of moral good and hatred of moral evil, quickened by meditation on eternal things. This dependence of motives for their practical force on the moral character, on the state of the heart, is taught alike by heathen moralists and the word of God. The maxim — "Trahit sua quemque voluptas," has its counterpart in the weighty text: "All we like sheep have gone astray; we have turned *every one to his own way.*" Man's choice of his own path determines, to a great extent, the class of motives which have the nearest access, hour by hour, to guide and determine the separate acts of his will. The temptations and urgencies of evil thicken and crowd around him in a downward path, till they hold him in a bondage like the chains of fate. The beauties and the joys of virtue, the good land of hope and heavenly blessing, open around him, in brighter and brighter vision, in that "way of life" which is "above to the wise." And they issue in that service which is perfect freedom, and in the liberty of that perfect law of moral goodness, whose seat, in the words of Hooker, is the bosom of God, and her voice the harmony of the world.

A second cause which has obscured the certainty of the ground of morals, and therefore the fact of man's responsibility, is the disputes of moralists themselves on the exact nature and definition of moral right and wrong. Some make the moral rightness of actions depend wholly on beneficial consequences without, others on conformity to a sense, an instinct, or a natural pre-eminence of conscience, within; others, again, on obedience to the will of a Supreme and Absolute Lawgiver. If moral distinctions, it may be asked, are a self-evident and fundamental fact, how can there have been such persistent debates on their grounds and true nature for two thousand years?

To this objection, without plunging into the thick of those controversies which have raged so long and so fiercely, there is a simple reply. For let us assume the truth of moral distinctions, of moral good and evil in human actions, and three results must surely follow. Actions good and right must be best suited to man's own nature and constitution; they must tend, in their result, to the general happiness and welfare; and if there be, as all but atheists believe, a Being supremely good, on whom all created goodness depends, they must be in agreement with His good and acceptable and perfect will. Their fibres and rootlets may be manifold, but these are the three main taproots by which they fix themselves deep in the whole system of actual things.

Now since, on every sensible view, these three main attributes of all right action must co-exist, is it surprising that there should be diverse views of their priority and dependence, and their exact relation to each other? Such discords are like those of political schools, whether King, Lords, and Commons,—Lords, King, and Commons,—or Commons, Lords, and King, is the truest and soundest form of expression, and order of precedence, in a constitutional monarchy. Each view, when urged to the exclusion of the rest, tends to a fatal issue. One would blot out the conscience, and degrade men into slaves of an immoral superstition; another would puff them up with self-conceited and vain-glorious pride; another tends rapidly to a democratic tyranny of sensual pleasures. But when these extremes are set aside, even should we fail to see clearly and define exactly the order and dependence of the three truths, they will still conspire and agree together in their main lesson. They form a threefold cord, which cannot be broken, to confirm the moral responsibility of man, and the reality of the eternal contrast between moral good and moral evil.

Another source of moral scepticism has been the immense diversity on particular questions of right and wrong, among different classes, in various countries, and in different ages of the world. Such facts have been urged by Locke against innate ideas, and Hume and others have carried the argument still further. But a full reply may be drawn from the parallel case of bodily vision. Take the case of some building or landscape. In spite of Berkeley's inferences from a theory of vision, now abandoned, no one seriously doubts the existence of such objects, and our power of actually seeing them and tracing their real outlines. Yet on how many varying elements does this vision depend! To what a number of mischances or hindrances it is exposed! We see the building in clear daylight, but at midnight we cannot see it. In twilight, and at a distance, its outlines are dim and faint, and almost disappear. Its appearance varies with the point of sight, the direction and level, of each observer. We fail to see it, even in the daytime, in thick fog and mist. The blind cannot see it at all, the short-sighted, the blear-eyed, see it confusedly. It is hard to see it plainly when the eyes are weak, or dazzled with excessive sunlight, or even when some deep emotion has filled them with tears. Yet amidst all these casualties and disturbances, and partly by means of them, we believe without doubt in the reality of the fields or the building on which we gaze.

The same explanation will apply to seeming contrasts and incongruities in the diversities of moral judgment. More is needed than a real object alone, to secure harmony of view, and perfect vision. The eye must be single, that the body, the whole moral being, may be full of light. The atmosphere must be so clear as not to hinder a healthy eye from discovering the real features of the object. And even when the means of vision are perfect, the same object may be seen in different aspects; and the elements that compose it, and form its moral features, will thus be grouped in varying proportion and perspective to different minds.

The perceptions, then, of conscience are no less real than those of sense and outward vision. There is a right and wrong in actions, no less than a contrast of straight, and curved or crooked lines. The laws of moral duty, which men endowed with choice and reason ought to obey, are higher in kind, but not less real, than the law of gravitation which guides each planet in its orbit, and which it cannot choose but obey. The world of moral thought and action, based on these higher truths, is not less wide, and still nobler and worthier of our research, than that world of space and mechanical force in which geometry makes its discoveries, and where physical laws of attraction and repulsion bear rule.

Man, then, is responsible, but to whom? First of all, to his fellow-men. This is a truth confirmed by the whole structure of society, and the enactment of public laws both in ancient and modern times. Man, by his actions, can benefit or injure his fellow-men. In one case there is a wrong and offence that demands reparation; in the other a benefit, to which, except in special cases, the recipient has no claim. But outward law can act decisively in the former case alone. It can forbid injuries, as a direct wrong. But the obligation of direct well-doing it can ratify in the case of contracts and promises or definite family relationships alone. Man cannot read the heart. And hence responsibility to our fellow-men, that of which they have right to take cognizance for themselves, does not extend to the secret thoughts, but only to the words and actions, by which we affect their state for good or evil. All the complex literature of jurisprudence, the codes of Roman and modern law, the acts of senates and parliaments, the byelaws of countless associations, bear witness in a thousand ways to the same doctrine, that man, as a social being, is and must be responsible to his fellow-men.

But the law of duty has a wider range, and a further claim. Each man can know for himself what his fellows cannot know, the secret thoughts and desires of his own heart. The obligation which lies on his conscience, and to which it responds, whenever it is not sunk in the stupor of vice and sin, is to seek for himself the highest attainable good, or the moral perfection of his whole being. Now this must include the cleansing and maintaining in purity all the hidden springs of thought and feeling within. For this, and nothing less, he must be responsible to his own conscience. The voice which speaks to him dimly from his own heart, more clearly in a divine message, is this: "Whatsoever things are true, whatsoever things are honest, whatsoever things are pure, whatsoever things are lovely, whatsoever things are of good report, if there be any virtue, and if there be any praise, think on these things." This grand, unalterable law of duty bends down over his spirit wherever he goes, like the blue firmament, and shuts him in on every side. He makes answer, and cannot help making answer, to himself. Remorse for dark and evil deeds awakens a bitterness of anguish beyond the worst torture of physical suffering.

> " Infected minds
> To their deaf pillows will discharge their secrets,"

and desperate suicide seems often too weak a form of self-punishment for hideous murders. On the other hand, the graceful Epicurean poet of Rome rises beyond his own level to the stern dignity of the Hebrew prophet, when he describes the calm, firm dignity of conscious uprightness in the midst of thickening dangers.

> Justum et tenacem propositi virum
> Non civium ardor, prava jubentium,
>   Non vultus instantis tyranni,
>   Mente quatit solidâ . . .
>   Si fractus illabatur orbis,
>   Impavidum ferient ruinæ.

Man is responsible to himself for what he has thought and done, whether of good or evil. A still small voice from his own conscience speaks to him in solitude, and sometimes, in slumberings on his bed, visits him even in his dreams. It speaks to him in silent, lonely hours of night, whether in the cottage homes of the poor, or in halls of courtly pomp and luxury;—

> In watches in the dead, the dark, when clocks
> Throb thunder through the palace floors, and cry
> On flying Time with all their silver tongues.

That voice tells him of duties neglected, of ill words spoken, and ill deeds done. It brings in review before him the follies of childhood, the vices or crimes of later years, and passes sentence upon them. It reminds him, like a judge, of golden hours misspent, and noble opportunities wasted and misimproved. And whenever the misdoing has been gross and flagrant, the guilty past pursues the soul with its warning and condemning voice, like the avenger of blood, till it cries out in the bitterness of its anguish, and looks round in vain for some city of refuge.

Man, then, is responsible for his actions to society, and both for thoughts and actions to his own conscience. But is he responsible to himself alone? Have we reached the limit in our upward ascent; when man, being lord of nature, sees above him a firm and sure law of the good and right, a "categorical imperative" which he may transgress, but still is bound to obey? Is it or is it not a truth of reason as well as revelation, that there is a Moral Governor, "who sitteth in the heavens over all from the beginning," so that "every one of us shall give account of himself to God"?

The starting-point of all science is that absolute ignorance to which the Positive Philosophy, as defined by its founder, would condemn us, when it excludes cause, force, and substance, as metaphysical ideas, and would confine us to note and register phenomena alone. This is the stage of infancy or idiot dreaminess, when Chance reigns without, and ignorance and utter nescience within. The first stage of ascent is reached by its wiser English disciples, when one forbidden idea, that of physical force, the cause o. motion, and perhaps a second, that of substance, has been welcomed back with honour. The research after forces is no longer proscribed, but made the very definition and key of true philosophy. This is the stage of Physical Science. But when attractive and repulsive force, performi.g a masquerade of ceaseless transformation, is made the key to vital action, and even to human reason and intelligence, this Science turns to foolishness, and is found in league and partnership with Moral Nescience.

We rise higher, and enter the field of Moral Science. The "must" of natural compulsion is replaced by the "ought," "thou shalt," and "thou shalt not," of moral duty. We escape from a tyranny of force and blind fate into a higher realm of moral freedom, where pure affections, virtuous deeds, high imaginings of hope, and free actings of love, are attainable if not attained, and have their proper home. The dreary wilderness is passed, where mere THINGS are whirled about, like the sand-drifts of Arabia, by forces as blind as themselves, and we seem to gaze on a better land,

> Where bright aërial spirits live insphered
> In regions calm of mild and serene air,
> Above the smoke and stir of this dim spot,
> Which men call earth.

But our upward journey is not ended. We must reach the third and last stage of Spiritual or Theological Science, before the doctrine of man's responsibility can be seen in all its solemn grandeur, or the deeper instincts of the conscience can be fulfilled, and the longing of man's spirit for light and truth can obtain a haven of intellectual repose.

And first, all Physical Science is founded on the conception of force or power, the cause of motion and physical change, which we are conscious of in ourselves, and perceive in persons and things around us. But the force of which we are conscious, and the other forces we observe in all nature, are limited, local, variable. The persons and things which have force not only act, but are acted upon; they are passive and dependent. The same law of reason, which carries us on from phenomena to causes of motion, that is, forces, carries us on from these limited causes or forces, these mutable, passive things around us, and from ourselves, who are feeble and passive also, to a great First Cause, the Fountain of all power, the Almighty, on whom these finite forces and causes depend.

Again, we are conscious, not only of force or power to act, but of reason and will. By this we feel raised to a higher level of being than the lifeless things which move and are moved without choice, or even than those lower forms of animated life, where acts of choice seem due, not to reflection, but to sensation and instinct alone. But our reason is imperfect, our wisdom like a mote in a great world of truth that lies undiscovered around us. Our weakness and our ignorance force on us the conception of a higher wisdom than our own, of a Being All-wise, on whom all the streamlets of human wisdom depend.

In the third place, we are conscious in ourselves that the actings of our power are guided and controlled by thought, reflection, and knowledge, by motives and aims that have gone before the decision. The most natural form of action, to our judgment, is not blind, capricious, and without motive, but such as knowledge and wisdom are guiding to some chosen and worthy aim. Now the things around us contain in themselves no signs of choice or final causes, and the choice in the actions of animals has limits far narrower than in human agents. Yet how small a part of the universe, in point of physical force, are all mankind! It has been said, perhaps truly, that the electric forces concealed and balanced in a drop of water, are enough to create a terrible thunderstorm. Now take our planet, and divide it into a thousand parts. Take one of these, and divide it a second time. Take one of these and divide it a third time. Do the same a fourth time. Take this homœopathic fragment and divide it a fifth time. Then at last we have come down to the quantum of matter which makes up the whole race of mankind. Divide this cosmical speck into a thousand parts. Do this a second time, and do it a third time. Then only we have reached the amount of the corporeal organism of a Bacon, or a Newton, or a Herschel, who can weigh the earth and measure the sun, probe the depths of the starry spaces, and unlock the secrets of the universe. In this little speck of matter force is united with and guided by thought, and we feel how it towers immensely in dignity over whole worlds of matter alone.

> Mind, mind alone, bear witness, heaven and earth,
> The living fountains in itself contains
> Of beauteous and sublime . . .

But shall we associate force with mind and reason in ourselves, and leave it blind and reasonless in its whole range, except this infinitesimal point of matter which belongs to mankind? Sound reason, true philosophy, repels the fancy with disdain. It sees a beauty and wisdom in the universe, which it denies to the material, chemical elements themselves. It speaks by the lips of its greatest discoverer: "This most beautiful system of sun, planets, and comets, could only proceed from the counsel and dominion of an intelligent and powerful being." And thus we have a third line of light, which leads direct to the throne of an All-wise God. The vast forces and powers of the material universe cannot be separated in thought from all design and reason, without violating and reversing the lesson of our own consciousness within. But the wisdom is not in the material elements, which we feel to be lifeless and unintelligent. It must then be above them and beyond them, the mind of an Almighty Creator, who is "wonderful in counsel and excellent in wisdom."

We pass on still higher. Conscience, like sense, by a clear intuition, reveals a moral law, which prescribes what, in the exercise of choice and reason, we ought to do. Man is conscious to himself that he is higher and nobler than all the visible objects around him, than animals, and still more than lifeless matter. He feels that the power of reasonable choice is the highest within him, and elevates him above a whole world of passive motion or mere instinct. But the law of right, the original incentive of duty, is still higher than what he feels highest within him, and claims over it a kingly authority, which he finds it vain to dispute. Is this, then, the true Highest in the universe, an impersonal, abstract law of duty, possibly never realized by one child of man; lofty and pure as the blue firmament, but, like that, vague, diffused, impersonal, undefined? The conscience and heart of man protest against such a view. The consciousness of force and causation leads up to a First Cause, which is Almighty. The consciousness of reason within us, and our conviction of the absence of reason in the beautiful world around us, point doubly to One All-wise, from whom our own reason is derived, and on whose wisdom the mighty Cosmos depends. And now the sense of a moral law above us, overshadowing and encompassing all moral agents, like the blue vault of heaven, leads our thoughts, with resistless force, to the vision of One All-good, as well as All-wise, in whom that law abides as the uncreated light of perfect, essential goodness; and from whom it diffuses itself, in its application to created moral agents, with all the rich and varied hues of light in the bow of heaven.

Still further, the Moral Law, in its very nature, speaks of something unfinished and imperfect, and leads the thoughts, if intelligent, to some further truth which lies beyond. For physical laws and forces *must* be obeyed. The Moral Law is one which *ought* to be obeyed. This is its higher dignity, as referring to higher and nobler beings, who may be persuaded or commanded, but not compelled. It *ought* to be obeyed, but then it may be disobeyed. In this it falls below the level of physical laws, just as in its own nature it rises high above them. It is "weak through the flesh." Perfect in one sense, as a standard, it is most imperfect in another. It has no power, like a physical law, to insure its own fulfilment. It reveals duties, and not facts or results. And thus it leaves a most weighty question behind. Is the law of perfect right, in this our world, always obeyed? or is it, in part or altogether, broken and disobeyed. Moral Science, when joined with Spiritual Nescience, recognizes the Law, but denies or evades the fact of its constant breach, so as to escape from the conclusion that this is a sinful world, which needs some remedy for sore and wide-spread moral disease. And this it may do in two different ways. If sky and earth are to meet, there must either be a thick mist to bring down the sky to the earth's level, or some illusive mirage, which translates earthly objects into the sky. Thus men may conceal and blot out the contrast between human practice and the law of eternal Right, either by lowering the standard into some shifting, misty substitute of worldly expediency, or by yielding themselves to the self-delusion of the Pharisee or the flattering voices of Stoical pride.

But when the contrast between what is and what ought to be is clearly felt and fully owned, this wicket gate of humility opens before us the wide field of spiritual science; a field higher than even that moral science which simply tells of duty, but can provide no security for duties being fulfilled, no remedy for long and repeated moral failures. The famous couplet of Pope is a curious example of the self-contradiction whereby fatalism sometimes attempts to conceal unwelcome truth :—

> And spite of pride, in erring reason's spite,
> One truth is clear, whatever is is right.

In other words, in spite of two enormous evils—pride,

the worst of wrongs in the heart of man,—and error, the fountain of all wrong in his understanding, it is perfectly plain that no evil or wrong exists! But when we see that the moral law of right is and has been continually broken, and the world has thus been filled with evils and miseries, a further conclusion must follow. Either the moral world must lapse below the physical into chance, chaos, anarchy, and darkness; or else there must be, above and beyond the moral law, a still higher and more wonderful law of Divine foresight, of righteous control of all evil, overruling all things by some secret counsel of goodness and love. As far as creatures, imperfect, sinful, or perverse, have come to fall below the standard of right, so far the goodness of the All-perfect Being, in whom that standard is enshrined, must exceed the perfection of the mere lawgiver; and include higher elements, the justice that executes righteous judgment, and the mercy that pours upon the sin-laden and the weary its floods of heavenly grace.

True philosophy, then, rises from phenomena to physical force, the key of all natural science, and thence to reason, choice, will, and duty, the ground and firm basis of moral science. It then discovers the humbling fact that duty has been transgressed, and its laws forgotten, despised, or widely reversed, by the Positive philosopher's " new Supreme Being," the highly gifted, but erring and guilty children of men. Thus it reveals three great wants, that must be felt by every thoughtful mind, dwelling in such a world of moral disorder and confusion, and which need to be supplied from a higher source. These are, a scheme of Divine Providence, by which all the moral disorder of a sinful world may be controlled ; a Righteous Judgment, by which the law of right may be enforced with effectual sanctions ; and some full display of Divine Grace, or of that goodness which delights to overcome evil with good, and that mercy which rejoices against judgment.

Human philosophy, if left to its own resources on these mountain heights, must soon grow weary, and be ready to faint and expire. Such knowledge is too wonderful and excellent for it to attain securely by its own efforts. The ascent is steep and hard, which brings it so near to the Divine footstool. Its limbs are feeble, and its eyes are dim, through its own share in the world's moral disease. And hence many of its sons may turn back, and dwell only on the fields of natural science which lie beneath them. It is easier for pride to look downward than upward, and to count up exultingly its triumphs over the secrets of nature, rather than to sum up its own debts against this law of perfect love. But if Philosophy in this stage of her ascent be still willing to look upward, " One like the similitude of the sons of men" touches her with his finger, sets her on her feet once more, and then leads her gently by the hand.

Divine Revelation, in the Old and New Testaments, supplies at once to the simplest reader those three great wants, which lie beyond the range of mere human science. It sets forth clearly three main facts: a Sacred History reaching through all ages; a Law of moral duty confirmed by the sanction of judgment to come; and a Gospel of mercy and divine love. Out of these facts flow at once three great aphorisms of spiritual wisdom. All evil, while it lasts and seems to prevail, is controlled by the counsel of One who is perfect in wisdom. Evil too strong, and too stubbornly evil, to listen to the authority of holiness and the persuasions of heavenly grace, will be judged and sentenced by One who is perfect in righteousness. All evil that owns its shame, and looks up for Divine help in its weakness, danger, or misery, shall be lost and swallowed up in a vast flood of Divine goodness and heavenly blessing.

We have now reached those highlands of thought, that land of Beulah, where human philosophy is married to heavenly wisdom, yields its hand to a higher guidance, and fears while it enters into the cloud, and stands on the holy mount of God. The doctrine of man's responsibility is now transfigured from a lesson of conscience into a direct message from heaven, and appears in its most august and solemn form. For here the Moral Law, proclaimed by the great Lawgiver with new sanctions, claims from every child of man a perfect and sinless obedience. Death, such as experience has made it known for ages, is the sentence for the breach of that law, and visits all men, for all have sinned. But for this death, so incurred, a full release and remedy is provided in One who is the Seed of the woman, the Conqueror of death and the grave. The sentence due to moral evil, simply as coming short of the perfect standard of right, is thus, by an act of Divine mercy, reversed and put away. "As in Adam all die, even so in Christ shall all be made alive." But the moral contrast remains between the upward path, in which Man owns the authority of God's law, laments his own departure, and seeks Divine help to regain God's image once more; and the downward course, when Man rejects the offered aid, and abandons himself either to sensual vice, or to self-righteous and unbelieving pride. On the choice of one or other of these two pathways his accountableness, under the present economy of Divine Providence, mainly depends. It stands out in full relief in all the promises and threatenings, connected with the revealed doctrine of judgment to come.

"God hath appointed a day, in which He will judge the world in righteousness." From the days of Enoch, when it was first proclaimed, to those of St. Paul, and onward to our own age, this great truth, in which natural conscience and supernatural revelation both agree, has been exposed to the "hard speeches" and frequent mockeries of the unbelieving and the profane. Doubts and perplexities of all kinds may be started to obscure its evidence. But the laws and jurisprudence of all nations, and the voices of deepest poetry in every land, while they recognize the moral contrast of right and wrong, the need of social justice to keep nations from ruin, and the depths of remorse and fear in the hearts of guilty men, re-echo and confirm in a thousand ways this firm and irrevocable message of judgment to come. The conclusion of the Apostle is drawn from a thousand converging premises, in the facts of social history and the voices of the human heart:—"So then every one of us shall give an account of himself to God."

But how far does this account extend? Scripture includes in it the thoughts and intents of the heart. Does philosophy make a different and opposite answer? With this inquiry I will bring this very brief and summary treatment of a vast subject to a needful close.

There is a well-known saying of a great departed statesman, some forty years ago:—"The doctrine has gone forth, that man is not responsible to man for his belief, over which he has no more control than over the height of his stature, or the colour of his skin." Is this doctrine true or false? If true, we must reverse nearly all our reasoning, and convict Christ and his Apostles of mischievous ignorance of the laws on which man's responsibility depends.

Man, it is true, is not responsible to his fellow-man for his thoughts, but for a wholly different reason. God alone can search the heart. Men may take cognizance, by laws, of the words and actions of their fellows; though even in these they do wisely, from the knowledge of their own faultiness, to limit their criminal code to definite cases of social misdoing. They need to make a clear distinction between sins against God, vices to be condemned with moral censure, and crimes to be repressed by the stern hand of human law. Many speeches and many actions may be morally wrong, which it would be most unwise to make the objects of penal legislation. But the inquisition which forces its way into the human heart, and strives to force hidden feelings and beliefs into daylight, in order to visit them with the penalties of eclesiastical or civil law, is an odious tyranny. It usurps a Divine prerogative, breeds hypocrisy in its victims, and cruelty in magistrates and inquisitors. Thus it turns judgment into wormwood, and tends to bury social confidence, intellectual life, moral freedom, and Divine truth, in one common grave.

But the maxim just quoted goes much farther. Man is responsible neither to God nor man for things wholly out of his control, the height of his stature, or the colour of his skin.* If the maxim, then, be right, the moral teaching of the New Testament on faith and unbelief must be wholly wrong. The actions of men, it is further plain, flow from their convictions of what is desirable, and are determined by them. If they are not responsible for their convictions, then they are not responsible for their acts, and must be wholly free from real obligation to every law, whether human or Divine.

How false the doctrine is, however, must be plain on the least reflection to honest minds. It is true that men cannot fix their belief, suddenly and directly, by an effort of will, so as not to believe whatever they dislike, or to believe whatever they wish to be true. But it is no less plain that a moral bias within has the greatest influence on the decisions of the understanding. The two powers, though distinct, are closely united, and react on each other.

Men can choose or refuse to listen to evidence. They can stop their ears, and refuse to hear. They can shut their eyes, and refuse to see. In the court of the soul, as in those of justice, they can play the part of the advocate, and not the judge; can bully and browbeat witnesses whose evidence they dislike, and swallow blindly, unsifted, all that favours the issue they desire to establish. In their array of cavils and objections to unwelcome truth, sceptical minds can swell mole-hills into mountains, and vault with ease over mountains of evidence that stand in their way. Their heart brings a large bribe to their understanding; and, even in the court of the soul, "a gift blindeth the eyes, and perverteth the words of the righteous." When the telescope is put to the blind eye of the spirit, nothing can be seen, no flag at the masthead, and no sun in the heavens.

The maxim, then, is foolish and false. One higher

than all modern schoolmasters, He who is the Truth, has proclaimed its falsehood. Light is come into the world, and men are guilty, He tells us, who shut their eyes against it. Whenever they "love darkness rather than light," it is "because their deeds are evil." The darkened understanding obeys the secret bias of sinful desires in the heart.

Man is responsible to his Maker for the whole state of his moral being, his beliefs, his habits, his desires, his words, and his actions. A moral unity runs through the whole. The understanding guides the volition, and the bias of the will reacts on the understanding. The disposition leads to the act. Acts form habits of action, and these habits strengthen and confirm the disposition. And the future account, revealed in Scripture, answers to this voice of sound philosophy. The process is not maimed and partial, but entire. The word, by which man is judged, pierces "even to the dividing of soul and spirit, of the joints and marrow" of man's inward life, and is a critical discerner of the thoughts and intents of the heart. All things alike, the actions, the words, the secret springs on which both depend, are open to the eyes of the Righteous Judge with whom we have to do.

Man, we thus conclude finally, is responsible, not only to his own conscience, but to the Most High God, the Supreme Creator, from whom all his high and noble gifts were at first received. It is the parting voice of the wisest of men—"God will bring every work into judgment, with every secret thing, whether it be good or evil." This great truth has, doubtless, its solemn side, on which it has been assailed with many doubts and strong aversion, and on which the space and object of this lecture forbid me to dwell. But, seen from a truer and higher point of view, it is cheering, blessed, and glorious. Man is not the sport of Chance, the slave of some blind and heartless Fate. The world is not abandoned to the hopeless anarchy of human passions, to the despotism of selfish and brutal tyrants, or the clamorous and suicidal follies of ungodly multitudes, who despise all authority, and scoff at laws both human and divine. One who is perfect in wisdom and goodness, One who is supreme in might, sitteth upon these waterfloods, and remaineth a King for ever. He is Judge of all the earth, and He will do right. The dark shadows, that veil His uprightness from sinful eyes, will be cleared away. Man, by the fact that he is called to stand in judgment, will assume the dignity which a false philosophy obscures, of a being made in the likeness of his God. The mystery of the long-endurance of evil will then be explained. The fragments of Providence, that seemed trivial and worthless, will be gathered up, and none be lost. No tear of repentant sorrow, no breathing of desire after the good and right, will be forgotten. No cup of cold water, given in genuine charity, shall lose its due notice and reward. The moral gems that were hidden in darkness will be brought to light, and help to form a royal diadem for the King of kings. The flowers of tender affection and loving thoughtfulness, the gentle charities of domestic life, with every variety of the delicate fragrance of Christian love, shall blush unseen no longer, nor be buried in the darkness of the grave; but will shine in garlands of immortal beauty, transplanted to the Paradise of God. The light that has been sown for the righteous in the painful discipline of this mortal life, and watered so often with tears of bitter sorrow, shall then yield its full harvest of blessing. That solemn account must be to every child of man most deeply humbling; to the sinful and unholy it may be solemnly severe. But it will be, and must be, worthy of Him who is wonderful in counsel, spotless in holiness, and perfect in love. From the thick clouds and darkness which now surround His throne, a light surpassingly wonderful will break forth on an admiring universe. Then will be seen inscribed on the arch of this world's dark history, as in letters of celestial fire, a glorious inscription, to be repeated with wonder and admiration by all the moral and intelligent universe—" He is the Rock, His work is perfect, all His ways are judgment—a God of truth, and without iniquity, just and right is HE!"

POINTS OF SUPPOSED COLLISION

BETWEEN THE

SCRIPTURES AND NATURAL SCIENCE.

BY

J. H. GLADSTONE, Ph.D., F.R.S.

POINTS OF SUPPOSED COLLISION

BETWEEN THE

SCRIPTURES AND NATURAL SCIENCE.

BEFORE depicting a battle, it is well for the historian to describe the combatants as faithfully as he can, and to point out their relative positions. This holds good of intellectual as well as martial conflicts.

The Scriptures consist of a collection of writings by about forty different authors. They fall into two series: the one carefully preserved by the Jewish people as containing their history from the earliest times, their code of laws, collections of their poetry and proverbs, and the utterances of their religious teachers; the other and later series containing the memoirs of Jesus of Nazareth, and the writings, historical and epistolary, of some of His first disciples. The first series is almost wholly in Hebrew, the second in Greek. Each possesses remarkable literary value, and throws much light on the history, customs, and mode of thinking of ancient times; but the interest attaching to these books arises mainly from the fact that they profess to be the repository of a revelation from God to man, and that they unquestionably are the text-book of the most powerful religion of the civilized world.

Natural science is the sum of our knowledge of the physical universe. The impressions made on our senses are compared, corrected, and classified, and the conclusions arrived at are more and more generalized This science was very imperfect at the time when the Scriptures were completed, but during the last three centuries it has advanced at a wonderful and ever-accelerating speed.

No writer in the sacred Scriptures ever professes to teach any natural science. The single exception is the short account of the creation of the world and its inhabitants; and even here the history is related not so much to teach a cosmogony, as to show that the one God was the Maker of all things. Indeed these various books all serve a religious purpose; histories, poems, speeches, and letters are intended to bear on the relation of God to man, and in so doing they profess to tell what nature cannot teach, and assert that the message was confirmed by supernatural proofs.

Yet they do not shrink from natural things; on the contrary, for loving reference to the phenomena of nature we can scarcely turn to anything superior to the book of Job, Moses' Song of the Rock, many of the Psalms of David, the imagery of Amos, Isaiah, and Habakkuk, or the Sermon on the Mount, and its echo in the Epistle of James. Still these are not lessons in natural history or philosophy; they are used simply as illustrations of moral and spiritual ideas.

At first sight it would appear difficult, if not impossible, to conceive of a collision arising between such writers and the expositors of modern science; yet there are several ways in which collision is possible. Thus it is conceivable that the advance of knowledge may disprove the Mosaic history of creation; or there may be things which these writings assert to be facts, but which science shows to be impossible; or the writers in describing natural objects may exhibit such gross misapprehension of the phenomena as would lessen if not destroy our respect for their testimony in other things; or, finally, there may be an irreconcilable difference between their views of the Divine procedure and the higher deductions of natural philosophy.

Now it is affirmed in some quarters that in each of these ways there is an actual conflict. I propose, as a student both of the Scriptures and of natural science, to glance rapidly at these points of supposed collision. I intend to treat the matter somewhat historically, and to indicate how in my own judgment the several questions now stand. The most important, indeed the only important question, for us to inquire is whether these apparent collisions take place between the well-established facts of science and the clear teaching of Scripture. If a Scriptural statement is opposed by some crude hypothesis of science, the Christian may quietly await the issue; if, on the other hand, some established fact should run counter to a portion of that traditionary gloss which has in all ages accumulated round the Scriptures, the Christian may gratefully acknowledge the aid of science in sweeping it away. It may even happen that the strife is on both sides a battle of phantoms, an internecine combat between the crude deductions of the theologian and of the philosopher, for it must be remembered that while Holy Writ and nature are both unchangeable, man's interpretation of either is liable to error.

The attack has come from the side of science. It may be thought that this was necessarily the case, because when the prophets and apostles wrote, science in the modern sense of the term was unborn. There were, however, certain current explanations of natural phenomena, and certain classifications in natural history; yet no sacred writer ever showed the least mistrust of these. On the contrary, Job is sent to study the phenomena of the heavens and the animate creation; it is frequently through observing the marvels of nature, or of his own frame, that David is led to praise the Lord;* and of another of the writers it is on

* Psalms viii., xxix., lxv., cxxxix., cxlv., etc.

record that "he spake of trees, from the cedar tree that is in Lebanon even unto the hyssop that springeth out of the wall: he spake also of beasts, and of fowl, and of creeping things, and of fishes." The only appearance of opposition that I am aware of, is the attitude of Paul towards those views of the universe which were propounded by some who claimed an especial γνῶσις, and which afterwards developed into perhaps the wildest dreams that the human brain ever excogitated. It was against the rudiments of these Gnostic absurdities, or rather against their theological bearing, that St. Paul wrote an epistle to warn the Church at Colosse; but it is scarcely necessary to add that both the methods and the conclusions of these Gnostic philosophers were the very reverse of those of modern science.

Astronomy gave the first alarm. The early Christians of course participated in the scientific opinions of the day regarding the movements of the heavenly bodies; and their views of natural and divine truth were so blended together that when the old notions of the universe were sought to be overthrown, they felt a shock was given to their religious faith. It was stated that the earth was a sphere instead of a plane, and they believed that a wrong was done to Scripture, for did it not speak of the earth as being "stretched out," and of "the ends of the earth"? Afterwards it was also maintained that there were antipodes—men on the other side of the earth walking upside-down—

an idea not only preposterous in itself, but irreconcilable with the belief that at the last day all men upon the earth should stand up and behold their Judge. Then the doctrine that the blue vault of heaven was no solid crystalline arch came into antagonism with the use of the word "firmament" in the Scriptures.* At a later period, when believers in the Bible had become reconciled to these advanced views, a still more serious assault was made : it was contended, not merely that our globe rotated on its own axis, but that it also travelled round the sun, instead of the sun round the earth; yet how could they accept such a flat contradiction to the Psalmist's words, "The world is established that it cannot be moved"? or such expressions as "The sun is as a bridegroom coming out of his chamber, and rejoiceth as a strong man to run a race ; his going forth is from the end of the heaven, and his circuit unto the ends of it"? or, again, how could they understand on such principles the command of Joshua, "Sun, stand thou still upon Gibeon ; and thou moon, in the valley of Ajalon"? † It mattered little, or nothing, that Copernicus, Tycho Brahe, Kepler, and Galileo, like Newton who consummated

* That the Hebrew word has not the meaning afterwards attached to the Greek στερέωμα or the Latin "firmamentum" is well argued in the Rev. Dr. M'Call's essay in "Aids to Faith."

† Joshua x. 12, 13. The fact that the verses from the lost book of Jasher in which these words occur, are quoted in the book of Joshua, where the battle of Bethhoron is described, has generally been held to commit believers in the Bible to their literal truth. The other quotation from the book of Jasher in 2 Samuel i. is universally treated as a piece

their work, were religious men : the new hypothesis was preached against, and the Roman Inquisition passed two decrees,—" First : The proposition that the sun is the centre of the world, and immovable from its place, is absurd, philosophically false, and formally heretical, because it is expressly contrary to Holy Scripture. Second : The proposition that the earth is not the centre of the world, nor immovable, but that it moves, and also with a diurnal motion, is absurd, philosophically false, and, theologically considered, at least erroneous in faith," and poor Galileo, but for his recantation, had given to science a martyr for the truth. The Reformed Church sided with the Vatican in this matter, and had we been living in the beginning of the seventeenth century, we too should have felt that the difficulty was a serious one. Yet the Ptolemaic system had received its death-blow. The modern astronomy ceased to shock the minds of the devout ; in 1818 the Papal edict was formally repealed, and the Copernican theory is now taught alike in Protestant schools of divinity and in Jesuit colleges. How was this ? Simply because as religious men became familiar with the new ideas, they perceived that the Scriptural terms were still true expressions

of elegiac poetry, and no one feels under an obligation to believe that Saul and Jonathan were both "lovely and pleasant in their lives," or that they were really "swifter than eagles and stronger than lions." For an interesting inquiry into the nature of this miraculous incident, accepting the quotation as an historic statement, see a paper by the Rev. T. P. Dale in *Christian Advocate and Review*, Nov. 1871.

of the phenomena, indeed the only expressions that could have been employed by the sacred penmen to convey their meaning to their contemporaries. To make this clearer, I have tried to put "The sun knoweth his going down"* into scientific language, avoiding every term that merely describes appearances. The best I can make of it is this: "There is a law by which is determined for any particular day the precise time at which a line drawn from the sun to a given point on the globe will be tangential to its surface, and in what azimuth that line will fall." It would, I suspect, be hard to put that into old-world Hebrew; but supposing it had been somehow achieved, surely it would have sounded sheer nonsense to those who first listened to the Psalm, it would have remained unintelligible for more than two thousand years, while it would seem pedantic now, and perhaps a piece of antiquated folly in another century.

I do not at all imagine that the prophets of old had any special illumination in regard to the material universe; that has indeed been contended for, but the array of passages brought forward by Gaussen in his "Theopneustie" appear to me rather to negative than to sustain the idea. Yet supposing the inspired men had been made natural philosophers, they would certainly have done what philosophers do now—speak generally in popular language. Why, modern astronomers talk, not only of sunsets, but of the

* Psalm civ. 19.

ascension and declination of the heavenly bodies, as though the Ptolemaic system was still believed in at Greenwich. The *Nautical Almanac* itself gives the age of the moon at six, ten, or perhaps twenty-eight days, but never as much as twenty-nine; while a well-known observer commences a paper recently communicated to the Royal Society with this startling contradiction in terms, "A careful examination of the proper motions of all the fixed stars——."

Time, the great reconciler, has made these apparent collisions between astronomy and the Scriptures a thing of the past. It has also reconciled devout minds to the thought of the enormous magnitude of the universe, and the comparative insignificance of our globe; and while the telescope has given a profounder meaning to the cry, "What is man that Thou art mindful of him?"* the microscope has answered the question by revealing a world of minuteness unsuspected before, but equally the workmanship and the care of the Almighty.

Among the open questions of astronomy is the "Nebular Theory." My first acquaintance with it was in the pages of a pious astronomer, who held it as a fresh proof of the greatness and wisdom of the Deity; but afterwards I heard it seriously objected to as an infidel hypothesis. Since then, the discoveries of the late Lord Rosse have depressed, and

---

* See the whole of Psalm viii. The argument is admirably given in Dr. Chalmers' "Astronomical Discourses."

those of Dr. Huggins and other spectroscopists, with the analysis of meteorites, have raised its credit among scientific men; and whether it be looked upon favourably or unfavourably by theologians, depends in a great measure upon the attitude of their minds towards modern views of evolution.*

To the anxious question of the ancient patriarch, "If a man die, shall he live again?" science can return no answer; but the Christian religion rests its claim to acceptance in no small degree on the resurrection of its Founder, and declares that He is "the first fruits of them that slept." But while this resurrection from the dead was among the elementary principles of Christian doctrine,† and an essential part of the Christian hope,‡ the nature of it was a subject of much dispute in the earliest days of the Church's history. The majority of the fathers, however, countenanced the idea of the resurrection of the flesh, ἀνάστασις τῆς σάρκος, and it was included in that most ancient of symbols the so-called "Apostle's Creed."§ The objection seems to have been urged that portions of the body, such as the nails, were always being removed and entering into new structures,

---

* The accordance of Genesis i. 1, 2, with the nebular theory has frequently been pointed out; and if any one chooses to translate Hebrews xi. 3, in such a way as to support it, it is fairly open to him to do so.

† See Hebrews vi. 1, 2.

‡ See 1 Thessalonians iv. 13.

§ The English version has "resurrection of the body," which is nearer to the language of Scripture.

while, on the other hand, it was contended that, in order to preserve our identity, the body must be the same in this and the future state. Gradually, what we may without offence call the carnal view came to be considered the orthodox one; and Jerome merely expressed the opinion of many other divines when he asserted that every member should be restored from the grave, even the teeth, for in the world of woe there is to be "gnashing of teeth," and the hair, "for the very hairs of your head are all numbered."

> "Quod credimus, hoc est;
> Et totus veniam, nec enim minor aut alius quam
> Nunc sum restituar. Vultus, vigor, et color idem,
> Qui modo vivit, erit. Nec me vel dente vel ungue
> Fraudatum revomet patefacti fossa sepulchri." *

But the advance of physical and physiological science showed more and more how completely our bodies are constructed with a view to terrestrial conditions, and chemistry demonstrated that the materials which compose a human body at dissolution enter into fresh combinations, and become integral parts of other men, so that at the resurrection the same ultimate particles of matter might be claimed for many bodies; while on the other hand it was shown that a man does preserve his identity notwithstanding a constant change in the elements of his body. Science, therefore, entered into this theological controversy; many minds were distressed, for she sided against the

---

* Prudentius, quoted by Hagenbach.

opinion that was reputed orthodox, but now it will be generally if not universally acknowledged that her strong arm only brought back the religious world to a more strict adherence to the Scriptural statements, for the resurrection of the flesh is unknown to the sacred writers, and St. Paul, arguing on this very point, drew the strongest contrast between the natural body that is sown and the spiritual body that is raised, and asserts emphatically that "flesh and blood cannot inherit the kingdom of God."*

Though man had for ages tilled the soil, dug for precious stones, and split the rocks for metallic ore, he never till of recent times studied the superposition of strata, or the structure of the solid earth, and he seems to have been scarcely aware even of the existence of fossils. At the beginning of the sixteenth century, however, shells in the limestone of Verona drew the attention of the thoughtful, and initiated some of the most important controversies we have to consider. The remains of marine animals, which were now found in almost every mountain range, were naturally enough attributed at first to the Noachian deluge; and though Fracastoro argued that the explanation was insufficient, the flood was long considered to have played the most important part in the moulding of hills, valleys, and plains, fossils were constantly attributed to it, and a petrified salamander was described as "Homo diluvii testis." Voltaire

* 1 Corinthians xv.

tried to evade the argument by supposing that the shells found on the Alps were those of fresh-water lakes, or had been dropped there by pilgrims, and that the fishes found in Hesse had been thrown away by travellers and become fossilized. This explanation was of course utterly unsatisfactory, and even absurd ; but it was gradually recognized that the generally received view was inadequate to account for all the phenomena, and that the majority of these fossiliferous strata must have been deposited slowly during the lapse of ages. The progress of discovery ran directly counter to a universal deluge. It was believed, for instance, that no diluvial wave could have swept over the volcanoes of Auvergne, or the slopes of Etna, within four thousand years. Again, the improved knowledge of natural history showed that all the species of beasts and birds could not have found room in the ark ; while the fresh-water or salt-water fishes, with the littoral molluscs and zoophytes, and the plants in general, for which no provision was made, must have perished utterly. Besides this, the geographer has helped the geologist and naturalist in showing that different animals, such as the marsupials in Australia, or the sloths in America, have for ages kept to a limited region, and could scarcely be conceived as travelling across oceans or other obstacles to the ark in Western Asia, and back again. Then the question arose whether the Scripture really affirmed a universal deluge, and it was found that according to the ordinary use of Semitic terms a partial deluge destroying the whole race of man, or even perhaps only that race to which the survivors belonged, would meet every requirement. That such a flood was possible, even from natural causes, in those parts of Asia where Noah probably lived, is shown by the fact that the whole of an enormous tract of land is far below the level of the Black Sea, and part of this region of the Caspian exhibits comparatively recent evidences of the action of water. This conclusion has not been reached without much controversy ; and it is well said in the new " Speaker's Commentary,"—" The peculiar unfairness of the objections urged is to be found, not so much in the objections themselves, as in the insisting at the same time on an interpretation of the Scripture narrative on principles which would not be applied to any other history whatever. Not only are we required to expound ancient and eastern phraseology with the cold exactness applicable only to the tongues of Northern Europe, but moreover to adhere to all the interpretations of past uncritical ages, to believe that there was but a single window in the ark, that the ark stranded on the top of a mountain within sight of which it very probably never sailed, that the waters of the flood rose three or even five miles above the sea level, and other prodigies, which the sacred text, even in its most natural significance, nowhere either asserts or implies."

The deluge is not the only point of contact between Genesis and geology. The progress of this science was impeded for a century or two, not only by the attempt to ascribe almost everything to the Noachian deluge, but by the common belief that the world had been created about six thousand years ago, in six natural days; and still more perhaps by the wild cosmogonies and strange perversions of Scripture which were put forward as sacred theories of the earth by a series of writers whose names we would willingly forget. At length, however, from the crude hypotheses of the young science, two conclusions came forth with such irresistible evidence that all geologists, whatever be their conflicting views on other points, hold them as fundamental truths: 1st, that the surface of the earth has been subject to changes that necessitated for their production vastly more than six thousand years ; and 2nd, that the introduction or fresh genera and species of plants and animals has been very gradual. Many of these pioneers of geology, like the early astronomers, were Christian men, and it needed no small moral courage on their part to oppose the religious opinions of the day. And indeed it was manifest that the answer which met the astronomical difficulties would scarcely apply here, for the account of the creation was either the teaching of God or the worthless guess of some ancient philosopher. No doubt it was written in the popular language of the time, and allowance might be made for figurative expressions; still as it came forward with greater pretensions it had to abide a more rigid scrutiny. So when the lessons taught by the strata were held to be authoritative, a number of books were published with the object of reconciling the two records. Many of these had better never have been written, for, to bring about a premature correspondence, they wrest either the facts of nature or the words of Scripture. Yet some are worthy of all respect as honest endeavours to meet the difficulty.* The more general view of late has been that the six days represent six epochs of indefinite length, or rather six of the days of the Most High; and the advocates of this view generally contend, and with reason, that there is an agreement —or at any rate a general resemblance—between the order of creation as told in Genesis, and that revealed by the strata of the earth. It matters little in this argument whether the forces that have formed the lands and seas have been pretty uniform in their operation or have acted by cataclysms; or whether we accept the enormous drafts on the bank of time which some geologists demand, or the one hundred million years to which Sir William Thomson and other physicists would restrict them. The progress of physical and geological science, and of linguistic

---

* Among the better sort may be mentioned the works of the Rev. Dr. Pye Smith, Hugh Miller, the Rev. Dr. King, Professor Hitchcock, Archdeacon Pratt, and Mr. George Warington. Doubtless there are others with which I am less acquainted.

criticism, may be expected to give us in the future a more accurate knowledge of the two records of creation. Should it prove that they are contradictory, we shall have to put aside, not the Bible, nor even Genesis, but that ancient and sublime fragment which forms the first thirty-four verses of that book. Should, however, the substantial agreement between the two which now appears to exist be completely established, geology will furnish a very conclusive proof of the supernatural origin of the Scripture history.

The facts of geology claim our attention also in other ways. They necessitate the belief that pain and death were in the world long ages before man trod the soil. This also came into collision with the popular belief, such as is enshrined in the opening verses of the " Paradise Lost " :—

> " Of man's first disobedience, and the fruit
> Of that forbidden tree, whose mortal taste
> Brought death into the world, and all our woe."

It is enough to reply, that whatever may be the dreams of the poets, there is not in all the Scriptures a single expression that connects in any way the death of the lower animals with the fall of man.

It appears also that serpents of the same anatomical structure as those now existing have been found in the early Eocene strata long anterior to the birth of man. Now there is a belief that the serpent's legless condition was part of his curse, and in Scheuchzer's " Physica Sacra " there is a delicious engraving of the serpent in three stages: first, a dragon on four legs ridden by the evil one, next walking in the condition of a biped, and lastly crawling upon the earth. Whether we take the account of the temptation by the serpent literally or figuratively, it seems to me that the expressions "On thy belly shalt thou go," "dust shalt thou eat," "he shall bruise thy head," are common metaphors to denote entire defeat and subjection, as we see in the Egyptian drawings of a victor treading on his prostrate foe, or as we read in the later Jewish writers, "They shall be as mighty men which tread down their enemies in the mire of the streets," "His enemies shall lick the dust," "God shall wound the head of His enemies." Such also seems to have been the thought of the apostle: "The God of peace shall bruise Satan under your feet shortly."*

Some time ago it was frequently contended that the different races of men have not sprung from one common stock. This opinion seems to be in opposition not merely to the general belief, but to the teaching of the earliest records, and to some arguments adduced in the New Testament; for instance, that employed by Paul at Areopagus: "God hath made of one blood all nations of men, for to dwell on all the face of the earth." But the advocates of a plurality of races differed most widely as to their number; and, what was more perplexing, different

---

* Zechariah x. 5; Psalms lxxii. 9; lxviii. 21; Romans xvi. 20. See also 2 Samuel viii. 2; Psalms xviii. 39, 40; xliv. 5, 25; Isaiah li. 23.

criteria for distinguishing the races gave different results. The more recent progress of thought has been rather to refer varieties everywhere to a common origin, than to exalt them into independent species. Besides which, the large amount of attention which has recently been paid to comparative philology, and to the manners, customs, and beliefs both of ancient and modern, civilized and savage nations, has indicated rather a continuous ramification from one original stock.

While, however, the tendency of the age is decidedly in favour of the unity of the race, many of the arguments just alluded to seem to require a longer period than the four thousand years from the deluge, or even the six thousand years from the creation of man, in order to account for the modifications of bodily structure, mental habits, and language. A similar deduction has been made from the advanced state of several of the useful arts among the Egyptians and some other nations at the dawn of the historic period. The testimony of geology with reference to the antiquity of man has been, first, to show that he is among the latest born of the dwellers on earth, thus supporting the order of creation given in the book of Genesis; and then to insist, nevertheless, that man's tenancy of our planet must date further back than the commonly received chronology. This conclusion rests on such arguments as the co-existence of man with the mammoth, rhinoceros tichorinus, cave-bear, and other extinct animals, as seen in the stalagmite of Kent's cavern near Torquay, and in many other old dwelling-places in England and France; the changes of level in the height of Denmark, Sicily, and other countries since they were inhabited by man; the discovery of human remains in the delta of streams in Switzerland, under circumstances that indicate the lapse of several thousand years; and the existence of flint implements in the undisturbed gravel of the valley of the Somme at depths compared with which the Roman graves in the same valley seem but the diggings of yesterday.

It may be that not one of the arguments of either the philologist, the ethnologist, the antiquarian, or the geologist is absolutely conclusive, but together they form a strong cumulative proof of the inadequacy of the current chronology which is founded on the genealogical tables of Genesis, while there seem to be no arguments of weight on the other side Here then there is more than a supposed collision between science and the letter of Scripture. Yet it requires no great scholarship to satisfy ourselves that the computation of the date of Adam, as made from the received Hebrew, or the Septuagint, or Peschito versions, will differ by many centuries; that the figures in Genesis v. have been tampered with in early days; that genealogies even in the New Testament are purposely curtailed;[*] that one man is sometimes said to be the son of another, though elsewhere it appears that many

[*] Matthew i. 17.

generations have intervened between them; * and that the genealogical lists after the flood refer, partially at least, to the descent, not of individuals, but of nations, one nation being said to have begotten other nations.† As therefore it is evident that these lists of names are intended to indicate only the line of descent, and not every step on the road, as they have suffered in transmission, and as we cannot always in the earlier records distinguish between nations and individuals we need not consider ourselves bound to any chronology deduced from them.

I ought to mention, however, that another theory has lately been advanced which even saves the common chronology. It is argued that the first account of the creation relates to the whole genus Homo, but that the second, commencing at the fourth verse of the second chapter of Genesis, refers to the Adamic race, and that this branch of the great family is alone treated of in the subsequent history. Such a hypothesis has the merit of removing several difficulties at once; and if it raises others of a theological character, it is possible that these may eventually disappear.

Here let me pause to point out how valuable to the Biblical student are the cross-lights thrown by natural science. As Bishop Butler well says in his "Analogy" when treating of inspiration, "We are wholly ignorant what degree of new knowledge it were to be expected

---

* Matthew i. 1, 9; Ezra vii. 1—5; 1 Chron. vii. 7—11.
† Genesis x.

God would give mankind by revelation, upon supposition of His affording one; or how far, or in what way, He would interpose miraculously to qualify them, to whom He should originally make the revelation, for communicating the knowledge given by it; and to secure their doing it to the age in which they should live; and to secure its being transmitted to posterity." The reverential student of the Divine message should therefore welcome every influence from without which affords any clearer insight into the manner in which the Scriptures have been constructed, or in which they ought to be interpreted.

The correctness of the natural history of the Bible has generally been acknowledged. The only exception of any importance is, I think, that the hare and the coney (hyrax) are said to chew the cud, though they do not divide the hoof. If these are really the two animals meant, anatomical science renders it still more certain that they are rightly included among unclean animals in the Levitical Code, for they are not even ruminants; but as both the hare and the hyrax do masticate their food in such a way as has led even modern observers to think they were chewing the cud, Moses, in admitting this external appearance, warns the Israelites of the clear reason why these should not be eaten. The identification of the names of plants and animals is not always possible; but there is an unlucky mistranslation in Matthew xii. 40, which has added a needless difficulty to the story of

Jonah, for a whale's gullet is far too narrow for a man to pass. Κῆτος means any large fish, and on the shores of the Mediterranean was often applied to the tunny or the shark.

Yet the science of biology has recently caused no small anxiety to some believers, and afforded no small triumph to some unbelievers. I allude to the doctrine of the evolution of living things. How this question presents itself to my mind will be best explained by putting myself into the confessional. When Darwin's book on "The Origin of Species" made its appearance, I read it with great interest and pleasure. Previous theories of development had appeared very unsatisfactory to me, but the additional arguments in that book, and the exposition of natural selection, made me entertain a different idea of the probabilities of the case. Though Darwin in that work treats only of the lower animals, it was perfectly plain that the argument must also include the genus Homo, as far as his bodily frame and instincts are concerned. Nevertheless I felt no shock to my religious faith : indeed the progressive development of animated nature seemed to harmonize with that gradual unveiling of the Divine plan which I had loved to trace in the Bible, while it offered a satisfactory explanation of those rudimentary or abortive organs which had puzzled me as a student of natural theology. But presently I heard around me many voices opposing the theory, not only as untrue, but as irreligious, while some of the other voices were loud in its praise because it was reputed anti-Christian. On listening, I seemed to distinguish two principal grounds of supposed antagonism between the development theory and Scriptural theology :—

1st. It cannot be true that God created all the different plants and animals if they only descended from other pre-existent forms.

2nd. This view removes God further from His universe, and only allows of His operation in the primitive forms or form at some incalculably remote epoch.

Now the first of these objections turns on the meaning of the Hebrew word *Bara*. I failed to discover any philological reason for supposing this word means necessarily to make out of nothing, and I examined all the places—about fifty in number—in which it occurs in the Old Testament. In each case it refers to a Divine act, but in not one is there any suggestion that the Divine action was exerted upon nothing. While in Psalms lxxxix. 47 [*] and cii. 18, the men of the present and of a future generation are said to be created; in Isaiah liv. 16 we read that God created the smith who forges the weapons of war and the devastator of countries; and in Ezekiel xxi. 30 the idea of creation by ordinary birth is distinctly expressed, where the Lord says of the nation of the Ammonites, " I will judge thee in the place where thou

[*] Translated "made" in the authorized version.

wast created, in the land of thy nativity." The Greek word κτίζω and its derivatives seem to be used in the New Testament just as *Bara* in the Old, with only one exception,* in which it bears the more classic meaning of a human institution.†

As to the second objection, that of banishing the idea of God to an incalculable distance, that objection is strong or weak according to our conceptions of the Most High. If we believe in the God of Epicurus, who set the world a-spinning, and then retired into inactivity, we certainly lessen the little interest we can have in such a Being by widening the distance that separates us from the period when He handed over His creation to the guidance of physical laws. If, however, we believe in the God of St. Paul, in whom "we live and move and have our being," and "by whom all things consist," the sustainer as well as the giver of life, it becomes a matter of no theological importance in what way He created each species, and development or evolution, if established, becomes merely the gradual carrying out of His mighty scheme of creation.

Yet we need hardly wonder at the attitude which religious men have generally assumed towards this

* 1 Peter II. 13.

† The son of Sirach says that the physician ought to be honoured because the Lord created him: He also created the drugs out of the earth (ἐκ γῆς, Ecclesiasticus xxxviii. 1, 4). In another place (Ecclesiasticus xvii. 1) it is said that out of the earth man himself was created. In the so-called Wisdom of Solomon (xi. 17), we read that the Almighty hand created the world out of amorphous matter (ἐξ ἀμόρφου ὕλης).

theory, when we recollect how eagerly it has been caught at by opponents of Christianity, and how some of its ablest advocates, especially on the Continent, have wrested its teachings in support of materialism.

There is however another aspect of the argument. Every student of the Bible is familiar with the continuous revelations of religious truth through the patriarchs, Moses and the prophets, Christ and the apostles, and the dependence of the later on the earlier; and he may fairly expect to find an analogous continuity and correlation also in nature. Law and order imply design; sudden transitions might be due to chance.

When the Darwinian theory of the origin of species is extended to the human race, there arise other objections. It is clearly inconsistent with a literal interpretation of Genesis ii. 4—24; but from time immemorial many Jews and Christians have taken this second account of the creation of man in a more or less figurative or allegorical sense, and in the present controversy few seem to have felt themselves bound to a literal exegesis. Far more potent against this theory as applied to ourselves are an unwillingness to recognize the monkeys, apes, and gorillas as our poor cousins; a sense of the enormous gulf between them and us; the impossibility of imagining at what stage a transition could take place from the brute to the "image of God;" and a fear lest the admission of development to account for man's bodily frame should open the way to dangerous opinions regarding his moral and spiritual nature.

However, I must continue my confession. During the early controversies on this theory there came into my mind certain objections to the influence of natural selection of a similar nature to those which have been so ably brought against it by St. George Mivart. That the "survival of the fittest" plays an important part in the economy of nature, seems to me beyond question; but that it has been the sole or even the principal means of bringing about the wondrous variety of organized beings, is quite another matter. Glancing to the best of my ability over the whole of animated nature, I am disposed to say as the Duke of Argyll says with special reference to the humming-birds: "If I am asked whether I believe that every separate species has been a separate creation—not born, but separately made—I must answer, that I do not believe it. I think the facts do suggest to the mind the idea of the working of some creative law; almost as certainly as they convince us that we know nothing of its nature, or of the conditions under which it does its glorious work." * The problem of the method of creation is a grand one, and modern science lures us on with the hope of a solution. At present we are in the early stage of crude guesses, or at best of partial glimpses: yet whatever further insight may be gained, we may rest assured that the Christian will continue

* "Reign of Law," chapter v.

to exclaim as the Psalmist did when reviewing the animate world, but with an ever-widening intelligence, "O Lord, how manifold are Thy works; in wisdom hast Thou made them all!"

It may perhaps be expected that I should say something about spontaneous generation, the vital force, or the physical basis of life, or that I should consider whether any people has ever raised itself to a civilized condition without influences *ab extra*; but however interesting these questions may be in themselves, I do not know any declaration of Scripture that is affected by their solution one way or the other.

Far otherwise is it with the use that has been made of the uniformity of natural laws as an argument against miracles, special interpositions, and the efficacy of prayer. The constancy of law is everywhere recognized by students of nature, while the doctrines impugned stand on every page of the Bible. It is the connection between the premiss and the conclusion that is doubtful. To discuss it fully would lead us into metaphysical arguments, and in regard to prayer would necessitate a theological inquiry as to the legitimate objects of supplication. I will simply observe that this permanency of the order of nature is no new doctrine. Common observation has always affirmed it. The Scriptures assume it, else a miracle could have no meaning; and while they assert that the ordinary sequence has at times been changed, they assign a special cause (generally the accrediting of a Divine messenger) to produce the new effect. Nor is the impossibility of a deviation from the general laws a new doctrine of science; it is only the modern form of the old question whether Jupiter was subject to Fate, or Fate to Jupiter. Yet the great attention lately paid to physical laws has certainly rendered men less disposed to believe in miracles; but on the other hand it has rendered the evidence from miracles more conclusive where they are believed. It has also a depressing effect upon religious faith unless we bear in mind that there may be influences which we cannot measure with our galvanometers, or weigh in our most delicate balances; and that while our wills are constantly modifying the manifestations of force, there may be a Supreme Will more free and more potent to act in a way which no experience of ours can possibly predict.

It may be said that, independently of these special points of collision, there is an irreconcilable opposition between natural science and the Scriptures in their general view of the operation of God: the one refers everything to His agency, the other is impatient of the supernatural; thus science, instead of hearing in the thunder "the voice of the Lord," strives to gain a clear conception and a measure of atmospheric electricity; or, instead of acknowledging life as the gift of the Almighty, she endeavours to show its correlation with the chemical and physical forces. I admit the difference, but not the contradiction. The world is not viewed from the same standpoint by science and by religion, but each view is correct in itself. They may be the opposite poles of thought, but like the two poles of a magnet each is a necessary part of the entire system. There are, no doubt, scientific men who, entering the very presence-chamber of the Most High, turn their back upon the throne; but there are others who in pursuing their studies feel themselves treading

> "Upon the great world's altar-stairs
> That slope through darkness up to God;"

while others, again, believe that for a full conception of the universe, it is necessary to gain ever a clearer insight into the action of physical laws, and at the same time to trace in them the thought, and to feel the presence, not of a great Unknowable, but of an ever-bountiful Father.

In this brief and imperfect sketch, I have necessarily confined my attention to points of supposed collision, and have said nothing about those points of contact between the Scriptures and natural science in which accordance is beyond question. Yet it must not be forgotten that such harmonies exist, and are ever increasing in their significance; for instance, the oneness of God, as taught by modern views of force and by the prophets of Israel. It also deserves notice that some of the scientific ideas which at first appeared as the opponents are now the allies of the Christian religion; thus the enormous extension of time which we now recognize for the Divine process of creation, reconciles our minds to the apparent slowness both of the Divine manifestation in the kingdom of grace, and of the triumphs of the Gospel.*

While making this rapid survey we have seen that the progress of scientific knowledge has frequently come into collision with the traditionary beliefs of Christendom. Some of these may have been impressed upon us in our childhood by those we loved most dearly, and may be now intertwined with our holiest feelings and our highest hopes; but if clearer light has shown us that they are no part of God's revelation, loyalty to the Truth demands that we should dismiss them from our creed. We have seen, too, that the progress of scientific knowledge has compelled theologians to inquire more carefully into the objects and nature of the Divine communications to man—a thing which, as Butler strongly and repeatedly insists, cannot be determined *a priori*†—and in so doing it has corrected some erroneous impressions. What we have not seen is, that the progress of science has rendered incredible, or even improbable,

* See the Hulsean Lectures for 1867, by the Rev. C. Pritchard, F.R.S.

† His language sometimes sounds prophetic, as when he says, "Since, upon experience, the acknowledged constitution and course of nature is found to be greatly different from what, before experience, would have been expected; and such as, men fancy, there lie great objections against; this renders it beforehand highly credible, that they may find the revealed dispensation likewise, if they judge of it as they do of the constitution of nature, very different from expectations formed beforehand, and liable, in appearance, to great objections."

anything which is clearly taught in the sacred writings as the word of God.

Nor has it been for want of will on the part of opponents of Christianity that this continues to be the result. The storehouses of natural science have often been ransacked for weapons against the old book; the defenders of the faith have sometimes shrieked with alarm, and the assailants have sung their pæan in anticipation of victory; earthworks which formed no part of the original fortress have been easily carried, but the citadel itself has remained unshaken, and the very vigour of these repeated attacks has proved how impregnable are its venerable walls.

It may be replied that I can only claim the victory for the Scriptures by showing that they do not profess to teach science, and by requiring full allowance for popular language and Eastern modes of speech. Granted: but this abstinence on the part of the writers is a fact, and it is also unquestionable that they were Easterns making use of the Hebrew of their day. I might look upon my task as accomplished, content if I have succeeded in removing that idea of the antagonism of modern science and the Bible which presses so heavily on the minds of many seekers after truth. But I am not content to leave the matter here. It seems to me a question worthy of consideration, How did it come to pass that these writers did not profess to explain the phenomena of the universe? So completely is this the case, that it is rarely possible to ascertain their own views. Thus I once took the trouble to examine every passage in the Bible relating to light or the process of vision, but I found nothing beyond the mere external facts, or such poetic metaphors as "the eyelids of the morning." If I had turned to the contemporary Greek writers, I might have found observations on the course of direct or reflected rays; learnt that we see by means of rays proceeding in straight lines, not from the thing seen, but from the eye, just as a blind man feels the form of an object with his staff; and made acquaintance with such dark definitions as that light is "the transparent in motion," and colour is something added on to "the absolute visible."

But in order fairly to understand the significance of the fact that these writers avoid scientific explanations, it is necessary to turn to other professed revelations, or to the commentators on the Bible itself. It is well known that the Phœnicians, Babylonians, Persians, Indians, Greeks, Chinese, and other nations had wonderful cosmogonies in which a mundane egg generally appears, and that the Puranas give a large amount of such information as that India is surrounded by seven oceans, composed respectively of salt water, sugar-cane juice, wine, clarified butter, curds, milk, and fresh water.

The books that grew up alongside of the sacred Scriptures are still more to the point. There was an oral tradition, carefully handed down by Jewish doctors, intended to supplement and to "fence the law." This was reduced to writing by several of the later scribes, and the books thus produced abound in fanciful conceits and etymological follies; for instance, it is said that the Bible begins with the letter *Beth*, which as a numeral stands for *two*, because God created *two* worlds, the material and the spiritual: but sometimes their speculations are more capable of being tested; thus, where the Royal Preacher says, "All the rivers run into the sea; yet the sea is not full: unto the place from whence the rivers come, thither they return again,"* the Targum has the gloss that the rivers flow into the ocean that surrounds the world like a ring, and that they return again through the subterranean channels. Then there are the books that compose the Apocrypha. They are moulded very closely after the model of the Hebrew Scriptures, but in reading them they do impress me as containing a larger amount of human theories of nature. Tobit indeed teaches the efficacy of a magical incantation, and gives a cause and a cure for blindness that are certainly unknown to the medical profession. The author of that barefaced forgery, 2 Esdras, recapitulates the account of the creation in Genesis with some enlargements,† especially that on the third day the dry land was made to occupy six parts and the waters the seventh part of the earth,

---

* Ecclesiastes i. 7.   † 2 Esdras vi.

and on the fifth day, instead of "He created great whales," or "great saurians" as some now render it, we learn that two living creatures were ordained called Enoch (or Behemoth) and Leviathan, and that to the first was given one part of the land, and to the other the seventh part where the water was gathered together. So where 2 Esdras departs from the Scriptural account he falls into manifest error. The pretended book of Enoch treats of "the stone which supports the corners of the earth," and other things unknown to modern physicists, while the seventy-first chapter begins thus: "The book of the revolutions of the luminaries of heaven," which the angel Uriel is said to have fully explained to the prophet; and then follows an elaborate account of the movements of the sun, whose chariot blown by the winds starts each month from a fresh gate in the east, and travels to a corresponding gate in the west, thus causing the varying length of day and night—"the year is precisely 364 days;"—and in succeeding chapters there is a still more complicated revelation of the movements and phases of the moon.

In the fourfold memoirs of Jesus Christ we never find Him accrediting His mission by any superior knowledge of nature; but this was so unlike the thoughts of men, that in the mythical gospels we cease to find this abstinence. Thus, in the Gospel of the Infancy, we read a long conversation of Jesus with the doctors in the temple about astronomy, physiology, and kindred subjects, which savours of the astrological and medical opinions of the period.*

Let us turn from spurious gospels to genuine but uncanonical epistles. Clement, the companion of St. Paul, wrote also a letter to the Corinthians, in which, like his master, he discoursed, among other things, of the resurrection of the dead, using the old simile of the buried grain of wheat, but adding also that of day and night alternately rising, and the resurrection of the phœnix. He tells the story of the bird rising from its ashes at considerable length, and with evident credence. In the epistle of Barnabas there are ascribed to the hare, hyæna, and weasel, habits which certainly do not belong to them or any other quadruped. Space forbids my tracing the scientific errors

---

* "When a certain astronomer who was present asked the Lord Jesus 'whether He had studied astronomy,' the Lord Jesus replied, and told him the number of the spheres and heavenly bodies, as also their triangular, square, and sextile aspect; their progressive and retrograde motion; their size and several prognostications; and other things which the reason of man had never discovered. There was also among them a philosopher well skilled in physic and natural philosophy, who asked the Lord Jesus 'whether He had studied physic.' He replied, and explained to him physics and metaphysics, also those things which were above and below the power of nature; the powers also of the body, its humours, and their effects; also the number of its members, and bones, veins, arteries, and nerves; the several constitutions of body, hot and dry, cold and moist, and the tendencies of them; how the soul operated upon the body; what its various sensations and faculties were: the faculty of speaking, anger, desire; and lastly the manner of its composition and dissolution; and other things which the understanding of no creature had ever reached. Then that philosopher arose, and worshipped the Lord Jesus, and said, 'O Lord Jesus, from henceforth I will be Thy disciple and servant.'"

of succeeding fathers of the Church, or of the Gnostics, or of the later Jewish writers. Suffice it to say that Maimonides lays down with the greatest precision, as part of the "foundations of the law," the doctrine of the four elements, and the Ptolemaic system of the universe, with its crystalline orbs each composed of unchangeable matter and form, and animated by a living soul possessed of greater knowledge than the sons of men. The Koran has a special claim to be considered, since it professes to be inspired. I must admit, however, that it lends little support to my argument, for it copies the Jewish Scriptures so closely that it avoids falling into scientific errors. Still, Mohammed would clearly have it understood that men were made of black mud or dried clay, and angels of subtle fire, and that the constellations are only lights set in the lower heavens.*

I have already had occasion to refer to some of the scientific opinions expressed by modern Christian commentators. If any one should desire to learn more of the difficulty of divesting oneself of mythic science, let him turn to the "Paradise Lost," that great poem of Milton, a man of capacious mind and vast erudition, fully conscious too of the fact that what he was writing would be judged by posterity;† or let him consult the headings of Cruden's Concordance under such words as Serpent or Ostrich. In a family Bible which I daily use—a handsome volume published in

---

* Koran, chapter xv., and elsewhere.
† See especially Books vii., viii., and x.

1846, by a firm well known for its splendid editions of the Scriptures, there are numerous marginal notes, philological and explanatory, of which these are two specimens taken almost at random. Psalm xlii. 7: "A waterspout is a large tube formed of clouds by means of the electric fluid, the base being uppermost, and the point let down perpendicularly from the clouds. It has a particular kind of circular motion at the point; and being hollow within, attracts vast quantities of water, which it frequently pours down in torrents upon the earth." Job xxxviii. 25, 26: "Water is composed of two elastic airs or gases, called oxygen and hydrogen, in the proportion of $88\frac{1}{4}$ of the former and $11\frac{3}{4}$ of the latter in 100 parts; the electric spark, or matter of lightning, passing through the atmosphere, ignites and decomposes those gases, which explode; and the water falls down in the form of rain. This explosion, as well as the rushing in of the circumambient air to restore the equilibrium, will account for the clap and peal." Suppose these explanations had been found in the text instead of the margin!

Enough of these illustrations, which might be multiplied *ad infinitum*. My object in adducing such examples from other professed revelations, from apocryphal books, and from Jewish or Christian commentaries, is to bring into greater prominence the remarkable fact that the canonical Scriptures themselves abstain almost wholly from human theories of nature. But in order to feel the full force of this argument, it is necessary to bear in mind that the Bible is the work of about forty human authors, extending over a period of at least one thousand and perhaps two thousand years, marked by a wondrous advance of civilization—men living in different countries, speaking different languages; some illiterate, and others the most learned of their day; kings, warriors, and legislators; priests, poets, and chroniclers; a physician and a gatherer of wild figs; the prime minister of Babylon, and the fishermen of Galilee. When we reflect that none of these ever professed to reveal the mysteries of nature, or claimed the authority of inspiration for anything that later science has shown to be false, we find an additional reason to believe that a higher intelligence than that of man has presided over the composition of this wonderful book.

THE ALLEGED MORAL DIFFICULTIES

OF THE

OLD TESTAMENT.

BY THE REV.

THOMAS POWNALL BOULTBEE, LL.D.,

PRINCIPAL OF THE LONDON DIVINITY COLLEGE, ST. JOHN'S HALL, HIGHBURY.

THE ALLEGED MORAL DIFFICULTIES

OF THE

OLD TESTAMENT.

IN approaching a subject so grave in all its bearings as the one now before us, it is peculiarly needful to define as closely as may be the matter proposed for debate. These supposed moral difficulties of the Old Testament need to be localised. They might be conceived to be inherent in its general system of morals. Or they may be lurking here or there in isolated facts or commands. If the former of these could be demonstrated, it would be absolutely fatal to a reception of the older Scriptures. And if it could be seriously argued, it would be of vital importance to discuss it. But we conceive the idea of a fundamentally false system of morality in the Old Testament to be simply absurd and unworthy of notice. It remains that the alleged moral difficulties are to be found in certain narratives or precepts of the Old Testament, which are singled out, and objected to, not as parts of a vicious whole, but as being thought inconsistent with the higher standard of the whole.

If this be accepted as a true statement, it becomes necessary to draw a further distinction. An objection may be made to the record of an act of the Almighty Himself, or to a command or permission asserted to have been given from Him to men to do certain acts. The first of these is scarcely in any sense open to our criticism. It must be accepted as a fixed point in all human reasoning that we are absolutely incompetent judges of the Divine acts. The ways of Providence, as displayed before us in the pages of history, and the story of human life passing before our own eyes, are in truth less intelligible to us than His ways marked out in Scripture. Scripture uniformly declares that His "ways are not as our ways," and are "past finding out." And this is no more than the bewilderment of all ages has been practically forced to confess. Therefore, acts of Divine severity recorded in Holy Scripture concern us no more, in point of debate of moral fitness, than acts of Divine severity elsewhere recorded, or passing under our own observation. I do not say that the believer in Divine revelation has no more light on the course of Divine judgment than the unbeliever. God forbid! But for the purpose of a complete defence, as for the purpose of a criticism, of the Divine proceedings, we are absolutely incompetent. We believe them to be a grand whole, symmetrical and complete, and to judge of a few isolated parts of such a whole, extending through many ages, and possibly worlds, we hold to be simply irrational. We have enough at least of the judicial faculty to decline the office of judge in a case which is scarcely before us even in part, and which, if it were before us, we have not intellect to grasp.

We decline, therefore, to assume the office of judge involved in the attempt to vindicate the ways of Divine Providence. We decline it from no unworthy cowardice, nor from alarm at supposed consequences, but from a profound consciousness that as yet the ends, aims, purposes of that Providence are to a great extent veiled from us; and that those ways in Scripture are simply a part of the very same mystery which day by day is being enacted before our eyes.

But to discuss the Providential acts of the Almighty is one thing; to examine precepts, injunctions, or permissions which He has given to man on any specified occasions is quite another. Of these last we are, to a certain extent, competent judges. Human conduct, and the rules which govern it, are of necessity, to some considerable extent, under our cognizance; and there can be no question that if there are in the Old Testament records of human conduct, and notes of rules for that conduct, which are honestly objected to on definite moral grounds coming within the scope of our knowledge and experience, we are bound to give a careful consideration to them, for they raise the critical question, Can this be the Word of God which either directs, orders, or commands things to which it is objected that they are not in strict consonance with high morality?

In further opening our subject it is of primary importance that we should state fairly the real issue. There is a vast deal of cavil, and of misrepresentation, which we must resolutely put on one side. The world of the Bible is no Utopia, nor is it in any way an idealized world. It is just the world in which we live; a strange, mixed condition, abounding in evil. That narratives of iniquity find place in Bible history is just as inevitable as that they find place in the great world of which it is a picture. We may turn away from them, we may dislike them finding a place there; but it is the sober truth of our evil state which the Bible sets before us, and it will not bate one hard line, or one harsh colour in the often revolting picture. Therefore, that there are narrations of evil things in the Old Testament, I put aside as being no part of our present argument, so long as there is no pretext for saying that there is any expressed or implied note of Divine approval. And I take the liberty of saying that an age which admires the licentiousness of French novels—an age which finds itself day by day photographed in the records of its doings, such as they are, in the daily newspapers — has not outgrown the homely plainness with which such things are held up before it by the ancient Scripture, however prudishly it may profess to avert its eyes from it.

These then we put aside; and we turn to the supposed case of *Divine direction or approval* of human acts conceived not to be consonant with high morality, which we have asserted to be the real issue now before us. That there must be some, however few, cases coming apparently under this description is certain; they have been the favourite ground of objection these 1,600 years from Porphyry downwards. They have been variously handled by Christian apologists. The old school of exegesis dealt in a very summary, not to say arbitrary, manner with them. All such matters, it said, were to be taken figuratively.* But this mode of disposing of questions will not satisfy the honest inquirer now, even if it will satisfy ourselves. We must grapple with this question more closely than by offering the changeable Proteus of figure and symbol to a searcher after truth. Otherwise he will certainly decline the contest on such terms, or persist in holding us fast like the Proteus of Virgil.

"Donec talis erit mutato corpore, qualem
Videris, incepto tegeret quum lumina somno."

And then, after all, the difficulty in its own form will have to be faced.

In attempting to offer something tangible to the thoughtful mind on this subject, the very first question

---

* "Quidquid in sermone divino neque ad morum honestatem neque ad fidei veritatem proprie referri potest, figuratum esse cognoscas."—Augustine de doct. Christ. iii. 10.

which seems to meet me is this.—"*Moral* difficulties" must arise in reference to some moral standard. In the case before us what is it? What is moral truth? Is it that which a man *troweth* to be right? We wish to raise no cavilling question about this. For simply and absolutely we cannot proceed with our argument until we have arrived at some definition on which we may rely. If the rule is to be conscience, we must needs ask whose conscience, for that will make endless variations. If the rule is to be some recognized authority, we must run over in dismay a few leading names of those who have exercised sway over men—Socrates, Aristotle, Mahomet, Spinoza, Hegel, Comte. Who is to be our standard? Or we put it nationally. Is it England or France, America or Germany, India or China, which shall give the standard for which we seek? In this perplexity probably the nearest and closest answer we can receive may be this—the standard shall be the enlightened European judgment. We accept the definition in spite of all its vagueness and imperfections, and we reply,—"Well, in point of fact that has been formed by the Bible, and more particularly by the New Testament." For since Jesus lived, whatever men may think of the truth of the record which tells of Him, or of the Divine honour claimed for Him, He must be still and for evermore the example, type, or ideal (whichever it is that men admit) of man's noblest and best. And if the enlightened European judgment to which appeal is made does present a higher and purer moral tribunal than elsewhere has been known, it is because that judgment has been moulded and swayed and taught for centuries in the school of Divine revelation.

We hold, therefore, that if any European section, considerable enough to be met in grave argument, alleges that there are moral difficulties in the Old Testament of the kind so far described, it is really a case of the disciples condemning, or at least questioning, their Master. But we acknowledge, if this be so, it does not absolutely end the contest, though we think it blunts the edge of the weapon which assails us. For it is certainly possible in some things that a disciple may improve on his master's teaching. But it seems to result that the worst now possible in the case before us is that some portions of that which we revere as Divine revelation fall short of the high standard which other portions reach. Nay, more precisely still, for it will indicate the line of argument we are about to follow, some of the earlier revelations are alleged not to reach the same high level as the later unquestionably do. This then is the real point before us, as it seems to me, and this the true nature of the difficulty fairly stated, after all needful process of elimination.

If this be the case, how shall we meet it? Shall we oppose a simple negative to it, and deny that there is any such difference of moral level? Shall we attempt to disprove the alleged fact broadly and absolutely, and contend that every detail of the Bible, from first to last, is precisely, and in every mode of measurement, and by every gauge of estimation, on the same moral level? We think no thoughtful reader of the Bible will say so for a moment. We think no school of Bible interpreters has ever maintained it. The Bible itself denies it. For thus does one of its later portions speak of one of its earlier and principal developments—(Heb. viii. 6, 7, 13)—" He is the Mediator of a better covenant, which was established upon better promises. For if that first covenant had been *faultless*, then should no place have been sought for the second." "That which is decayed and waxeth old is ready to vanish away." There is, therefore, in Scripture itself the admission, nay, the assertion as a ground of argument and of faith, of the very thing which we need in the further handling of the subject before us.

If, therefore, there are some matters in the older Scriptures not thought to be precisely on the same height of moral level with the later revelation, this is not of necessity a thing to be denied, or a thing to create alarm in the believer's mind. It is, however, necessary first to examine closely such alleged cases, to see whether haply our moral barometer was out of adjustment—the vacuum at the top of its mercurial column imperfect, by the admission of some deceptive air. For then our estimate of moral level will be proportionally defective, and that which seemed to be lower was in reality at the same elevation as the higher. But if after such careful inquiry there still seem to be in parts of the older revelation a lower level of morality, then it is simply a case for a careful inquiry into the plan of revelation and its progressive nature; it is a case for a wise and cautious study of the plan of God in giving to man successive degrees of light in the knowledge of virtue, just as the Christian believes He has given successive degrees of doctrinal knowledge as the ages passed onward in their course.

Thus allowing for such differences, accounting for them, showing their place in the plan of revelation, they may even cease to be "DIFFICULTIES," and become almost aids to faith. For the consistency and coherence of the manner of revelation from first to last, its growth and development on one system through many ages, surely betrays the hand of the one Divine Artificer even more marvellously than a rounded completeness of an absolute moral and doctrinal system once for all and for ever given could possibly have done. The heathen might fable a Pallas springing forth fully grown and armed from the head of Zeus; but we know of nothing in the dealings of the Eternal One with us which suggests any parallel. The mushroom may spring forth in a night, but even that transitory vegetable product counts hours for its development. Growth, accretion, slowness, belong to the ways of God with us; and Time, howsoever little it may influence the Eternal, has place in all that He does with us.

But granting that in some sense most of us may admit that morality, whether revealed or not, may gradually come to perfection, we must at once meet a possible objection. Is morality then a variable thing? May the right of one age be the wrong of another? We hope to show that we repudiate warmly whatever of this may be inconsistent with the Supreme Good. Principles can never change; they exist for ever, the Eternal Idea in the Eternal One. Evil is never good. The false is never true. We admit no paltering with the fundamental verities. But in a world of strange disorder and of darkness, athwart which the light dimly falls, and on which it dawns only gradually, it comes glimmeringly and doubtfully at first. In this matter of which we speak, measured by the age of mankind instead of the age of the individual, "the path of the just is as the shining light, *which shineth more and more* unto the perfect day."

I do not know that this position needs to be fortified any more before we proceed. It seems to me one of the first principles which we discern in inquiring into the dealings of the Creator with His creatures, whenever we search into the actual and ascertained *facts* of His proceedings. To the fifteenth century He gave printing. To the eighteenth He gave the steam-engine. For the nineteenth He reserved the electric telegraph, and that marvellous boon to His suffering creatures, chloroform. Call it Providence; call it a result of a law of nature; call it what you will,—this is the method of His procedure. And what we simply say is, that He, ever self-consistent, gave certain degrees of moral light in times of old ; not the same degree to each age, but progressive light. If anyone question the procedure, it is not for us to reply ; we have *facts*, not *reasons*, to guide us in our search. And when we shall know why the shrill cry of anguish rose under the surgeon's knife but a few years since, and is now stilled under the blessed torpor of chloroform, we may begin to try to answer why the light which God by any means gives is not always the same. Nay, observe this, these differences of which we speak belong not only to the successive ages. In the same age the perception of the bearing and degree of obligation of revealed truth is widely different in different individuals. Yet the truth itself changes not. Its *relation* to the intellect and the conscience changes, as everything that is *relative* must change.

Now let us draw more closely to the subject of our investigation. Only let us note that we are to investigate *facts*, not *opinions*. We are not to be guided or misguided by preconceived opinions of our own or of others. We have seen enough so far of the analogies of the Divine proceedings—whether again you call them *Law* or *Providence*—to repudiate any expression of mere opinion that He will or will not bestow this, that, or the other degree of light on any given century. Our inquiry will be simply into the *fact* of the degree of the moral light He is declared to have sent into the darkness; and how far, in certain cases, that degree is consistent with the development of the age and with what is claimed to be His completed Word. I know not in what other shape the question can be made and issue raised on grounds susceptible of fair argument.

How, then, does the fact stand about the revelation of moral truth to man? Those patriarchal ages of which we have a rapid review in the book of Genesis come first in order. We may have individual opinions, or even convictions, of a moral law revealed objectively or in the conscience which was the guide and the measure of responsibility in those ages. But we have nothing to do with that. As far as the *facts* of revelation go, we are compelled to affirm that the amount of moral law externally given was small indeed. And accordingly of moral difficulties such as we have here defined, and understand them, I think in the book of Genesis we have but few. There is the record of certain crimes with which we are sufficiently familiar. But as we are not concerned to approve or defend the morality of all that the patriarchs did, still less of what we are told of various unrighteous men, I do not see that much remains for our review here, after we shall have said something on the injunction to sacrifice Isaac, and something about the marriage customs of early ages. For, as we have urged, no record whatever can be found fault with for facts truly reported, however evil, of which it expresses no approval, and which for a sufficient reason it may be needful to report. We have required, for the purpose of creating a *real moral difficulty*, that the act or injunction, supposed to be immoral, shall have the Divine sanction.

The Books of the Law which follow do, I suppose, raise more of questions of this kind. And as it is impossible in the scope of a lecture to deal textually and closely with many individual particulars, we will at once group together the principal classes of subjects which seem to require treatment. I may enumerate them thus:—1. the marriage law; 2. the law of slavery; 3. sanguinary punishments; 4. the injunction to sacrifice Isaac, together with some matters in the subsequent history inviting notice.

With regard to all these classes of subjects, I shall thus state the question before us in close accordance with the principles so far laid down. In the age to which these records and these regulations belong, those parts of the world and those races of mankind with which we are for our present purposes concerned, and Israel in particular, had attained to a certain condition of enlightenment and of civilization. They possessed (whether by tradition or otherwise) certain usages; they had deeply-fixed habits of thought and of reasoning, and a standard of humanity and of morals, of which I will only now say that it was essentially Oriental. In all this they were separated from any known modern European standard by a wider gulf than we, except by study and careful consideration, can well estimate. Now the problem before us is this :—Israel being in that particular stage of moral development, it was (as we believe) the will of God to commence a series of revelations to them, which should at first be local and national. But it was also the will of God that in a marvellous manner those earlier Israelitic revelations should contain the germ of higher and world-wide revelations which should ultimately be based upon and grow out of the particular and national. Just as the original Abrahamic covenant, beginning with the national and the local—" I will make of thee a great nation ; " " Unto thy seed will I give this land;" advanced to the universal—" In thy seed shall all families of the earth be blessed."

Still, with this element of the universal and perfectional in it, the first draft of that revelation was eminently temporal, local, national. Now comes the question :—This being so, what was the will of God in giving a revelation ? Would He aim at bringing that race, that chosen race, out of the then existing stage of civilization, of science, of morals ? And if so, how far would He be pleased to bring them ? And would it be by a code which should bring them *per saltum* into a higher state, or by one which should contain germinal principles, rather than rules, which might fructify in the minds of the people ; and being developed by the thought and studies of successive generations, lead the nation gradually, wisely, and safely to higher moral levels, from which they might the less easily relapse ?

I may illustrate the question before us thus :—If we ourselves, having made the long ascent, are rejoicing in the elastic air and the clear vision of the mountain summit, and are witnesses of the early toils of a party far below us beginning to scale the same heights, we shall by no means despise them. They may seem at that distance scarcely above the plain with its fogs, or the subjacent marsh with its miasma. But our recollection of the severity of the effort required to reach that first range of summits, and evade the first barrier of lower precipice, is too fresh and vivid for us to feel otherwise than interested in their progress, or to doubt that they have attained a very sensible elevation above the valley. But if, habituated to the vast sky-line around us, and the lighter atmosphere of the heights, we never knew or had forgotten the delights and the toils of the lower elevations, we might scorn the position of those who had merely reached them, and say, are they indeed at all above those grovellers in the marsh?

These judgments from higher points of level—these *à priori* conclusions of what was fitting to be done in the way of measure and degree of Divine revelation, I wish entirely to shake off. Those early revelations, in which some think they can see some blots and blemishes, I wish to look at in strict relation to their own times, and in their own fixed and ascertained place in a progressive scheme. I am not listening to John, I am listening to Moses. Does the fact (which we believe) that both John and Moses were taught of God, and sent by God, after the previous fact of the different chronological place they occupy in the great progression? Not in the least, unless you assume—the very thing against which I am struggling—the prejudication that all God's teaching in revelation, contrary to all His other teaching, shall always reach the same level. But if it is found that the moral and spiritual teaching of Moses develops naturally into that of John by a process which the whole Christian world for many centuries has held with certainty of deduction, both of reason and of conscience, then the Christian rests upon their combined teaching without hesitation; he sees the same Divine Spirit in both, and he almost forgets, until the unbeliever forces him to think of the points of difference, that there is any difference at all. Therefore it is, that to one who is at all filled with the Spirit of the Scripture, these *alleged moral difficulties* of some parts scarcely bring any difficulty at all. Nor, so far as we can see, has the persistent urging and canvassing them for all these centuries produced any perceptible result upon the general reception of Holy Scripture.

So, then, in the inquiry now before us we reject the form into which—as we contend—objectors really cast it. How far *will* God, in commencing a revelation of moral law, be pleased to conduct it? What precise line of moral level *will* He lay down in the first, or in the second instance. We repudiate the tense in which the question is put. We thrust aside the *future* and insert the *perfect*. How far *has* God, in commencing a revelation of moral law, been pleased to conduct it? What precise line of moral level *did* He lay down? If we are told that this begs the question, we reply, No! The very shape the argument of our opponent takes is this: "I see moral difficulties in these statements, and they make me hesitate, or even refuse, to accept as a revelation from God that which contains them." We are not called upon now to look at other difficulties, but at these. And we, therefore, feel entitled to assert on the contrary: "Well, taking for granted all other matters which are not now in question, and assuming that otherwise this would seem to be a revelation from God, there is no sufficient ground for rejecting or doubting it on the score of difficulties of the class now before us. And in this point of view we have insisted on the right form to give to our inquiry, as one into *facts*, and not into matters of *à priori* opinion.

That this mode of investigation may lead to true results, I think may thus be made clear to any capacity. Supposing that a system declared to be of Divine origin should prove on investigation to produce results on a lower level than that of contemporary civilization, or even a level no higher, or only partially higher in a few excepted parts of no great moment—supposing it to prove a dead, inert system, scarcely serving as a basis, and not proving to be fruitful and germinant of higher and higher principles and practice, even to the very highest—supposing this to be so not only in theory and in the judgment of some who have examined into its probable results, but also practically shown to be so in the history of a nation or even sect who adopted it as their rule, and who have shown in their want of moral and spiritual development that the thing was dead and inert, and therefore not Divine; —such an examination, I say, would lead to a true condemnation.

On the other hand, suppose the system should on similar investigation prove, indeed, to be in some respects kindred to the type of the prevalent civilization of the age, but everywhere elevated above it—suppose it to introduce into what may have been local, temporal, and national usages a remarkable something which differentiates them at once in themselves and in their actual issues from similar existing practices—suppose that most fruitful germs of higher and higher moral and spiritual truth are discovered in the system—and then, lastly, suppose further that the career of the nation to which these laws were given should thenceforward have been marvellously distinguished in moral type from all others, and that in course of time and after many and almost fatal defections from those laws, the highest known type of spiritual and moral advancement should have been developed from among them, and should thenceforward have been the guide in whatever progress towards moral perfection the most advanced nations of the earth have known;—then I say such an initial system of asserted revelation, so characterized, cannot be discredited as to its Divine original simply because, in the judgment of some, a few of its incidental particulars may not reach the moral height which those objectors think it ought to have done, and to which the perfected whole ultimately led. This is the position to which we think we have reduced the matter in debate.

Let us now attempt to illustrate the mode of treatment which we think may be applied to some of those portions of the early Scriptures which may appear most defective, judged by the more advanced standard since given to man. That which strikes me, at least, as most defective and most open to grave objection, is the whole subject of the connexion of the sexes. I shall not, and I need not, enter into many particulars; but I desire, before offering a few remarks on the general question, to fortify my position by the highest authority a Christian can invoke. Our Master said, speaking of one branch only of this subject, "Moses, because of the hardness of your hearts, suffered you to put away your wives: but from the beginning it was not so." I hold this to cover the whole of the position I have taken up in this debate. It is there laid down as a fact, that a certain provision of the Mosaic law, bearing on the marriage relation, and, as it seems to me, by no means the most objectionable of regulations affecting the relation of the sexes, was not in itself admirable, and was not thenceforward to be continued—that it was simply a concession to those who could not bear a stricter law, and that it was not in harmony with the original intent and institution of God Himself. I do not know that we could well have a case more in point, and more suggestive as to the right view to be taken of various other early regulations which may seem to fall below the higher standard of Christianity.

If this be so as to the law of divorce, how much more may we affirm it as to some of the other laxities in the marriage tie, which occur in the narrative of the Old Testament. For instance, we must remember that polygamy, if it is not inconsistent with the Mosaic law, on which I shall offer no contention, at least receives no sanction there. It stands there in the narrative, but it has no place in the law. It is conspicuous, moreover, in the narrative itself as the hateful thing, which we, looking at it from a higher level, judge it to be; the fruitful source of hatred, contention, jealousy, and contamination of the race; the destroyer of the original blessings and purposes of the marriage bond, viz., the godly, pure up-bringing of generation after generation in the fear of God and in undivided family love. In no other light is it ever depicted. Abraham himself broke not the primitive usage without this penalty, though no lust allured him to the infraction. Jacob's history is deeply tragic from no other cause. The kings of Judah adopted the hateful Orientalism, and suffered or exhibited the full measure of the curse which has always followed the sin, and which has darkened Eastern history with a fearful cloud of crime. I think the lesson of the Old Testament is clear as it is terrible, however silent it may be as to the precept. When, therefore, we hear the last of the prophets (Malachi ii. 15) appealing against the corrupt usage of his age, thus, "Did not He make *one*? Yet had He the residue of the spirit. And wherefore one? That He might seek a godly seed," we have in truth the lesson of the Old Testament, set forth in Eden, illustrated by the terrible intervening corruptions. If we object to this, and say surely a revelation from God will speak more clearly than this, and will not permit men to fall into such immoralities unwarned, I might deny that they were unwarned in many ways. But without urging that, you must observe it comes to this, either God has left us unwarned, uninstructed, on this matter which lies at the very basis of all human society and improvement, and has abandoned us merely to the uncertain deductions of experience, which never hold men when their passions are concerned ; or else He has given the instructions of revelation to us in this behalf. If, therefore, in some of the earlier stages of His Word those instuctions seem not to be so distinct as some may think they might have been, even then our race has been in far better condition than it would have been had God in this matter withdrawn Himself into Epicurean silence.

Thus I bring this subject to what I have held to be the right ground of investigation—not to the question, Is there now, might there have been then (abstractedly considered), a higher, purer standard? but to the fact how far does it appear that it pleased God to lead men at that time towards that higher and purer?

We reserve some general considerations on the state of things thus disclosed for subsequent comment, and we notice next the law of slavery. I observe here, as in nearly all the usages of society in the Old Testament, no violent, revolutionary handling of them. It appears as a fact that a certain stage of advance in civilization has entailed the condition of slavery and the possession of slaves. I know of no exception to it in the ancient world. Now comes the question, Is that relation in itself so infamous and abhorrent as to demand instant excision in all cases and in all ages? Must the Almighty at once denounce it as a thing everywhere and always abominable? Such an opinion cuts very deeply. St. Paul did not hold it when he wrote to Philemon about Onesimus. And if it obtains even now, in this absolute shape, any general currency, such prevalence is certainly not yet fifty years old. I am not going to indulge in a pro-slavery argument; on the contrary, I yield to none in the sincerity of my conviction that slavery stands condemned by the genius of Christianity, and that the destruction of that most abominable form of it which has prevailed in modern times has been one of the brightest trophies of the power of Christian *principles* in a case upon which Christian *precept* spoke only by inference.

Well, then, the *fact* again is this, the law of Moses recognized the possession of slaves; as I should hold, because it always recognized the universal and inevitable in human usages. How did it deal with them? It surrounded them as far as possible with tender care. "Tender," I mean, in comparison with that hard age, and those unsympathetic natures. "As far as possible"—I mean, because there was no policeman at hand to watch the hard pressed slave or the churlish master—none of those checks and counter-checks to which we are accustomed. Resolve society into its elements—give us that simple patriarchal form which Moses contemplated, and tell me what more you could do. These boons were given to the slave. One day in seven was his, on which his master might exact no labour : the ox was to stand still from the plough and the threshing—"that thy manservant and maidservant may rest as well as thou." Oh! if we could call up an Israelitish slave purchased from an Egyptian master, and ask him what he thought of that blessed rest sealed to him by the covenant, enshrined within the very Holy of Holies in that golden ark! Then there were varied precautious both for life and limb, and for redemption money, and for personal honour. If they seem not all that a higher stage of civilization might require even for the slave, I should be disposed to ask, by way of testing the possibility, Was anything so good and merciful possible in the swamps of Carolina, or the Jamaica hills, among a people calling themselves Christian? I fear not; and the key-note of much of this ancient legislation of which we speak is just this—*the possible*. What! shall we thus speak of God, with whom all things are possible? Yes, for with man all things are not possible! And unless it had pleased Him miraculously to change the course of human society, more than this we are bold to say was not possible.

But before we leave this subject I feel bound to notice one of the laws which has been the cause of much hostile comment. In Exodus xxi. 20, it is laid down that "if a man smite his servant or his maid with a rod, and he die under his hand; he shall surely be punished." Nevertheless it proceeds—" If he continue a day or two, he shall not be punished: for he is his money." Upon which much indignation has been lavished. And in a certain point of view I am ready to join in it. Am I to look upon one who is made with me in the image of God as so much money, a purchased chattel? We shall spurn the idea. But, observe, all this is beside the question. Here is slavery, an existing, recognized institution throughout the whole world—impossible as yet to destroy—nay, not to be destroyed till even Christianity had run its course for 1,800 years and more! Well then it is a simple fact. It may be a hateful one, but it is a fact, the slave was his money. And though it might be an inadequate punishment in many cases, and though human brutality might not meet with all its due meed, it was perhaps in that age all that could be done. If the slave died under harsh treatment, it might be susceptible of proof and the master might be punished. If he died after an interval of some days, who in those days could well prove it? The loss which the master suffered when his slave died was after all probably the best protection to the poor slave. Of this I am sure, that if in our day we are calling out for the lash to protect poor women from brutality which beats even to death's door, we may well hesitate before we pronounce too surely that we could give a practically better security to the slave of Moses' days.

I pass on to some general observations on sanguinary punishments. Some of these belonged to civil, some of them to religious offences. Some of them on a more wholesale scale occurred in the course of desolating wars. The same line of thought will lead us in the first place to observe that a very large part of the amelioration in respect of sanguinary laws and usages has only become possible by the appliances and organization of an advanced civilization. We are very liable to forget this. But without defining how far the principle may extend, we may see at a glance that where there is neither policeman to watch over our property and apprehend the marauder, nor gaol in which to lodge him, but society has simply to take care of itself, the defensive proceedings must be, and will be, sharp and decisive. And there would be no difficulty in showing how the Mosaic laws interfered with those early and rude usages, so as to temper as far as was possible in that age, consistently with security for life and property, the wild and irresponsible revenge. This is very conspicuous in the interposition of the city of refuge between the vengeance of the kinsman of the slain man, and the investigation of the actual degree of guilt of the manslayer. This was the first step—a wise step, probably the only possible step, in that semi-patriarchal development of society—towards the extinguishing of the terrible blood-feud, and the substitution of the calm and neutral hand of justice.

Similar considerations hold good as to a great deal that is horrible in that Eastern warfare. It requires the severe pressure of the code of honour which has gradually grown up in modern ages. It requires yet more the appliances of modern civilization—the means of transport, the roads, the conveyances, the accumulations of large magazines, the great fortresses where prisoners of war may be secured, the system of taxes which raise from large and flourishing populations the resources from which all these things are maintained. It requires, I say, all this complex system to ensure, and barely to ensure, that which we call, in somewhat grim antithesis, the humane method of modern warfare. How very nearly this was strained to the very edge of a catastrophe beyond measure horrible, at which the very world would have stood aghast, we cannot but remember. When 100,000 Frenchmen fell suddenly into the hands of the Germans at Sedan, a very little more deficiency in the provisions, and a few degrees of frost, might have left their bones, as of old, whitening the marshes. When Paris surrendered, had it not been for the facilities of modern conveyance, and the residue of her own provision beyond what was expected, she might have been in a week one huge charnel-house. In the Indian Mutiny, when a few small bands of English heroes were traversing at wide intervals the vast plains, it was a terrible strain to know how to dispose of prisoners. If you cannot feed them, if you have no spare soldiers to guard them, if to dismiss them is simply to reinforce an enemy already overwhelming in numbers, and you are fighting for dear life, and the honour of kith and kin and country, I fear there might even now be, and sometimes then was, no word but *Death!* If, then, with these thoughts I turn to the contemplation of ancient border warfare, with all the horrors wherewith it was made to feed itself, and with none of the appliances which scarcely even now are able to stave off some of war's most revolting features, I, for one, dare not say what brutalities were in great measure inevitable when once the war-trumpet was blown. Here, then, again, I shall judge with the greatest caution as to *the possible* in that ancient warfare ; and I shall apply with care this question of the degree of development the world had reached when I have to decide upon things which are not eternal principles, but things *practically done* in relation to the existing state of society.

Passing on to the punishment of religious offences, I am well aware that in the explanation we must offer we can scarcely have with us the assent of those who do not accept the ground on which it is based. But, possibly, we may show that from our point of view at least there is a sufficient account to be given of these things. If so, that reduces the debate between us to another question, viz., this, Can our ground be accepted? Is this the Word of God? If it is, we think our explanation of these things scarcely assailable. For if it is the Word of God, if the account in the Pentateuch is true, then there subsisted on the part of God towards Israel such a peculiar relation as never before or since has subsisted towards any other people. Under that relation God placed Himself towards them as a lawgiver, and as the immediate foundation of all right and duty. He was the fountain of all power, executive or judicial. Hence the peculiarity of the history of the covenant-people. God in it interferes promptly and palpably when either ruler or nation rejects or disobeys Him. This was not a hierarchy, as the Papacy is. It was very partially dependent on the priesthood. Nor was it in their power to modify it. And during a large part of its existence the independent order of prophets vindicated its claims against a corrupt priesthood as well as apostatizing princes.

We are aware of the danger of fallacious reasoning here. We know that we may be charged with reasoning in a circle, and with arguing thus : 1st. This is the Word of God ; 2nd. The Mosaic system was a pure theocracy, as above described ; 3rd. Therefore the punishments and bloodshed under it must have been of a perfect moral standard. But this is not at all a true representation of the position we assume. We simply say this. If there was such a theocracy, then the rightfulness of such punishments and severities at once results. If there was *not* such a theocracy, I know not that we are much concerned to discuss the morality and rectitude of these things any more than if they had happened at Athens. But if there was (and this believers accept, though probably they may somewhat vary in their mode of expressing their appreciation of the fact), if there was a theocracy, I say, of this nature, then we have the key to what might otherwise perplex us ; and to what does perplex those who reject the key.

I am aware, again, that even on the admission of the existence of the theocracy much will depend on the idea we shall have formed of the will and nature of God towards man. They who readily assume that He is indulgent, easy, placable, and what in man would be somewhat inert, may think that He would not administer the prompt severity of the Mosaic law. But I confess that I am unable thus to picture the Most High I see Him the Lord of life and death, and I behold

Him inexorably taking the forfeit. I see the world rebellious against His law, and I behold it filled with misery, anguish, and countless fears. And the distress and degradation seems to bear no inexact proportion to the departure from Him, if not always in individuals, yet in societies which have cast off His allegiance. There is, indeed, the other side. There is the rich beneficence. There is the longsuffering. But then it is just that—it is longsuffering, not careless indulgence. Whether, therefore, I look at what I can see of that aspect of God's nature which made the inspired writer say of Him, " Our God is a consuming fire ; " or whether I think of the special purpose of vindicating His sovereignty and maintaining His obedience under that special system, I think that few believers feel much perplexity about the severities on the score of religious offences which God Himself enacted. To others it seems to me that the difficulty is rooted in a greater and antecedent one, viz., the reception of the system in which alone these things can find their right place and their due interpretation.

I am conscious that I am to a certain extent only touching some of these great questions. Yet in the scope of a lecture no more is possible ; and I hope it is a touch that to a certain extent adjusts them into their places. I have neither time nor inclination to allow the debate to drop into a mere petty wrangle about individual opinions as to the right and wrong of certain details. The tactics of opponents generally lead them to rend from their context and their position some few facts or words, and then to challenge their morality or rectitude. Very possibly this may be questionable, and very possibly it is open to indignant moral denunciation when thus handled. That which is first needed is quietly to place back the facts or words into their true position, their true chronological place in a great system. Then look at them, and weigh them well, as tested by what we can learn of the facts of God's dealings with this earth, and not simply by the opinion of the nineteenth century, and we are persuaded that no difficulty will usually remain beyond what is inherent in the very nature of the case, when man is attempting to judge the mysterious ways of God.

To illustrate this point we may briefly notice an instance which it is impossible, within our limited space, to treat with any approach to its importance—the command to Abraham to offer up Isaac. To Christians generally, I believe that no Old Testament narrative is of more unmixed edification. To them it seems to illustrate so clearly and instructively matters of doctrine and practice of the most transcendent importance that the notion of *moral difficulty* being connected with it would come upon many of them with unmixed surprise. Yet it is the favourite difficulty of a large portion of modern sceptics. How does the difficulty arise? many thoughtful Christians would ask. Precisely as I have just described—by making a bald statement of a portion of the fact severed from all that qualifies it. Thus, for instance, it has chanced to come before me recently. "Is it immoral to bind one's unoffending son upon an altar, with the view of putting him to death?" Could there be a more signal instance of misrepresentation under a mask of literal truth? We replace that fragment back into its place in the narrative, and its proportions and relations become instantly changed. We first glance at certain historical facts. Human sacrifice was one of the abominations against which the revealed system of Moses struggled, and for which the Canaanites were cast out. We can only hurriedly place in a note* a few references to all this. How far Abraham himself was free† from some misguided persuasion on this head it is impossible to say. The narrative is introduced by our being told that God by this means tempted or tried Abraham. What was the result? That such a deed was repudiated by God, who taught His servant, as men needed to be taught, the practical lesson how He would be approached. Again, the bare act of "slaying one's son" is one thing, but that highest devotion which withholds nothing from God, not even one's child, is another thing. Were it not for that devotion it is an open question whether Druids might not have been burning human victims in some oak-grove on this spot at this moment. Therefore—if I may say it without

---

* Deut. xviii. 9—12; xii. 31. 2 Kings xxi. 2—6. Jer. vii. 31; xix. 5, 6.
† Josh. xxiv. 2, 14.

risk of misrepresentation and misunderstanding—there is an element of something noble, something lofty, something true, even in that horrible travesty of the grand truth which led the misguided Canaanite to offer his dearest to his terrible God. And that something, that elevation of faith, that self-sacrifice, which lifts man above himself, for his country, for his kind, and —highest of all—for his God, is taught in Scripture, is embodied in Christ, is imparted by the Spirit of God. And the first elementary lesson on this true nobility of man is delicately, exquisitely set forth in the narrative of which we speak, in which some so strangely stumble upon a moral difficulty. I merely touch upon a point or two here. I am not at liberty, even if time allowed, to do more than allude to the doctrinal matters we find illustrated here, and the foreshadowings with which Infinite Wisdom indicated herein the Gospel of the grace of God in man's salvation. " Moral difficulty," forsooth ! No morals so high and pure—no light from eternity shining on the spiritual darkness so brightly — nothing that illustrates sinful man's true relation to his God so clearly, can be found in those early centuries as in the conflict, the agony, and the deliverance on Mount Moriah.

A further distinction I feel it needful to lay down which arises out of our principle of the gradual development of the moral system, and which may conduce to a right view of some actions which may appear of dubious or mixed morality. I allude to such trans-

actions as those of Jael, Rahab, Jehu, and others.
Need I remind you of the fearful admixture of evil
which the enlightened conscience recognizes in our
own best doings, so far as they are the outcome of
human motive and human modes of action? And of
old there must have been yet more of this evil admixture more palpably displayed, more visible to human
perception, when the standard of morality was less
clearly defined, when the perception of truth, honour,
and charity was far less marked and distinct than it
now is under the Gospel. And so, when certain things
had to be done to carry out the providential purposes
of God by persons in very obscure states of enlightenment, some of them (I might instance Jehu) scarcely
enlightened at all, are we likely, are we required, to
approve altogether of the mode of action? There
may be a grand principle of obedience, of faith, or
some other Scripture requisite, which receives even
the more emphatic approval from the mixture of
human defect in the performance. But it is the principle involved in the transaction, not the possibly
erring human element, which the Christian instinct
unerringly seizes on, and from which he derives deep
instruction. And if the unbeliever selects these things,
in order to hold up to scorn the human performance
as though that were falsely represented as the Divine
example, we can but say, What is to be expected from
hostile and unappreciating criticism?

In conclusion, I would say again, the question

seems to be simply one of historic fact, not at all of human opinion, how many steps towards a perfect moral system it has pleased God to lead mankind at different stages of the world's history. We look at the early Scriptures, and we answer, according to our perception of the distinctness in detail of their moral teaching,—"So far." If objection be raised to this, and the query be suggested: "Why? Why no further?" the ultimate answer is the same as that which must be given, when it is asked why at this present moment the world is not delivered. And that is the same answer which must be given when it is asked how came it that the All-Holy One ever permitted evil to come into the world at all; or that, having come, He did not at once and utterly destroy it. We are simply in these things face to face with the great mystery of evil, and it is but playing with its awfulness to ask, Why not this, or not the other mode of dealing with it by the Divine power and will?

But if we cannot give the *ultimate* answer when challenged with the question, Why this degree rather than any other degree of moral enlightenment in past ages? we may answer it *sufficiently* by asking again, Was anything higher and better possible, consistently with that age of the world and the state of that people? Look at them as they are photographed before us in the Bible story. Mark their relapses into idolatry—their utter failure to escape the polytheism or pantheism that reigned around them. Mark well the direful reign of lust. See the hard Eastern cruelty. Could you in that age and for that people strain the standard higher? Why, as it was, it was too high and pure for them, as every indignant word of their ancient prophets shows. Is it possible to mould a people's morals as you mould clay? Let me ask one short question, which will suggest nearly all we need:—Can we here, whatever our moral standard may be in this nineteenth century, abolish brothels and regulate our public-houses? Why not? Why not have a higher standard of morality and enforce it? We hang down our heads. We know we cannot.

So then we look over that marvellous history of the Old Testament, and the more we think of the Oneness of the Great King—one in the principles, though manifold in the details, of His actings—we learn that we have there the history of His Providence in the world illustrated in a pictured series. Object to it, and you object to the whole course of Providence. Nay, even if the word Providence be disliked, then you object to the course—call it by what name you will—fated, arranged, ordered by law. There it was—there it is.

If there are in that pictured series some things that are startling and shocking—even so! But we cannot evade the facts, nor must we call them other than startling and shocking. These facts are necessary parts of the development of sin, and misery, and redemption. They belong to that history of mixed Divine interposition and human faulty instrumentality, which when evolved will be the wonder of eternity, and, perhaps, the security of the redeemed. Meanwhile their character, considered as a model for imitation, must be judged by no lower standard than that of the Gospel. Let our judgment of some of the details be that they belong to a lower elevation, and an obscurer light than ours, then the more blessed are we who have been led higher, and into a clearer light. But even for us, do not we who believe feel well assured that we shall one day behold a clearer day and a purer light, which when it glances over what now seems to us bright and good shall show in it manifold imperfections?

Yes, this question is eminently one of adjustment, rather than of debate and dispute. And how grand it becomes thus to contemplate the Eternal One leading on this world which He has made by His own path and at His own measured rate of progress, steadily towards that end which to Him from the first was manifest! The unbeliever who receives not this together with the marvellous part which Holy Scripture plays in the gradual evolution, may, and must, cavil at parts which to him have no meaning. But that system which led up to Christ, and which has been developed in Christ, and shall find its issue in Christ, is to us a unity of moral and spiritual perfection. Not yet complete, for the mystery is not accomplished, the measure of the stature of the fulness of Christ not attained. And if of old time there was even greater immaturity, we know that it could not be otherwise, for Christian teaching tells us that "the law was weak through the flesh," and that until Christ came to show us the very ideal of human perfection, and until He gave that Holy Spirit which is the only true and effectual source of purity, and until His atonement removed the obstructive sense of guilt, men could not rise nearer to God. Yes, "our life is hid with Christ in God"—there is the ideal, there the vital power, there the ultimate perfection of that moral and spiritual life of redeemed man, of which it is written, "It doth not yet appear what we shall be, but we know that when He shall appear, we shall be like Him; for we shall see Him as He is."

ON THE CORROBORATIVE EVIDENCE

OF

OLD TESTAMENT HISTORY

FROM THE

EGYPTIAN AND ASSYRIAN MONUMENTS.

BY

W. R. COOPER, Esq.,

SECRETARY OF THE SOCIETY OF BIBLICAL ARCHÆOLOGY

ON
THE CORROBORATIVE EVIDENCE OF
OLD TESTAMENT HISTORY
FROM THE
EGYPTIAN AND ASSYRIAN MONUMENTS.

BEFORE directly entering upon the topic with which your Committee have favoured me, the corroborative evidence of the historical truth of the Bible from the Egyptian and Assyrian monuments, it will a little simplify the investigation of the subject if it be first considered what class of evidences may be reasonably looked for, and what not. Among general readers, and Bible-quoting people, the most extravagant expectations are awakened, and the strangest kinds of relics are believed to remain somewhere or other, beneath the ruins of ages, and the tumuli of deserted cities. A bas-relief of the whale ingesting Jonah, or Nebuchadnezzar eating grass, the yoke of Jeremiah, or the reed of Ezekiel, are still with them among the expectanda and desiderata in Assyrian archæology.

Among the antiquities of Egypt, others again have great hope to find the rod of Moses, or the wheels of Pharaoh's chariot—a jar containing the water which was turned into blood, or a mural painting representing Joseph and his brethren before Pharaoh—à la Gustave Doré. Others, not less sanguine, subscribe to the Palestine Exploration Fund, believing that still beneath the Haram-es-Sherēēf lies the ark of Jehovah, and the Tables of the Law—the Golden Candlestick and the mystic Ephod. Nay, so nearly do the extremes of ignorance and superstition meet, that in the nineteenth century any tolerably crafty impostor who could bring from Mount Ararat a rib of Noah's ark, or from the Moabitis an autograph memorandum of Moses, from the salt moraines of the Bahr Lūt (or Dead Sea) a fragment of the skeleton of Lot's wife, or from the deserts of Beer Sheba the pitcher which Hagar carried, with "Agar" in *modern* Hebrew inscribed upon it, a cast from Solomon's seal, or the necklace of the Queen of Sheba, his success would now be as great, and the credulity of faith as manifest, as when in the twelfth century diseases were cured by scrapings from the cave of Elijah, and the Crusaders defeated an army by the grace of the shift of the Virgin Mary and a less delicate relic attributed to our Lord.

Now therefore at the outset let this truth be borne in mind: such classes of miraculous relics may not be reasonably expected; and further, that the expectation of such is an insult to common sense, and an injury to religion. Facts, places, and things, to which time has given an adventitious value, would be deemed of little import when they first originated; and would therefore be the less likely to be preserved. Thousands of Roman tradesmen paid for garlick in the forum of Antioch with the denarii of Pescennius Niger, yet now such coins are worth triple their weight in gold. The halfpenny ballads of the reign of Queen Elizabeth have been preserved, not by design, but by accident, and from the very nature of a certain class of evidences anticipated, their preservation would be most unlikely, and if produced, such evidence most suspicious and unreliable.

What, then, is the class, and what are the objects which we may reasonably expect, either in detail cr in degree, to be corroborative of Biblical truth? Few in number, and often apparently contradictory in their testimony, these are, statues, inscriptions, instruments and implements for offence and domestic use, memorial stones, and natural objects. Yet even here difficulties present themselves. Great nations preserve no records of their defeats, and events of vast importance to one people, are but petty incidents in the history of another, lightly referred to when necessarily mentioned, and often from policy, pride, or prejudice, misrepresented. The massacre of St. Bartholomew, which ensanguined the annals of France, and originated our silk manufactories, is indeed commemorated in the frescoes of the Vatican, but it is as the *defeat* of the Huguenots. The victory of Waterloo is simply, in French history, the retreat of Napoleon; and Lord Macartney's embassy to China, intended to display the importance, magnificence, and civilization of the British Empire, was, and is represented, in the official records of the Flowery Land, as " Barbarians bringing tribute to the country of China."

One lesser difficulty remains to be stated, the want of synchronism, and of chronological succession, in the history of the Bible itself. My hearers will, I feel sure, pardon me if I assume that they, in common with the best and most orthodox critics and archæologists of modern times, will admit, that prior to Solomon there is no true chronology, that nearly throughout the genealogies are selective, the succession of events is often inverted; and that the writers, while faithful historians, yet are so in the manner of episodic narrators rather than that of systematic annalists.

This premised, to commence with the corroborations supplied by the monumental remains of the oldest nation first, there is no country which has yet been so abundantly illustrative of Old Testament history, as the country of Egypt, whose ruins, the most ancient and colossal the world contains, are almost vignettes to the text of the Pentateuch, whose literature, rich in Divinity, History, Poetry, Science, and Romance, is yet extant and intelligible before us —whose liturgies preceded by many centuries the

Hymns of the Vedas, and whose poets wrote epics four hundred years before Homer, and odes and antiphonal lyrics ages before Hesiod theorized in Greece, or Orpheus civilized the inhabitants of Thrace.

When it is borne in mind how early commenced and how long continued was the intercourse between Israel and Egypt—when it is recollected that the father of the faithful himself sojourned and dwelt as a nobleman in the court suburbs of Egypt—that the compiler of the Pentateuch was an Egyptian priest, and, according to Josephus, a successful Egyptian commander, offices which the hieroglyphic monuments assure us were in that great empire compatible with each other,—when these facts, I repeat, are borne in mind, it will be seen that Egyptological study has become as necessary for the interpretation of the Old Testament as that of Greek philology is to the New, and that so far from having to explain doubtful passages and obscure words by searching for imaginary Hebrew roots, a reference to the language and the theology of the Egyptians, whose influence for many generations pervaded the Israelitish mind, will render the most difficult sentences easy, and will, still more in the future as it has to a great extent done in the past, make the Bible its own expositor, and the word of God consistent with its history, its theology, and itself.

Perhaps the strongest of all evidences, monumental or historical, are the implied or incidental ones. Let me, therefore, now give an illustration of these as afforded by the most beautiful of all inspired episodes, the History of Joseph. When throughout this history Pharaoh has occasion to speak, it is always in the first person singular, with a most sublime and unconscious egotism, and without any reference to any person except himself, as in such passages as "*I* am Pharaoh," "*I* have set thee over the whole land of Egypt," "Who is the Lord?" "*I* know not the Lord," etc. etc. Now this was quite in accordance with a principle of the Egyptian theology, only recently revealed to us. According to the tenets of that faith, the king, from the moment of his accession, became hypostated into the deity, and thenceforth existed, not as a symbol of, or a medium immanated from, but the very essential and eternal deity himself. "I am Ra in the Land of the Living," says the king, in an inscription yet preserved to us. "The king is as God," declares another papyrus, that of Prisse d'Avennés. "Even from thy birth thou hast been as God," attests the inscription of Karnak to Rameses II. Agreeably to this dicta, Pharaoh is represented as worshipping himself on a slab preserved in the British Museum—"Adoring his own name" on another in the Musée de Louvre—"Is the third in the great triad" at Elephantis—"Stands coadjutor with Amun Ra" among the divinities in another shrine—"Claims divine worship" on the stéles of Rosetta and Canopus, and "is numbered among the gods" in the Hall of Ancestors and the tablet of Thothmoses. These are features in the Egyptian monarcho-theology which, while they existed in full force in the time of the earlier books of the Bible, had lost much of their earlier potentiality and effect in the time in which recent sceptical critics consider those very books to have been written. Let me guard myself ;—I do not assert that in the Ptolemaic period the king, although of Greco-Egyptian origin, was not still a god; but then he was *a* god—one of many; not THE God—"the soul of the world." The Ptolemaic sovereigns were only by legal fictions Θεοι Αδελφοι (Theoi Adelphoi), but the Pharaohs of the eighteenth dynasty were by the authority of two thousand years sole, supreme, unconquerable, and illimitable God. True, Rameses II. affirms, when fighting the Hittites, he alone led his disheartened army into the very van of his innumerable foes : "Aman, my father, helped me, and Mentou gave me strength;" but then, in the very sentences which precede that statement he likens himself in nature and being to God, not profanely either, since with the assumption of the double crown of Egypt came also the insufflation of the divine essence itself.

When Joseph appeared before Pharaoh, the Bible asserts that he was vested in a chain and collar of gold, and garments of fine linen. True in even its smallest details is this wonderful narrative, for the Egyptian monuments have shown us that what we should call the blue ribbon of a military official, or of a distinguished civil officer, was a golden collar. This king Amenophis I. is reported to have bestowed on his servant Aahmes ; in whose tomb at Beni Hassan there is a picture, which has been several times engraved, representing a similar investiture. In the Berlin Museum, the very collars themselves are preserved, and in the upper Egyptian room of the British Museum, there are portions of similar decorations.

Again in this same history, one of the most affecting and the most minutely accurate of all Biblical narratives, which has charmed children by its simplicity, and delighted the aged by its dramatic unity and consummate knowledge of the human heart,—Joseph swears "By the life of Pharaoh." Let me beg my lady hearers not to be virtuously indignant, nor my reverend friends to declaim against the error of a man who sinned against a precept not promulgated for two hundred years after his time, for Joseph, as an Egyptian, swore the official oath, and that very act of his, which has been explained away by some commentators, palliated by others, and been a stumbling-block to all, is in itself an inferential evidence of the truth of the narrative which contains the adjuration.

M. Chabas has shown in his Hebræo-Ægyptiaca, lately read before the Society of which I have the honour to be the Secretary, that among the Egyptians, as among the Greeks and Romans, certain oaths were judicial, others were conversational, and a few official. The common ranks of Egyptian society swore by their namesake or local gods, and I dare say they were quite vulgar enough to avail themselves of the privilege as often as anything interfered with their domestic arrangements. Priests not being in themselves State functionaries, swore by the deity to whose worship they were devoted; and all military, lay, or cleric, who filled an official capacity, swore "By the life of Pharaoh," an oath which varied with the name of every sovereign, and after the period of the Psammetichi went out of fashion, and whose very existence has only been known within the last three years. Among the papyri in the Musée de Louvre, there is one which states that the slave Mesu, one of the many labourers employed on the canal executed by Rameses in the Delta, on almost the same route as the present (Suez Canal), being ordered to do some work by his superior officer, refused to work, and swore at that official. The words of his oath were as follows—(the phrase in which they occur has not, however, been preserved): "The August, him whom Amun enlarges, the Royal Sovereign, Him whose wishes are stronger than death, the life of the king, the Ra."—So indignant was the official to whom those words were addressed, that, uncertain in what manner to punish a menial who had blasphemously dared to take the king's name in vain, and to *swear like a nobleman*, that he wrote to his superior officer, who in his turn copied the indictment upon a slip of papyrus, and sent it to the superintendent of the district, awaiting his decision. The words of the report which follow are curious: "I have sent this report of the slave Mesu to my lord, not being willing to, and not knowing how to, act till I receive his instructions upon it; for it is no part of my duty to punish him for his oath by 'the life of Pharaoh.'" Hence from a mutilated fragment of papyrus is derived a wonderful explanation and a singular attestation of the veracity of an event in Joseph's life, which inutilitates some volumes of commentational divinity.

Another of these incidental circumstances cannot be altogether passed over. In the Pentateuch, the king of Egypt is *the* Pharaoh, for none other bore that title, as in the eighteenth century the name "Emperor" was always understood to refer to the Emperor of Germany, and therefore his personal name was not generally used. In the book of Kings (2 Kings vii. 6) the passage occurs "the kings of the Egyptians," implying a plurality of governors; and this again is strictly consonant to monumental testimony, for at that later time a foreign incursion and its concomitant intestine troubles had severed the empire of Egypt into several petty kingdoms.

Take we now another example, or class of examples. The Egyptian priests are reported in Exodus vii. 10, to have thrown down their sticks, which instantly became serpents. A painting in the British Museum represents certain Egyptian priests carrying serpent-shaped sticks in their hands, for with them the cobra or basilisk was the emblem of eternal life, and hence that reptile was called "the serpent of immortal years." To this day, in India, the serpent-charmers possess the art, by pressure on the nape of the neck, of throwing the Naja, or spectacle snake, into a rigid cataleptic position. Be it granted, then, that the Egyptian clergy knew of a similar art four thousand years ago, as the Indians have for three thousand, and the whole mystery of the magician's enchantments becomes apparent, for the act of flinging the serpent on the ground, would restore it to its original consciousness and vivacity.

Again, we are told in Judges viii. 27, that the Israelites went a-whoring after the ephod of Gideon. The term is one which is used throughout the Bible to imply a kind of spiritual fornication, and has not a little puzzled many expositors, who generally, like most critics, give an inferior sense to the author, (which sense being the product of their own brain, they afterwards praise him for possessing,) and suppose that the intrinsic value of the ornament itself excited the avarice of the people. The monuments of Egypt and Assyria alike afford a very good reason for believing that *that* was not the case. The ornament in question appears to have been a magnificent collar (or Askh), having, as was usual with all ancient jewellery, many elaborate pendants—all, more or less, representations of idols, or objects used in idolatrous worship. Now many of the Egyptian and Assyrian symbols were afterwards adopted by the Israelites, but others were absolutely impure, and were representations of the triads of Egypt. The jewelled objects containing these figures were often wrought with exquisite skill, and of very great value, were *sacrasanct*, and acted as talismans to preserve the wearer. Proud of his mighty victory, Gideon in his simple-hearted faith wanted common sense, and warped by his very integrity of purpose, did not foresee that by wearing these and similar impious figures around his neck, he was in some sense encouraging the naturally strong tendency of the Israelites towards a representative or symbolic idolatry. Hence the thing became a snare to Gideon and all his house, and was the cause of the ultimate destruction of his family, since the command given by God to Moses was "The images of their gods shall ye burn with fire."

As the political, so the social and religious life of the Egyptians, the Canaanites, and their contemporaries is recorded upon their monuments. Direct mention of human sacrifice is found in the Assyrian records. The sale of families and children occurs again and again on the tablets in the British Museum, which form a class by themselves. That the bulk of the people were themselves unable to write is proven by these documents being signed by the indentation of the finger nail of the vendor and purchaser, attested by the counter-signature of the scribe. The kings of Egypt, in other respects some of the most enlightened sovereigns the world ever possessed, were but slave-dealers on a larger scale, and many of their wars were undertaken for no less brutal a purpose. The early intercourse which in the book of Genesis is shown to have existed between Egypt and Palestine, was not a little increased by this nefarious traffic, while the corrupt manners of the period, to which so many allusions are found in the Pentateuch, are fully proven by an Egyptian romance written to entertain king Rameses II., and recently translated by M. Chabas. This novel, probably the oldest in the world's literature, turns entirely upon the affection of two brothers for each other, the wife of the elder of whom, Anepou, endeavours to seduce the younger into an adulterous connection with her. On his resistance, her guilty passion, artifice, and hatred, all the story turns, and the interposition of the gods is at last necessary to avenge the innocent and to punish the guilty. Drunkenness, incest,—one of the Pharaohs, the same Rameses II. if a doubtful authority is to be credited, marrying his own daughter Bent-anat,—lying, and fraud in all its manifold forms, are recorded in the papyri as Egyptian failings. Despite of much that was good in their religion, yet the bulk of its precepts being confined to the royal family, the higher clergy, and the initiated alone, the bulk of the people were left to substitute a ceremonial for a spiritual religion, and to condone by the extravagances of sensation for the errors of sense.

Perhaps on no one group of subjects has more information been obtained from the monuments of Egypt than on those terrible calamities which are detailed in the seventh to the eleventh chapters of the book of Exodus, and are popularly called the Ten Plagues. Much *trifling* criticism has been bestowed by infidel critics upon the *trifling* character of many of these judgments; but that very circumstance attests the authenticity of the narrative, for things deemed of little consequence in later times held then no unimportant rank in the book of Egyptian theology. Permit me, therefore, very briefly to notice these events in their succession, bearing in mind that the purport of all those inflictions was to show the Egyptians that " I am God," for "against all the gods of the Egyptians I will execute judgment, saith the Lord." (Exod. xii. 12.)

The first and most significant of these ominous plagues was the conversion of the waters of Egypt, local or general, into an apparently sanguineous fluid, revolting to the sight, nauseous to the taste, and offensive to the smell. To Moses and the Egyptians, the purport of this miracle of vengeance was obvious, for the Nile was not only the gift of a deity, but a deity itself venerated under the form of a corpulent young man called Hapimou. The very kingdom of Egypt was considered as the gift of the Nile, and at the annual festival of the Niloa, Pharaoh, attended by all his court, paid in the name of all his people divine worship to the river, the Father of the Land of Egypt.

Popular tradition supposed the bounteous Nile to flow from heaven, and a lustral power was attributed to baptism in its waters. Many of its fishes were themselves venerated, and one species (the Oxyrhynchus) was so extensively adored as to have one of the seven districts of the Heptanomos named after it, the inhabitants of which province wore its figure around their necks as an amulet and an ornament. At the touch of the rod of Moses the water of that river, famous for being the sweetest and purest in the world, was rendered loathsome and impure; unable to preserve their sacred lives, the deified fishes died under the shadow of their own temples; the celestial river attested the hand of a celestial messenger, and in its blood-stained waves was contained an omen of the destruction of the people who stood around its banks, and whose fathers four hundred years before had reddened its stream with the carcases of the Hebrew children.

Nor was the second, the plague of frogs, less significant. Pthah, the creator of animal life, was venerated under the special form of a frog, that creature being supposed to be spontaneously generated from the mud of the Nile, by the vivific rays of the sun. From its immense fecundity, the frog and tadpole were used as the hieroglyphics of a million, and the titles "Lord of Life" and "Lord of the Land" were frequently engraved upon the statuettes of this Batrachian. Hence the people of Lower Egypt venerated the frog, and hence their animal worship was rebuked, and the very creatures they venerated were made a torture to them, so that even Pharaoh himself was compelled to exclaim, "Take away these (gods though they be) out of the land."

In the third infliction, the plague of lice, a no less important warning was conveyed. The sand of the Nile, (holy as is to the modern Jew the earth of Jerusalem,) scattered by the hand of Moses in the air, brought forward this most offensive plague. According to both monumental and historical testimony, the strictest care was taken by the priests to avoid defilement by any unclean insect. For this purpose the whole of the body was scrupulously shaved, vestments of woollen were especially forbidden, linen, or linen and cotton united, often washed, and oftener changed, were alone allowed to be used. Stated and repeated ablutions formed a part of the routine life of the sacerdotal orders, and the touch of an unclean insect rendered them ceremonially impure. That plague, therefore, the magicians or clergy did not attempt to copy, for they dared not perform an act which wou'd defile themselves, and thereupon came from their lips the reluctant exclamation, " *This* is the finger of God!"

In the fourth plague, that of flies, or as the word implies "beetles," the Ateuchis Sacer, or Sacred Scarab of the Egyptians, was selected as the minister of vengeance. This insect was a beautiful little beetle, very harmless, and very abundant, which from its habit of laying its eggs in a ball of mud, and then rolling it to be hatched by the heat of the sun, was supposed to represent the care of the Creator over the world both in forming and preserving it, and was therefore representatively worshipped as the emblem of Kheper Ra, the formator of the world. The multiplication of figures of this insect in all sizes and all materials, from the huge specimen in basalt, nearly five feet across, in the British Museum, down to another in crystal, scarce a quarter of an inch in diameter, in the same collection, was something almost incredible. Every one wore it—sometimes not only one, but as many as fifty—in chains around the neck. It was wrought in the cheapest as well as the costliest stones; from the tender steatite to the stubborn jasper. Figures of the scarabæus were used interchangeably with rings for currency. The living wore it on their fingers; the priests upon their breasts; and the dead, protected by the sacred amulet were expressly said by the Egyptian liturgy to " pass through the place of dangers, and to await in safety all their transformations." But now, at the word of Moses, all this was reversed. Willingly or unwillingly, the people in self-defence were compelled to slay their own divinities, and the twenty-fourth verse of the eighth chapter of Exodus shows that Kheper Ra, instead of preserving the land which worshipped the beetle, by the myriads of those very dead insects corrupted it.

But still the awful signs proceeded, and in the fifth, the plague of murrain, Apis the bull-god suffered, with all his bovine tribe,—that Apis, the first of animal deities, one of the incarnations of Osiris the god of agriculture, and the most popular deity throughout the land of Egypt,—that Apis which was stalled in a golden manger, and fed to the sound of music, with perfumed oats, and straw from golden plates,—that bovine deity, who bleated oracles, and whose very excrements were holy—who was supposed to be born of a virgin cow by the direct influence of the rays of the moon, and upon whose life depended the welfare of Lower Egypt,—that same Apis then became hopelessly smitten with the same murrain whereby the less sacred domestic cattle of Egypt were destroyed. So important was the birth of the Apis, that his discovery was a triumphant festival,—his death, a national mourning. Civil and domestic occurrences were dated by the years of its life; and stored away in the vast subterranean catacombs of the Serapeum, near Memphis, in lofty granite sarcophagi, lay all the *sacrasanct* mummies of the Apis gods of Egypt. These sarcophagi have in the last few years rendered a most important service to Biblical chronology, for M. Marriette Bey in his excavations for the Pasha of Egypt discovered the entrance to the catacombs, and was the first European who for many centuries had read the hieroglyphical epitaphs upon those tombs which had been closed since the rise of Christianity.

The sarcophagi, sixty-four in number, when discovered, were all dated; and further, had around them no less than six hundred funeral tablets in honour of the priests of the different Apii, dating from the eighteenth dynasty, 200 B.C., to the very rise of the Christian era. These were not only consecutive, but contained many historical facts, and by the aid of these tablets, or stèle, much of the later chronology of the Bible has been synchronized. But time presses.

The sixth plague converted the ashes of blessing into the instruments of curse. The clergy, by supernatural power the prescriptive doctors of the people, fled from the infliction, and were powerless to cure or to avert it, and hence they and their gods were shown to be inutile. Of the extent of their real knowledge of medical science, students are now themselves enabled to judge more correctly than any former commentators, for three treatises on medicine written in ancient hieroglyphics exist; of one, an account has lately been published by the learned Dr. Birch, who has shown that it contains prescriptions ascribed to king Cheops, the founder of the first pyramid, 4000 B.C. A second, published by M. Brugsch, and ascribed to the time of Rameses I., treats of the cure of diseases by the use of amulets, incantations, and sympathetic remedies,—analogous to those used in England two hundred years ago, when a man who was knocked down by a club, or stabbed by a knife, simply bathed the part afflicted and put himself to bed, and sent for the doctor to anoint the stick or knife with which the injury was inflicted with Fryer's Balsam, tallow from the altar candles, and extracts inspissated from plants gathered when the planets were in trine, or the sun in Jupiter. Of a like class were all the Egyptian remedies—superstitious, empirical, and absurd to an extreme degree; when therefore, in the sixth judgment, both physician and patient were attacked by the plague of boils, neither charm nor prayer availed them, no rank excepted, or amulet protected,—all suffered alike.

The seventh act of the drama of the Dies Iræ commenced with a fearful storm. Rain, though not unknown in Egypt, was the particular attribute of the feminine deities—of Isis, queen of heaven, of Saté, goddess of the material sky, and of Neith, the spiritual heaven, and goddess of wisdom. The souls of the dead, which were supposed to ascend to the heavens, were by Isis and Neith especially protected, and from them all blessings descended. But in this plague, regardless of, and restraintless by, feminine deities, the hail and lightning descended, and, terrified by the awful judgment, the king, *disowning his own divinity*, declared that he was wicked, a concession of a nature which only those who well understand the Egyptian theology can duly appreciate.

As the seventh with storm, so the eighth with locusts, devastated the land, and the trees, which themselves were sacred, the vegetable gods, despised by Juvenal and ridiculed by Pliny,—the pine, the tree of life; the tamarisk, that of knowledge; the lotus, sacred to the dead, the papyrus to the gods, and many lesser vegetables to lesser deities,—all were smitten then, and finally the locust, rarely seen, and scarcely, from its rarity, even dreaded in Egypt, devoured all that the hail had left.

As the curtain closed upon the awful tragedy, the stage of the theatre became darkened, for when the hands of the prophet were extended towards heaven, a darkness that might be felt covered the land. This, as it was the last directly theological, so it was also, in one sense, the most conclusive; for after all, at the root of all the Egyptian theogony lay the divine truth that there was one unbegotten God, sole, existent, and eternal. "The creator of all existences and the unbegotten." He, the great deity, or Amun Ra, was believed to inhabit the heaven of heavens itself—to produce all the other gods by direct emanation; as most of the deities were originated from him, so most of their names were compounded with his, and he the invisible and beneficent God was symbolized by eternal light—the sun was his representative, and all living things were but his manifestations. In the conception of his power and dignity the extremes of materialism and pantheism united. But then at the word of the servant of a greater god, a dark veil passed between him and his creatures. A *three*-days' curse, because of his three attributes, as Amun Ra, father of divine life, Kheper Ra, the father of animal, and Kneph Ra, of human, then he, the god of the heavens and of the Egyptians, was by the God of the Israelites blotted out.

Last of all, descended the horrors of the tenth plague. The Egyptians having felt, and the Israelites having witnessed, the powerlessness of the gods they had been accustomed to venerate, the long-delayed retribution fell upon *the* Pharaoh and his servants ; and those who had made the Israelites childless, were by an invisible and irresistible executioner rendered childless themselves. Fancy cannot imagine, artist cannot paint, nor poet describe, the scene which produced the cry which rang throughout all the land of Egypt, when under the very shadow of the gods whom he worshipped, with their amulets upon his heart, and their adorations inscribed in the bracelets upon his hands, the first-born of every Egyptian lay agonized, paralyzed, dead ! To say more, belongs to the province of the theologian, and perhaps I have already said too much; but as this is one of the subjects which has received most light from the researches of Biblical archæology, I have ventured, despite its necessary length of detail, to bring it before your notice.

Nor are the corroborations of Old Testament History to be taken from Egypt alone, for, as might be expected from the monuments of Assyria, fresh confirmations avail us there, and that mighty empire has witnessed for the truth of the Bible in an unexpected manner, and with no uncertain voice. From the ruins of her palaces has her history been disinterred, and from the mutilated walls of her temples has her theology and poetry been restored.

The conquest of Palestine is recorded on the annals of Sennacherib, and the cylinder of Tiglath Pileser describes his invasion of Palestine. The names of Jehu, of Amaziah, of Hezekiah, of Omri, Ahaz, and Uzziah, have been made out. The very clay which sealed the treaty between the kings of Judah and Assyria, with the impresses of their joint seals upon it, is preserved in the Nineveh gallery. The library of Assurbanipal, in 20,000 fragments, contains, among other scientific treatises, such as astronomical notices, grammatical essays, tables of verbs, genealogies, etc., an historico-geographical account of Babylonia and the surrounding countries. As far as these fragments have been translated, the district and tribal names given in the Bible correspond very closely with them. Here and there occur discrepancies, but they are such as vanity might suggest, or shame originate. Babylon, and not Jerusalem, is the centre spot of the world, and the house of the Assyrian king is the garden of Eden. These variations are trifling; every nation has its romancers, and without the hand of inspiration the history of every people commences in fable.

Although so nearly allied, politically and chronologically speaking, yet the idiosyncrasies and mythological ideas of the two empires were as widely different as were their territories and their peoples. The

Egyptian gods loved their worshippers. In Assyria the worshippers loved their gods. In Egypt the Pharaoh venerated himself, but the Assyrians never lost sight of the two great truths of all primitive theology, the fatherhood of the Supreme Being, and the sinfulness of all, from the highest to the lowest, of the human race. In Egypt the king was in a manner independent of God, but among the Semitic Assyrians even the armipotent Nebuchadnezzar was the servant of his Bel and Assur, "who gave him victory, and set him to rule over nations."

Agreeably therefore to these national distinctions, stands out in prominent relief to a careful reader, who is willing to suppose that his ignorance may really be not *quite* equal to the task of ridiculing the collected wisdom of thirty generations, the reserved and almost reverential manner in which the kings of Assyria, Tiglath Pilesser and Nebuchadnezzar, spoke of their personal relation to their God. With them, and their successor Assurbanipal, all victory, all grace, were ascribed on their records to "Nana, the delight of Babylon," to "Ishtar the strong," to "Assur the great," and to "Bel the protector," among the gods of Babylonia. While the proud monarch of the southern kingdom claimed equal deity for himself, and as on the sarcophagus of Oimenepthah I. declares that he is in very nature like unto Osiris, to Ra, to Set, to Horus, and all the other greater deities, the less presumptuous sovereigns of the East personally besought the favour and entreated the forgiveness of their gods. In Egypt, the king, being a god, could not possibly commit sin, but the Assyrian Assurbanipal besought "May the look of pity that shines in thy eternal face dispel my griefs; may I never feel the anger and the wrath of the God; may my omissions and sins be wiped out; may I find reconciliation with him, for I am the servant of his power." The prayers of other Assyrian potentates have also been preserved, and through these runs a spirit of dependence, submission, and inferiority, far, very far differing from anything to be found in the liturgies and supplications of any other contemporary nation except the Jews.

It was while worshipping Nisroch, the eagle-headed deity of Assyria, that the blasphemous Sennacherib was slain, and Nebuchadnezzar set up an image of gold, not to himself, but to Bel, and the proportions of that image agree perfectly well with those of the stéle and altar of Assar-nazir-pal at the British Museum. If my hearers will read carefully the thirty-sixth of Isaiah, for I see they are anxious to interrupt me, they will find the blasphemy of Sennacherib consisted, not in the assertion that "I have with the soles of my feet dried up all the rivers of besieged places," but in the lie that "the *Lord* said unto me, Go up against this place and destroy it." There was nothing in the passage itself that claimed divinity for the speaker, while the phrase employed is the Assyrian official one, for in a well-known slab in the national collection, often engraved, but oftener forgotten, Sennacherib sits in his state chair with the arrows of divination in his hand, and the inscription around and before him reads, "I sit before the city of Lachish —I give permission to destroy it."

One of the most curious of the Assyrian inscriptions lately discovered is that which has been translated by M. Charles Lenormant, and relates to the construction by Vulnarari (or Bin-narari) of a golden temple to the great god Bel. Erected in seven stages, analogous to the present ruins of Bin Nimrūd, the walls, the roof, the columns, and the sanctuary, the vessels, and the statues of the gods, were all alike plated, or composed of solid gold. It was founded, so runs the inscription, "To the glory of the great god Bel, my lord and master, whose servant I am, who has placed me on the throne of this people." That such an edifice could be erected of materials so costly and so rare, at a period very near to that of king Solomon, removes at once all dispute as to the credibility of the Biblical narrative concerning his temple, and affords a justification of the means employed by the wisest of kings for storing up a metal not then used as an article of currency. Of this magnificent structure, only the indications of its site remain. Voltaire and Tom Paine would have said it never existed, but it *did* exist; and it is not probable that the son of David, confessedly the richest monarch of his time, who inherited from his parsimonious father the accumulated wealth of the conquered Palestinian kings, would have had less resources at his command than an Assyrian monarch whose empire was at that time little superior to his own, and who possessed a far less universal reputation.

Not the least interesting of the ancient inscriptions before mentioned are those which, dating from 1200 B.C. to 600 B.C., are called Boundary Stones. These were set up to mark the angles which circumscribe the limits of fields of various landowners. Upon them were generally inscribed the names of the parties, the value and limits of their properties, and dedications to different deities, whose emblems were inscribed upon the summit of the stone. Thus, as in many instances in the Bible, the same pillar partook of the nature of altar, deed, and milestone, and was reverenced accordingly.

A singular discovery has resulted from the translation of these and similar inscriptions, one which a few years ago was but little to be anticipated, namely, the employment of one species of character for the transcription of no less than three languages—the Persian, the Accadian, and the Median. Of these three, the second is the most important, for while it contains in itself many root words of Turanian origin, yet as a Semitic tongue it contains elements which enable us the more closely to realize the nature of the earlier Syrian languages, and the idiomatisms of speech with which the first writers of the Bible were most familiar, and therefrom we are enabled the better to understand certain passages, which if translated purely by Hebrew or Chaldee would prove at best obscure. Thus archæology has supported philology, and both have rendered important services to the cause of Biblical criticism. The incommunicable name of the Great Jehovah (Yahveh) Himself, has been found as the name of a Syrian deity of extreme antiquity, probably not in its spiritual character far remote from the God of the Hebrews. The names of the cities founded by he early Ethnarchs have been more or less identified, and their sites pointed out. Of these, not a few have names both Turanian and Semitic, in which case both names are purely translations of each other. This custom seems to have prevailed to very recent times, and many of the proper names in the Bible are now shown from contemporaneous inscriptions to be translations or corruptions, in the same way as Naples, Nablus, and Napulia are corruptions of the Greek Neapolis, the new city; in a manner precisely similar to that in which a French map of London would give Blancchapelle, for Whitechapel, Porte-neuf, for Newgate, Chartreuse, for Crutched Friars, and Mont Grenvich for Greenwich Hill.

Quitting the people of Assyria for their contemporaries the Jews, let me mention the investigations which have recently been made at a tumulus long known to travellers as Tell el Yehoudeh, or the

Mound of the Jews, which is known to cover the site of the ancient Jewish city of Onion, founded by the high-priest Onias in the reign of Ptolemy Physcon, one of the Greco-Egyptian kings of Egypt, as a place of refuge for his people who were expatriated from Judæa by the armies of Antiochus. There, as we are told in the book of Maccabees, and the historian Josephus, was erected another temple in character and detail analogous to that of Solomon. The Egyptian temple for some long period flourished, and the Jews were received with great favour by the Ptolemaic sovereigns. A college, a library, and various public buildings were founded, and the prophecies of the later prophets were fondly applied by the Jews to that city and its temple. At last, in the continued revolutions which ended in the destruction of the Egyptian empire by the suicide of the infamous Cleopatra, —the prostitute of her brother, of Cæsar, and of Antony, the murderess of her sister, the curse of her country—the city of Onion perished, its buildings were destroyed, and its temples ransacked. The dispersed Jews settled in Alexandria, in Marseilles, and the various colonies of the victorious Roman empire, beneath whose eagle wings all the world was ultimately gathered to prepare for the better and holier federation of the nations of the world in the empire of Christianity. Until recently, little attention has been turned to the preservation of Jewish antiquities, and the result naturally was that the temple of the pseudo-Onias became as completely lost to the world as its prototypes of Solomon, Zerubbabel, and Herod. Upon the restoration of learning, and still more upon the revival of archæology in the Augustine era of English literature, the reign of Queen Anne, a good deal of very ingenious conjecture was hazarded, and some exceedingly plausible theories were promulgated to the no little injury of good logic and better paper, as to the dimensions and construction of the temple at Jerusalem. From the almost visionary work of Villalpandus, in three volumes folio, and that of Solomon Bennett in a more modest quarto, down to the later conjectures of Messrs. Fergusson, Lewin, and Sharpe, who have been contented to speculate in octavo, the essays, both scientific and theological, upon the topography of Solomon's temple, have formed a library in themselves. Now, however, at last there seems some probability that the excavations at Tel el Yehoudeh, in Egypt, combined with the enterprise of Captains Warren and Wilson at Jerusalem, will settle the long-vexed question, for the Egyptian excavations have revealed two classes of antiquities—one, the fragments of a palace of the twenty-third dynasty, in pure Pharaohnic art; and the other a class of remains comprising the fragments of a column and architrave of a different, and wholly Semitic, type of architecture, such as more or less prevails in Central Syria, the ruins of Capernaum, and the cave tombs in the valley of Jehoshaphat,—a type, more-

over, wholly unknown in Egypt Proper, having much
in common with Herodian and Greek, but, except
in the materials, very little resembling Egyptian
work. This being so, there is every reason to believe, as the Rev. Greville Chester, who has brought
some of these relics to England, suggests, that
they are portions of the temple of Onias; and if
according to the writings of Josephus, and all contemporaneous and traditional history, that temple
was modelled after the one which was the glory
of Jerusalem, it is scarcely too much to conjecture that we are on the track of materials which
will enable us to construct a model of the costliest,
most contested, and most sacred edifice the world ever
beheld. But the subject of this paper, and the illu.-
trations and corroborations of the Bible, often direct,
but more frequently indirect, which can be obtained,
and are being obtained in abundance, from the
monuments of Egypt, Assyria, and Palestine, requires
not one, but many evenings to examine it. It would
tax the patience of the most diligent scholar, the
tongue of the most voluble expositor, the hand of the
most laborious amanuensis to dwell upon them. The
British Museum, and many public and private collections, may well be visited with no other guide-book
than the Bible; and to those who are content to
wait and hope, to study and to persevere, the richest
and most gratifying results may be predicted. As in
nature, so in art, directly or indirectly the works of God,

and of those whom God has made, are in harmony with His word and work. What science and archæology are *not* in harmony with, are hasty premises, predetermined conclusions, and superficial examination. The light of the antiquary's torch increases as the darkness of the ruins amongst which he gropes becomes more intense; and the student of the Bible will often find the strongest confirmation afforded by the patient examination of an apparently incontrovertible difficulty. The light of revelation, held by the hand of reason, will in due time dispel the obscurity of ages, and penetrate the most distant recesses of the past. Be it therefore the province of this Society collectively, and of you its members individually, to uphold that heaven-given light, and to work in harmony, and march in step, through the accumulated *débris* of time and change. Still in the future, as in all the past, shall the radiance of that torch increase, and the glory of the torch-bearers extend, for it is lit by the effluence of that Deity who, placing it in the hands of His servants, is Himself, as an ancient Christian lamp in the British Museum, in almost the very words of the Nicene Creed, attests, Φως, φωτος, "The Light of Light."

THE ARGUMENT

FOR THE

SUPERNATURAL CHARACTER OF CHRISTIANITY, FROM ITS EXISTENCE AND ACHIEVEMENTS.

BY

THE REV. HENRY ALLON, D.D.

THE ARGUMENT FOR THE SUPERNATURAL CHARACTER OF CHRISTIANITY, FROM ITS EXISTENCE AND ACHIEVEMENTS.

THE historical character of Christianity subjects it to peculiar and crucial tests. The metaphysical tests of theological dogma, the moral and spiritual tests of religious life, are subtle and evasive compared with the exact tests of historic time and circumstance. Their apprehension and power depend more upon mental idiosyncrasies and moral sympathies. Hence these constitute a higher kind of evidence than that of which I am now to speak, and demand a higher nature for its appreciation. To spiritual minds, moral evidence is of all proof the most conclusive.

The argument from final causes has its place and power in the domain of moral truth. The truth which meets and satisfies the deepest instincts, the greatest necessities, and the strongest yearnings of a man's spiritual nature, is to him the most conclusively attested truth. To truth-loving souls truth is its own light. The soul is made for truth, as the eye is made for light, and the heart for love. Augustine's great saying, "Thou hast made us for Thyself, and we cannot rest until we rest in Thee," is but the supreme expression of the soul's relation to all truth. Hence this is the note of the chief appeal of our Lord as a religious teacher, " He that is of the truth heareth my voice." Souls that are true feel the truthfulness of His great spiritual words. Instinctively they test them by the necessities and yearnings of their religious nature—as the artist tests beauty, as the poet tests language, as the musician tests melody. It is "the vision and faculty divine." In every department of life the criterion is held to be valid. As to the poetic soul, the only necessary, the only possible test of poetic beauty is itself, so to the spiritual soul, the supreme evidence of spiritual truth is its own inherent character.

According to every legitimate principle and analogy of human nature, therefore, we claim for moral and spiritual evidence—for the appeal to truth-loving souls of the inherent fitness and beauty of the truth which appeals to them—the supreme place of congruity and power. If there be any validity in the doctrine of final causes, then must the validity be admitted of those teachings which perfectly satisfy the instincts, necessities, and yearnings of our spiritual nature. It is a sufficient proof of spiritual truth that it approves itself to the spiritual sense. While he, whose unspiritual, unapprehending soul is incapable of such an appeal—to whom spiritual truths are unintelligible and unconvincing just in proportion as they are spiritual—who in the presence of Christ's greatest moral glory asks, "What sign showest Thou?" thereby proclaims himself as fundamentally incompetent to judge spiritual truth, as the man physically blind is to judge the light of the sun. Just as he who sees the sun needs no scientific demonstration of its light, so he who sees spiritual truth needs no attestation of external evidence. His experience is his sufficient proof. Like the man born blind, he replies to all objectors, "Whether he be a sinner or not, I know not; one thing I know, that whereas I was blind now I see."

This evidence of spiritual experience and fitness is, for thousands, their only and sufficient proof of Christianity. In the spiritual teachings of Christ, in the spiritual life and blessings which as the Redeemer of men He practically gives, they find all that they religiously need or desire,—the sense of the forgiveness of sins, the moral power of a new and holy life, practical rest in the moral and providential order of God, beatitude and joy in communion with God, and perfect satisfaction for all their instincts and hopes in the promise of immortal life. If these be delusions, they are wonderfully full of practical fitness and power. Those who realize them cannot demonstrate to others their absolute truth; they can only attest their own wonderful transformation by them, and their satisfaction in them. They cannot prove their beliefs, but they can die for them.

This is the supreme strength of religious faith; no intellectual arguments can prevail over indubitable experiences.

You may demonstrate to a man that it is a mere philosophic imagination to believe in a personal God, that it is an unhistoric delusion to put faith in Christ, that it is a scientific absurdity to offer prayer, that it is a gratuitous expectation to dream of a life after this. He may be utterly unable to reply to your arguments, but his own conscious experience neutralizes them all. He knows, and feels, that there is a God who forgives sin, and hears prayer, who gives holy inspirations to his soul, and holds spiritual fellowship with him. If these be delusions, if God be but a philosophical necessity, and man but a highly developed materialism, if religious intercourse with God be a natural impossibility, if immortal life be but the "baseless fabric of a vision," then is man the greatest solecism in nature, his nature the greatest failure, his consciousness and experience the greatest delusion.

So long as the religious nature of man is what it is, and so long as the religion of Jesus Christ so wonderfully meets and satisfies it, sceptical science has not the ghost of a chance; the facts are too terribly against it.

But while, as Christian apologists, we thus justify ourselves by asserting the legitimacy and supremacy of the moral argument, and the spiritual incompetency of men who cannot appreciate it, we are perfectly willing to abide by the appeal to external evidence, and to rest the case of Christianity upon the demonstration of its historic and scientific truth. No true spiritual system can be enshrined in mendacious history or imaginative science—in the manner and degree, that is, in which history and science are incorporated with Christianity. It is no accidental contact of metaphysical dogma and historical circumstance. The peculiarity of Christianity among the religious systems of the world is that history enters into it as a vital element. Scarcely any constituent of Christianity is pure dogma. Metaphysical dogma of the very highest kind is of the very essence of it. No scheme of thought soars to such transcendental heights, or penetrates so profoundly to the heart of things; but the dogma is so inextricably and vitally connected with the historic circumstance, that if the latter be proved fabulous the former is discredited. It is morally impossible to save the dogma of Christianity and sacrifice its history. No theory of fable, legend, or myth that human ingenuity has yet conceived can save either the New Testament writers or Christ himself from the imputation of a purposed and systematic falsehood of statement, which, by its extent, its deliberateness, its grossness, and its deluding effects, must utterly destroy their personal moral integrity, and discredit whatever dogma may rest upon their authority. The incarnation and the resurrection, the miraculous works and the death upon the cross, are much more than the ore of truth in a matrix of circumstance, they are essential historic facts, the significance and explanation of which is dogma; so that we cannot disallow the facts without destroying the dogma.

This subjects the Christian system to tests which are peculiarly searching. Men who deny its theological ideas, or who are insensible to its spiritual appeals, may yet question the evidence of its facts. Take, for instance, the resurrection of Christ. Men who can see no force in its theological congruity, and its harmony with human instincts and yearnings, are yet competent, on a purely historical basis, to appraise its evidence, and to pronounce upon the truth or falsehood of its assertion. With the incarnation the historic proof is necessarily less complete; but connected even with this there is an array of circumstantial and presumptive evidence which the spirit of history can appreciate, and which is sufficient to enable a historical verdict.

As Christian apologists, then, we accept this ground of debate; we freely and fully concede that if the Christian history be discredited, both its dogma and its moral authority are invalidated. Whether intrinsically true or false, it can derive no authority from its source. We can have neither confidence nor joy in teachings so vitally connected with personal mendaciousness and religious fraud. The ground of its distinctive appeal to our respect and acceptance is utterly destroyed.

This, however, does not commit us to any theory of the verbal infallibility of the history; nor does it involve us in untenable positions such as may have been assumed by its defenders. The vindication of the supernatural and authoritative character of the Bible has too often been embarrassed by speculative theories authorized neither by the statements of the Book itself, nor by a consensus of the judgments of its believing disciples. For our present purpose we claim for the Bible only the authority of the ordinary literature of history. But it is no reply to the essential claims of the Book to be a supernatural revelation from God, to show that certain speculative theories concerning the *modus* and degree of its inspiration are untenable. Apart from all theories of inspiration, or of its orthodox expositors, there are certain broad historical and religious characteristics of the Bible which appeal to the general student, and which must be accounted for before either its historical character or its supernatural claims can be disallowed. For the purposes of our present argument we put it on a level with other books of ancient literature, and submit it to the verdict of ordinary historic, literary, and moral tests. Nay, we will concede that from the extraordinary character of its contents it demands the severest and most conclusive historical demonstration.

Another admission to be made is, that the mere

existence and prevalence of a religious system is not, *per se*, a sufficient demonstration of either its supernatural character or its truth. Buddhism exists, Hinduism exists, Confucianism exists, Mahometanism exists,—the former far more extensively than Christianity. The peculiar character of Christianity, and the peculiar conditions of its success, are essential elements of the argument.

It is vital to our conclusion that these limits and conditions of our claim should be made clear.

Some religious system or other, men must have; the mere existence of such systems proves only the corresponding existence in human nature of the religious sentiment, which is as real, as valid, and as indestructible an element of our nature as any other. So also there are the sentiment of humanity, which is the root of human kindness, and the sentiment of patriotism, which is the inspiration of all service and sacrifice for one's country, and the conjugal sentiment, and the parental sentiment, and others the validity of which no one questions, and the actuating power of which all must admit. It is part of the philosophy of human nature to give account of these sentiments, and of their dynamic power. These various sentiments are fundamental in our human constitution, although they are capable of instruction and development. Most of the things that we do, as members of the human community, are prompted by them. In obedience to these human sentiments, men serve and sacrifice themselves, as patriots and philanthropists, as parents and children, as merchants and men of science. No one questions their legitimacy and value; without them, society would dissolve.

Among these the religious sentiment has the supreme place; of all our sentiments it is the deepest and the noblest. That it is a fundamental part of our human constitution is demonstrated by the analogy of other sentiments; by philosophy; by experience; and, not least, by the signal failure of Mr. Mill and Mr. Darwin to prove that it is developed or derived. No scientific *fiasco* of our day is so complete as Mr. Darwin's recent theory of conscience.

Apart from all theological dogmas there is nothing in the nature of man that in idea is so grand, and nothing in the social life of man that in practice is so influential, as the religious sentiment. It is essential to the wellbeing of society that men should be pure and truthful, upright and unselfish, honourable and benevolent. Compared with the sentiment that prompts these practical virtues, all other sentiments of our nature are practically unimportant. It is the religious sentiment which makes systems of religious thought and conduct imperative. It prompts too the religious propagandism which is so characteristic of men, and so obligatory upon them. For if men are deemed noble and worthy of praise when in obedience to their philanthropic sentiments they sacrifice themselves for the good of their country or of their fellow-men, to promote commerce, to advance science, to liberate slaves, or to reform prisons, much more when in obedience to their religious sentiment they sacrifice themselves to impart religious knowledge, to develop religious life, to make men moral and holy, devout and spiritual. Of all the superficial cavils at Christian men, of all the blind passionate wrongs done to human nature, surely that is the most ignorant and insane which reprobates religious missions on the ground of their fanaticism. If, while they obey all other instincts of patriotism and philanthropy, men refuse to obey the instinct of religion, they are simply recreant to the noblest sentiment of their nature, and enthrone selfishness and meanness in the holy place of the soul. And if, in addition to the mere promptings of the religious sentiment, any religious system that men have received teaches them that not only the weal of the present life, but that also of the life hereafter, depends upon their religious character here, they must either seek to apply it to the religious life of their fellow-men, or abjure all generous and gracious feeling.

If I think that the truth that I possess is higher or more cogent than that possessed by my fellow-man, that it will more powerfully and beneficially affect his present character and his future destiny, I am constrained by every consideration of duty and philanthropy to put him in possession of it. Religious propagandism has its root in the very noblest sentiment of human nature; it is independent of any specific religious system, and has been prosecuted under all. The religious sentiment can no more be disregarded without selfishness and moral degradation than can the patriotic or the philanthropic sentiment.

A religious system may be a false one. It may, that is, teach false gods, or false notions of the true God,—His character, relations, and claims; nevertheless the religious man will seek to propagate it in virtue of the religious sentiment that has received it. It is the highest religious truth that he knows. In every religious system there is something true—in most there is more of truth than of falsehood ; more or less therefore each ministers to the religious sentiment, even though the element of falsehood in it may, like poison, be working deleteriously. It is simply an attestation of the depth and strength of the religious sentiment that even under the falsest religious system it impels men to make converts. It may be mistaken in its methods, its zeal may become a morbid fanaticism,—religious persecution is simply perverted religious solicitude,—but the underlying sentiment is true and irrepressible. The founder of Buddhism—Sakyamuni, if we may trust the traditions concerning him, relinquished a throne, and for forty years propagated the religious truth that he had discovered, with an unwearying zeal and a magnanimous unselfishness that have scarcely ever been surpassed; Mahomet propagated his monotheistic faith, at first, from high religious motives, although his later life shows sad deterioration; and he effected an amazing and beneficial destruction of Arabian idolatry.

Nothing in men is stronger than the religious sentiment. To realize his own religious beliefs a man will make any sacrifices, submit to any discipline, perform any penance, even lay down life itself,—the fakeer of India and the devotees of Mohammedanism equally with the ascetic and martyr of Romanism. And to propagate his beliefs a man will make any sacrifices, and endure any hardships.

It is not therefore either the prevalence of Christianity, or the fact of its propagandism, that demonstrates its truth. These attest only the fact and the strength of the religious sentiment.

But then, just in proportion to the truth of a religious system will be the power of its inspirations, the manner and the degree in which it will excite the religious sentiment that receives it. If a religious system be false—a device of the religious imagination, a superstition generated by ignorance or fear, or a growth of priestcraft—it does not make it true that I sincerely believe it. Whatever the intrinsic strength of the religious sentiment, no theological falsehood will minister to it; or if it do, it will be only as the poison of fever makes men strong,—it will generate violence rather than healthy vigour. Like every other part of our nature, our religious nature is made for truth, not for falsehood; and only truth can healthily minister to it. Just as my physical nature can be made healthy and strong only by things really adapted to it, and not by things that I may ignorantly think so; just as appetite can be satisfied only by wholesome food, and disease cured only by fitting medicine—so my soul can be made healthy and strong only by true religious ideas. Things deleterious will injure body and soul none the less that I think them beneficial. False religious ideas are always injurious to the individual or to the community that receives them. Hence the perverted religious feelings, the disabling superstitions, the moral corruption, the social selfishness and cruelty, that we see where Paganism, Mohammedanism, or corrupt Christianity prevails. The religious and moral contrast of nations as they now exist upon the face of the earth is indeed a sufficient vindication of Christianity.

How then, it may be asked, may the Christian believer know that his beliefs are true? What criteria of the value of his convictions has he that are more certain than those of the Pagan or Mohammedan? A sufficient answer is, precisely the reason that a Newton has for believing that his astronomical theories are truer than those of a Persian astrologer—precisely the reason that a Lyell has for believing that his cosmogony is truer than that of the Hindu Shasters—precisely the reason that an Owen or a Huxley has for believing that his physiology is truer than that of Hippocrates.

Men cannot help knowing when theirs is an induction from a larger knowledge, the exercise of a higher reason, when their theories are truer than those of less informed men. It is the essential function of reason to appraise comparative evidence, and to know that it is not superstition nor savagery. Philosophers differ among themselves on more obscure or subordinate matters, but there is a consensus of opinion which makes them conscious of a truer general system than those of their predecessors. Truth is its own light, and the light of everything that comes within its sphere. So it is in the moral or religious domain, men know when they have attained to the highest truth. It commends itself to their reason, meets and satisfies their highest intelligence, their noblest aspirations. It "tells them all that ever they did." In the conscious presence of the truest lights, and in the exercise of the highest intellectual faculties and religious feelings, they judge the comparative claims of Paganism, Judaism, Mohammedanism, philosophical scepticism, and Christianity. In the light of our religious consciousness, and according to the highest tests of human reason, we know that in the Christian revelation we have the truth of God. We are as certain of spiritual truth in the moral and religious domain, as the man of science is of physical truth in the material domain. It is, therefore, neither ignorance nor arrogance that affirms the falsehood of other religious systems, and the truth of Christianity. It is the conclusion of enlightened reason ; else reason itself were an absurdity.

We have only to add to this exposition of the proper ground of our argument, that, in the very nature of things, no proof of Christianity, either moral or historical, can have the exactness or carry the necessary conviction of either mathematical or scientific demonstration. Moral truths do not admit of the exact treatment of either numbers or physics: their domain is reason and the moral consciousness ; their proof is strong probability,—intellectual and moral congruity. So far as the element of history enters into them they are amenable to the tests of historic science; but these, again, are less exact than those of physical science. It is part of the moral responsibility and education of men to exercise their moral judgment, and to determine truth in the conscientious spirit of truth.

Our claim is that the history of Christianity shall be subjected to the ordinary tests of historical science ; that the moral truths of Christianity shall be subjected to the ordinary tests of moral science ; and that judgment shall be given on the grounds of ordinary historic and moral probability.

I. In estimating the force of the argument from the existence and prevalence of Christianity, there is, first, *an antecedent history of Christianity*, which must be accounted for.

It is part of the claim of Christianity to be a supernatural revelation from God, that from the very beginning of human history it was purposed and prepared for; that it was gradually unfolded to men in successive dispensations and teachings, corresponding to their developing intelligence and character; and, finally established by Jesus Christ as avowedly the accomplishment and crown of them all. This of course has to be demonstrated by its own proper and detailed evidence, which cannot be attempted in a cursory reference like this. But it is part of our proper argument to note the scope and general coherence of the entire claim. If Christianity be not a supernatural revelation from God, it is difficult to conceive a claim more daring and embarrassing: if it be, it is precisely the arrangement most in accordance with our conceptions of divine plan and purpose. Nothing is more natural than that, in His dealings with men, God should have proceeded upon the basis of it, and by previous and progressive revelations, prepared men for the full manifestation of his remedial mercy in Jesus Christ. That there is this gradual development in the Old Testament and a singular harmony between it and Christianity will hardly be disputed. The Christian argument, therefore, is entitled to the strong moral presumption which arises out of this. If Christianity be an imposture or a delusion, it is so on a scale of vastness, and of varied and complicated harmony, which has no parallel in the history of human thought.

The claim of the antecedent history of Christianity

is this, that from the earliest records of history a remedial provision for sin was promised and prepared for, and that from the very beginning it met the yearnings and inspired the hopes of men.

It is admitted that in the earliest intimations of this, there are a necessary vagueness and faintness which render it possible for exacting criticism to question any particular instance, and difficult for faith to demonstrate it. But it is contended, first, that on the assumption of the supernatural character of Christianity, its earliest promise would necessarily be the faintest blush of light in the darkness, a nebulous mist gradually condensing into solid and definite prediction; and, next, that faith is justified in throwing upon these early intimations the after lights of prophetic utterance and historic fulfilment, and of thus explaining the meaning of phenomena otherwise unaccountable, which is precisely the method of all science; and that the entire harmony of these faint indications with the after history is a presumptive proof which no detailed exceptions to particular instances can set aside. Whatever the intrinsic meaning and evidential value of specific passages :—of the first promise of a deliverer to sinning man, of the intimations of a Messiah to the patriarchs, or to Moses—the fact is indubitable that the hope of a redeemer from sin did take possession of man in his early history in a way that the mere optimism of humanity, or mere dreams of a "golden age," are altogether inadequate to account for. The literature of the Bible, on the very lowest computation, extends over a period of 1,500 years. Its theological, religious, and historic harmony present phenomena which are not only unique, but are in themselves a miracle, and, I am bold to say, on any other than the supernatural theory are utterly inexplicable.

1. Take first the Book of Genesis. Admitting Ewald's theory of the composition of the Pentateuch, that its contents were contributed by four or five different narrators, and its present form determined by successive *rédacteurs*, of whom the latest lived in the time of King Josiah, say 620 years before Christ; or even Spinoza's wild supposition that it was written by Ezra or one of his contemporaries, say 450 years before Christ, we have a composition a century older than Plato, and coeval with Æschylus; the production of one of the most unscientific and illiterate nations of the old civilised world. But the extravagance of even Ewald's theory has discredited it among scholars of almost every school, most of whom admit that the Pentateuch must have existed before the division of the kingdom of Solomon, and that much of it, to say the least, was the production of Moses. It is hardly possible for it to be later than a thousand years before Christ, which is a century older than Homer. Now whatever the exact historic value of the Book of Genesis, there are in it theological and moral characteristics which, in its

relation to the New Testament, only the theory of the supernatural can account for. From any point of view it is a most remarkable part of the structure of Biblical theology, presenting precisely the characteristics of diversity in harmony which its assumed place in the development of the Christian system, and in the chronology of the Biblical writings demand. Its artistic place in the Bible is fully seen only when the whole is completed; and its fitness and harmony are unimpeachable. Passing over the numerous and singular individual counterparts between the teachings of this ancient Book and Christianity, such as the first and second Adam, the fall and Christ's redemption, the temptation of Eve and the temptation of Christ, I will limit myself to one or two broad positions, which will admit of ample allowance for alleged inconclusiveness of any specific features.

(*a*.) Take for instance its *conception of God*, and its objective presentation of His character and dealings with the sinful race of men. This is in perfect consistency with the entire Biblical idea, with the Christian representation of God, and with our present nineteenth century theology. Making due allowance for the anthropomorphism of these early times, and for imperfect modes of manifestation, there is nothing in the conception of the Jehovah of the Book of Genesis that the highest intellects of this nineteenth Christian century have difficulty in teaching. The spirit of the theology of the Bible, which has its supreme manifestation in Jesus Christ, undeniably pervades the book of Genesis.

Its Jehovah has none of the theological incongruities or moral inconsistencies of the Egyptian, Persian, or Greek mythologies. He is neither Osiris, Ormuzd, nor Zeus.

(*b*.) In like manner the *religious heroes* of the book —Adam, Noah, Abraham, Joseph—are none of them demi-gods, like Heracles for instance; their relations with Jehovah are intimate and peculiar, and yet they always appear as proper men.

(*c*). So again the *moral ideas* of the book of Genesis are homogeneous with those of the Sermon on the Mount. However corrupt the history narrated, however complicate the character delineated, the moral principles maintained, the moral tests implied are never dubious. Who can conceive of Abraham guilty of such an enormity as is attributed to Cato in relation to his friend Hortensius? Even in a character so tortuous as that of Jacob, we are never for a moment dubious about what is right. Whence a morality so far in advance of that of all other ancient literature?

2. The later books of the Pentateuch describe a peculiar national institution of ritual sacrifice and worship, with provisions so unique and restricted, that it is impossible to explain them as a mere Jewish variety of the general sacrificial cultus of the nations. And

associated with this ritual we find a moral code and a religious literature so enlightened, elevated, and philosophical that it is impossible to attribute the Leviticus to ignorant superstition. The rite of expiatory sacrifice practiced by almost all nations is in the Jewish temple service regulated so arbitarily and connected with a ritual so elaborate and minute, that if its typical character be denied, rational explanation of it is inconceivable. If its typical character be admitted, if the expiatory sacrifice of Christ has the vital religious importance which Christian theologians affirm, and the Jewish Leviticus be a supernatural preparation for it, then the correspondences between the two, so minute, so complicate, and so singular, are perfectly accounted for. On any other theory they are an inexplicable puzzle. The argument does not depend upon the ingenuity which discovers resemblances and types in every minute particular. The broad, general, undeniable characteristics of the Leviticus are amply sufficient to sustain it.

Here we have an entire national history and economy, maintained for nearly 1,500 years, which is an exact symbolical prophecy of the Messianic work of our Lord, as the New Testament writers expound it. Either therefore the facts of our Lord's life were more or less arranged, and the New Testament doctrine was constructed as an idealization of the Jewish Leviticus, or the accidental coincidence is so wonderful as to be virtually miraculous, or the two are purposed type and antitype. Marvellous are the credulities of rejectors of the supernatural. I must confess myself too much of a rationalist to be capable of them.

3. Further, during the first half of the seven centuries immediately preceding the Christian era, a series of predictions was uttered by a class of great religious teachers who sprang up among the Jewish people, which, if they do not relate to the coming and character, the atoning work and spiritual kingdom of Jesus Christ, are not only among the most inscrutable utterances of human literature, but are also a fresh miracle of fortuitous coincidence.

Had no such personage as our Lord appeared, no events, or personages, or tendencies of thought among the Jewish people could have furnished an explanation of these predictions. We can understand the visions of poets, the imaginations of romance writers, the utopias of philosophers, the metaphors of rhetoricians. These have their palpable characteristics, for which instinctive allowance is made. But here are, not only one or two, but some twelve or fourteen men springing up at a special period, and under precisely the circumstances which the theory of supernatural development requires, using language of an elevated, mystical, and cosmic character, which it is simply preposterous to refer to any Jewish personage, or event, or hope; and which, if it be not inspired prediction, must subject its authors to the suspicion of insanity. Men, too, most varied in character, education, social position, intellectual gifts, and literary form, and yet perfectly homogeneous in the great ideas of their prediction.

Then, as if to make doubt impossible, an august personage appears, whose character and teaching are described and expounded by eleven different writers in the New Testament, most of them unlettered men, writing biographies, histories, treatises, letters, and visions; and yet not only are their representations harmonious, but they correspond to these Old Testament predictions with such wonderful fitness and completeness that theologians, subjecting both to constant and crucial criticism, feel no serious difficulties of interpretation, encounter no intractable facts, or ideas, which they are compelled to eliminate from their harmony. Here, then, restricting ourselves as before to broad and unchallenged features, is another and independent set of harmonies to be accounted for and explained away; if the supernatural theory be rejected.

Either, again, the history and doctrines of the New Testament were by these eleven writers cunningly framed to fit in to the utterances of these dozen Jewish prophets, and both inexplicably adjusted to the earlier theological ideas of the book of Genesis, and to the singular and elaborate Leviticus of the Pentateuch and the temple, or the supernatural character of the whole must be conceded.

These various harmonies are not merely independent additions to the sum total of Christian evidence, they multiply into each other. Apply to them the doctrine of probabilities, and it is difficult to estimate their cumulative power. Here are independent lines of preparation—religious ideas, ritual institutions, prophetic utterances—any one of which would be remarkable, but which together are simply overwhelming. If any one of them fail, even if important elements in any one prove intractable, the Christian argument is discredited.

Assume the theory of Christian theology, there is in these a perfect and wonderful harmony of convergent evidence. Reject it, they are utterly inexplicable, and necessarily involve the historical student and philosopher in a chaos of unauthorized and contradictory conjecture.

II. The *historic occurrence* of Christianity has to be accounted for.

I can indicate only general lines of argument.

I may, I presume, take for granted the historic character of Jesus of Nazareth. Although almost every detail of the New Testament history of Him has been questioned, few have ventured to deny His existence. But whatever the ground of denial assumed, the difficulties of maintaining it are almost equally great. The conception of the person of Christ, and dogmatic and spiritual Christianity exist, and in some way or other both must be accounted for. I venture to affirm that no sceptical theory has yet been propounded for this purpose that does not involve difficulties of violent assumption and flagrant inconsistency, which if involved in the theory of faith would be regarded as fatal to it. If it be affirmed that Jesus never existed, it then becomes imperative to invent a plausible theory for the conception of His New Testament character, and for the origin of Christianity. If it be admitted that He did exist, then all the theories of conscious imposture, of unconscious delusion, or of mythical development, which have been adventured to account for His portraiture, His system of dogma, and His spiritual kingdom have signally failed. Some, like the theory of Strauss, have been abandoned by their own authors; others, like the romance of Renan, have expired beneath the moral indignation of some, and the inextinguishable laughter of others; frequently they they have refuted one another—as, for example, those of Strauss and Renan. While the theory of faith in the divine Christ has been maintained for eighteen centuries, and from the beginning has never lacked keen-witted and learned assailants, it would be difficult to mention a theory of denial that has survived the generation of its birth. Christianity indeed might well be contented to leave its vindication to its enemies, who like equivalent quantities in an algebraic equation neutralize each other. Such is their mutation and decay, that they " never continue in one stay." They are all " like the grass, and their glory like the flower of the grass; but the word of the Lord endureth for ever."

Sakya-muni may be a myth—Confucius may be of doubtful historical character; there is nothing in either Buddhism or Confucianism that may not be otherwise accounted for. Even Moses may be a fabulous personage, and the integrity of Judaism remain unaffected; but the historic reality of the Jesus of the Evangelists is inextricably bound up with any rational exposition of Christianity.

1. On the theory of Chrstian theologians, there is a profound and perfect harmony between the supernatural incarnation of Christ, and the redeeming work which he came to accomplish. Ideas superficially so remote and antagonistic as His sinless birth, His perfect life, and His shameful death upon the cross are philosophically and indissolubly connected by the profound Christian dogma of redemption. The dogma may be denied—its truth is to be vindicated by its own proper evidence—but its philosophical harmony with the incarnation on the one hand, and with the expiatory death of the cross on the other, cannot be gainsaid. The incarnation, in its supernatural and sinless birth is the only conceivable origin of such a personage, and His perfectly pure life is His only possible character.

2. There is a perfect and profound harmony between the dogmas of the Christian theory and the admitted necessities of our human consciousness.

(*a.*) There is no feeling of human nature more singular, more profound, or more universal than *the feeling of sin:* a feeling so far as we know *sui generis* —radically different from the feeling which calamity or folly occasions—a feeling that has its root in a latent sense of personal responsibility, and is occasioned solely by moral ideas—a feeling of self-reproach, of regret, of shame. There is no human feeling more mysterious, more sacred, and more indicative. A man's feeling about sin is the measure of his likeness to God. The most hardened criminal cannot wholly emancipate himself from it; the most sensuous of religious systems have recognized it. It has inspired Mythology with its sublimest conceptions, Paganism with its most dread immolations, and Christianity with its most passionate experiences. But this element of man's psychology is utterly anomalous and unaccountable on the theory that there is no God; or that man is the creature of mere material circumstance; or but a development from an ascidian mollusc. Sin being an impossibility, the feeling of it is a universal delusion. It is therefore one of the most flagrant anomalies in the doctrine of final causes. If man's conscience be the creation of mere experience, as Mr. Mill and Mr. Darwin tell us, no feeling is more inexplicable; and if God has made us just what we now are, an incongruous mixture of evil and good, of feelings that have no rational cause, of yearnings that have no destined satisfaction, what are we to think of His wisdom, goodness, or power, seeing that He has failed so egregiously in His creation.

This universal feeling of sin prompts all men to seek atonement for it. Every religious system, therefore, begins with a theory of forgiveness; if not, men turn away from it as idle dreaming.

Only in the redeeming work of Christ does the feeling of sin meet its full recognition and remedy. Whether the Christian dogma of sacrificial atonement be true or not, there is practically no force in Christianity or in human thought that in its peace-giving, sanctifying, and constraining power is comparable with it. It is the "power of God unto salvation."

(*b.*) The *sense of sinful disorder* and moral disability in men is equally strong: "the good that they would they do not; the evil that they would not, that they do." They "know the better, and pursue the worse;" the best men cry out with the deepest sense of helplessness, "Oh wretched man that I am! who shall deliver me from the body of this death." It is not teaching that men need, they have always known more than they could realize; It is help— "a strong son of God," to be their deliverer. How perfectly, again, the Christian dogmas of the perfectly holy Jesus, and of the renewing power of the Holy Spirit, meet and satisfy this feeling. And what amazing power of practical inspiration they have.

(*c.*) The *sorrows of human life* overwhelm men. From the days of Job until now, the hardships of toil and struggle, of oppression and pain, of disappointment and bereavement, have been the theme of moralists and poets, and the burden and prayer of weary men. Nothing has been sought more earnestly than the solution of this problem of human sorrow, nothing has been desired more passionately than consolation and help in its endurance.

Has any one unfolded the mystery of human sorrow like Jesus Christ, or been its comforter and helper, like Him who was crowned its king? He is our "faithful and merciful High Priest touched with the feeling of our infirmities," and under the influence of His teaching and sympathy sorrow is transformed into a Gospel, and is borne not only with amazing faith and patience, but often with a feeling of exultation and triumph, like that which Paul expressed when he spake of "glorying in tribulation."

(*d.*) And then there is *the great darkness and desolateness of death;* that wraps up life in mystery; "through fear of which we are all our lifetime subject to bondage;" "the shadow feared of man." What philosophy of death can be compared with that of Jesus Christ, who brought "life and immortality to light"? What comfort and hope in death are comparable to His? We think of Stoic and Epicurean; of the ghastly bravery of the old Alexandrine invitation to "supper and suicide;" and then we turn to Jesus comforting the sisters of Bethany; to Paul comforting the Thessalonians and Corinthians; himself having a "desire to depart," "ready to be offered up, the time of his departure at hand, and anticipating his crown of righteousness." We think of Stephen looking with angel face up into heaven, and praying for the men who were murdering him. And we think of the myriads of Christian death-beds since—peaceful, joyous, triumphant. There is scarcely a minister of religion who could not tell of many such. For myself, if the personal intrusion may be pardoned, I have, during the thirty years of my ministerial life, stood by hundreds of death-beds. In the majority of instances, faith has triumphed over all fear of death, over all love of life, even the tenderest affections have been overpowered by its hopes and visions. I have heard songs of triumph from lips faltering through pain, and seen rapture beam from eyes that the films of death were darkening—often a "joy unspeakable and full of glory." Never yet have I met the instance in which Christian faith was not sufficient to inspire perfect peace and comfort.

Now it may be that all these feelings are delusions; that there is no forgiveness of sins, no new life of the spirit, no divine comforter for our sorrow, no inspirer of hope in death; none the less do our human instincts, our religious consciousness crave them. And if it be so, if Christ be not a real Saviour, if the dogmas of the New Testament be untrue, then we get this astounding anomaly, that the falsehoods of Christianity meet men's conscious necessities and cravings, and minister to them more perfectly than all admitted truth. If Christianity be not true, we are "of all men most miserable." God has "made all men in vain." If it be true, we possess the greatest comforts, and are inspired with the loftiest hopes that have blessed humanity.

3. The subtle spiritual harmonies of our Lord's miracles constitute another argument.

First, speaking only of general characteristics, their utter contrast with the meaningless marvels of mere wonder-workers; next, their exquisitely adjusted relations to the miracles of the Old Testament. They present exactly that diversity which the development of the supernatural revelation demands, and yet are in such substantial correlation with them, that the unity of divine miracle-working is unmistakable. Not only is this adjustment of the miraculous elements of the two dispensations an achievement of singular prescience, which, the diversity and chronology of the alleged miracle-workers being taken into account, is little short of a miracle itself; but the exquisite conception of our Lord's miracles, in respect of their human benevolence, their parabolic significance, and their spiritual congruity, transcends all rational belief in mere inventive genius.

I have no wish to exaggerate the individual force of this argument; it is enough to say that it is the addition of another to the manifold and complicate harmonies of the Christian theory.

And yet, so far from parading His miracle-working,

our Lord rebuked those who demanded it, and upbraided them with the spiritual blindness, that could not recognize the truth of words, and the holiness of His character without it.*

4. I can hardly touch the argument to be drawn from the peculiar religious teachings of the Christian Scriptures. The profoundly spiritual, ethical, and philosophical teaching, first of our Lord, then of His apostles. The harmony of both with the alleged facts of Christ's history, and with the Christian theories of His person and work. The perfect adjustment of both to the natural development of the assumed revelation. Take first, the teaching of Christ Himself, and the progress of its spiritual thought; as indicated by the interval which separates the sermon on the mount from the great discourse of the "night on which He was betrayed." And next, the entire theological and ecclesiastical thought of the New Testament, which moves in steadily advancing idea from the first words of Christ to the last words of John:—through the preparatory words that preceded Christ's death; the unfoldings of the forty days before His ascension; and the subsequent development of the unapprehended facts of Christ's life into the grand dogmatic theology of Paul and John.† We are bold to affirm that the Christian system of theological thought, whether supernatural or not, is more spiritually true, and

* See Isaac Taylor's "Restoration of Belief," p. 225, *et seq.*
† See Bernard's "Progress of Doctrine in the New Testament," *passim.*

philosophically profound; and that in its ethical idea and force it is more elevated and influential than any hitherto conceived by human thought. And yet it was developed in this involuntary, complicate, and marvellous way.

(5) There yet remains the transcendent conception of the character of Christ Himself. A conception of which it has been justly said, that if a creation of imaginative genius, its inventor is greater than his hero. It is the greatest miracle of literature.

I can attempt no analysis of this wondrous character, this has often been done;* and I will not attempt to paint it by any poor rhetoric of mine. It needs no vindication. The moral and religious instinct of the world has confessed it. Eighteen centuries of the keenest criticism have only exalted it to the very highest place of human admiration and homage. The uniform verdict of friend and foe has been, " I find no fault in Him." Jesus Christ is the one perfect Man of the world's history; the one hope of a world of sinful men; so divine that the loftiest and purest do worship to Him—so human that the most polluted and lost can weep at His feet, and little children can smile in His arms while He blesses them. His was a life in which there was no fault to be corrected, no stain to be washed out. Other men *become* good, by learning, by growth, by suffering; Jesus *was* good, as pure when His life began as when it ended; advancing

* See especially Bushnell's "Nature and the Supernatural," chapter x.

maturity was His only change. All human excellences blend in Him in perfect proportion, an ideal of moral symmetry which has neither defect nor excess. His was a wise mature goodness; not as being ignorant of evil, but as being infinitely above it. His self-consciousness is altogether unlike that of other men. Moses and Isaiah may tremble before God, and acknowledge their sin; Jesus never confesses defect, never indicates any feeling of unworthiness; no tear of penitence rolls down His cheek, no prayer for forgiveness escapes His lips. When He speaks concerning Himself, it is to assert His own faultlessness, and to avow Himself the divine source of other men's spiritual life. So transcendent was He, that from the very beginning men revered His goodness as perfect, and bowed before it as divine. Virtues almost incongruous wonderfully blend in Him—greatness and gentleness, holiness and pity, strength and sympathy. He is nobler than the greatest man, more tender than the gentlest woman.

Earnest and absorbed in His work, with a passion that made Him a martyr, He never even suggests the impulsive enthusiast, the self-deluded zealot; He is always calm, clear, and wise. He verges towards no extreme. He is equally remote from asceticism and laxity; He repudiates no lawful enjoyment; He sanctions no single excess. He always preserves the golden mean. He wondrously holds the balance of life. He plants His spiritual kingdom, neither in convent nor cell, neither in church, nor in ritual observance, but in the market and the house, in the secret place of a man's solitude, in the inmost recesses of his soul. He does not call the world into His presence; He comes into the world, and sanctifies all things in it by accepting them as service to Himself. The very conception of His kingdom is a marvel. Making Himself its centre, He founds everything in it upon His own person and work. In His lofty self-consciousness He speaks as none of the world's instructors have dared to speak, prefers claims of which none of them have ever thought. Even Nebuchadnezzar, when he set up his golden image on the plain of Dura, never conceived of such a claim as this lowliest and calmest of men prefers. The kingdom that He conceives is so holy that the purest church ever falls short of it; it is so catholic that it includes men of every age, and race and character, "every nation, and kindred, and people, and tongue." And this conception originated among the mountains of Galilee, in the mind of a village carpenter, who knew little of the world—its books, its politics, its history, its geography, its races—who was brought up amid the notions and prejudices of the most illiterate and exclusive of ancient civilized peoples, and who was put to death at an age when Socrates had not yet become a sage. He put forth His conception moreover at the very beginning of His teaching. It did not shape itself gradually, as His thought was instructed and stimulated by experience. His first proclamation was of this spiritual, holy, and catholic kingdom of heaven. There is no indication of either growth or modification. The very first word of this young carpenter of Nazareth was that He was the spiritual King of a spiritual and universal kingdom; the progress of which He declared should continue through all the world's history; the consummation of which should be the conversion and the service of all its peoples.

And this He purposed to achieve—first, by disallowing all weapons but spiritual truth; next, by assailing all the intolerance and fanaticism, all the sin and selfishness of men; and next, by the inherent attractiveness of the cross upon which He died. It was to be a kingdom of pure spiritual truth—a kingdom of the poor and sorrowful—of which the most saintly are the most princely. What are we to think of the intellectual and moral grandeur of the nature in which such a conception originated? Upon any hypothesis it places its author transcendently above all the statesmen, all the philosophers, all the moralists that have appeared among mankind.

If our Lord never existed—if these four brief records, which so marvellously and yet so artlessly portray Him be spurious—whence this conception of Him? Was it the conception that created the life, or the life that created the conception? Had He never lived, could He have been imagined? How came it to pass that four obscure Jews, one of them a tax-gatherer, another a fisherman, should simultaneously conceive such a character, and individually contribute to it, with such diverse gifts and motives, and yet in such marvellous harmony?* If four, why not more? Scepticism has had its genius, why has it never produced a fifth gospel? The entire question of Christianity may safely be staked upon the mere conception of Christ's character.

III. There remains *the subsequent history of Christianity* to be accounted for. But my theme has proved too vast for me; I cannot traverse a field so boundless. What has been said already will however suffice to indicate the argument.

(1) There is the persistent discipleship of the twelve to be accounted for; their testimony to the miracles, and the resurrection of Christ, and their endurance of persecution and martyrdom in attestation thereof. Men have often died for false opinions, never in simple attestation of imaginary facts.

(2) The conversion of Saul of Tarsus must be accounted for. The rigid Pharisee; the fierce persecutor; the man of vast learning, of regal intellect, suddenly becoming a Christian convert, "counting all things that were gain to him but loss for Christ;" growing to be the chiefest Christian apostle; spending a long life as a missionary; and dying a martyr to his faith in Jesus Christ.

* See Bishop Alexander's "Leading Ideas of the Gospels." 1872.

(3) The New Testament itself must be accounted for;—its historical records; its incidental origin, its peculiar authorship, its diversified literary forms, and its marvellous unity.

(4) The rapid progress of Christianity in the first three centuries must be accounted for; then the subsequent conversion, first, of the northern nations, afterwards of various pagan peoples, by modern Christian missions. This, as I said at the beginning, is to be estimated in connexion with its peculiar conditions;—the lofty demands of Christianity, its utter intolerance of all forms of sin and selfishness, its absolute repudiation of all but moral means, its comparative failure when its own degenerate or mistaken disciples have had recourse to persecution, to secular coercion, or to any forms of worldly inducement; and the marvellous triumphs of its purely spiritual truths, pre-eminently of the truths represented by the Saviour's cross. The argument from the failures of Christianity is indeed almost as conclusive as that from its successes. The measure of failure has almost uniformly been the measure of departure from pure Christian ideas.

Putting it in the broadest way; what nations of the earth can be compared with Christian nations in general moral elevation? We know what Christianity did when it came into contact with the unutterable depravities of Greece and Rome—what it found its converts, and what it made them; we know what it has done in Pagan nations since; we know what just now Europe is in comparison with Asia, America in comparison with Africa. And the latest triumphs of Christianity have been the most signal. We need instance only what a few years ago the South Sea Islands, and Madagascar were, in comparison with what they are now. Wherever it comes, Christianity works ameliorations in literature and laws, in social institutions, in family and social life. Christian men themselves have often been unfaithful to their faith, they have corrupted its truths and abused its influences; and on the principle that the best things are capable of the grossest perversions, they have often become worse than the heathen; but in proportion as they have maintained its principles and realized its spirit, it has been a power that no form of human evil could withstand.

Nay, the proof is in every church, in every social circle, almost in every family; the phenomena of religious conversion are as indisputable, as they are unaccountable, save on the supernatural theory of Christianity. The truths of Christianity read in the Bible, or listened to from a preacher, work the most marvellous transformations; they put an arrest upon sinful habit and feeling, and often in a single day change the entire life of a man. Conversions as sudden and as radical as that of Saul of Tarsus, are continually occurring. A godless, profligate, hardened man, whose life has been given up to evil, and whose mind has scarcely ever been troubled about religion, is suddenly arrested by some truth of Christianity, subdued into thoughtfulness, and penitence for sin. Those who yesterday heard him blaspheme, to-day hear him pray. The impure has become chaste, the unprincipled has become upright, the liar speaks the truth, and the hard, grasping, selfish man becomes pitiful and benevolent; the sinner has become a saint; and between his old life and his new there has come to be in a few hours "a great gulf fixed." And the reality and thoroughness of the change are attested by a long subsequent life of humble holiness, consecrated service, patient endurance, and grateful love.

Writing to the Corinthian Christians, the Apostle Paul speaks of "thieves, and covetous, drunkards, revellers, and extortioners," and says, "Such were some of you: but ye are washed, but ye are sanctified, but ye are justified in the name of the Lord Jesus, and by the Spirit of our God." And there is scarcely a Christian pastor who could not speak of similar transformations in some members of his flock.

How are these to be accounted for? No other truths, no other books produce radical changes of spiritual character. Read to a man Plato, or Shakspeare, or Milton, or Bacon, they affect him but little; read to him the New Testament, he becomes "a new creature in Christ Jesus."

The argument does not admit of a formal summing up, it is a congeries of independent lines of evidence, wonderfully harmonious, and all conducing to one great demonstration. Scepticism has not done its work when its ingenuity has embarrassed any one of these—the harmonious correlation, and concurrent tendency of the whole must be accounted for. If Christianity be not of God, then is it historically and structurally a series of marvels unique in the world's history; a miracle greater than its assumed supernaturalism itself. In the light of these phenomena are we not justified in applying to its assailants the wise words of a calm observer of its earlier phenomena, " Refrain from these men, and let them alone; for if this counsel or this work be of men, it will come to nought; but if it be of God, ye cannot overthrow it; lest haply ye be found even to fight against God."

CHRISTIANITY SUITED TO ALL FORMS OF CIVILIZATION.

BY

SIR BARTLE FRERE, G.C.S.I., K.C.B., D.C.L.

CHRISTIANITY SUITED TO ALL FORMS OF CIVILIZATION.

I HAVE been requested by the managers of this series of lectures to state to you the results of observation and experience in other countries as to the adequacy of Christianity to meet the requirements of the varying forms of civilization.

It will be my object to tell you what is—what I have seen myself—rather than what I imagine ought to be. I wish to meet the theory which, in one shape or another, is not uncommonly propounded in this country, that Christianity is a Semitic variety of religion, suited to Syria and to a people of Jewish or Arab origin, but little adapted to men of other races and other climates. I wish to show you, as far as the brief limits of a lecture allow, that experience proves Christianity to be a religion perfectly adapted to mankind of the most various races, and in every stage of civilization, from the lowest to the highest.

We must first define the meaning we intend to attach to some of the words which we shall have to use. For instance, the word "Christianity" itself has a signification widely different as used by different Christians, and still more different as used by writers who can in no sense be classed as Christian writers. I shall speak of it in this lecture as the religion which is a rule of life to the majority of religious people in England calling themselves Christians. We may take the Apostles' Creed, as generally received and interpreted among us here in England, as the symbol of the belief whose adequacy to meet the requirements of all forms of civilization I hope to illustrate.

Further let us bear in mind, that however much we Christians may differ as to particular articles of doctrinal belief, or of discipline, we all regard our Christian religion as depending on a revelation of some kind—as being something told us from without, in contradistinction to the modern theory, "that people have their religion as part of their growth, and that a man is not more responsible for his religion, than he is for the colour of his hair, or the length of his arm; that, in fact, it grows as a part of himself." This is a convenient doctrine as getting rid of all personal responsibility in matters of belief, and is rather commonly met with in these days among many classes of professed Christians. We have not time at present to discuss it, or to show how fundamentally it is opposed to the idea of *any* religion as a rule of life. I will only therefore remark that we cannot recognize this description as applying to Christianity, which we regard as embodying truths and rules of conduct revealed to the intelligence of man from an external power—it may be through the senses, it may be through the conscience or the intellect, it may be recorded in books or handed down in traditions; but in whatever form, it is an *external* something, which is able powefully to modify the very nature of man, and all functions of his intellect and spirit, as well as his physical being.

As a further preliminary we must consider what we require a religion to do?

Let us leave out for a moment the consideration of all that relates to the world to come. Nor let us for the present even stop to discuss the question whether mankind might or might not be better off without any religion at all. Much ingenuity has been expended on proving such a position, just as it might be in proving that mankind would be better off without salt, or bread, or meat. But the general sense of mankind is all the other way, and our present purpose is comparative. Let us look on religion as one of the things which men generally think they require to aid moral and social laws in making men better and happier, more prosperous in life, and more able to promote the well-being both of believers themselves and of all in contact with and affected by them. To what extent is Christianity, as compared with other religions, adapted in these respects to the wants of mankind under various forms of civilization? This is the question which we propose to discuss, not by *a priori* arguments, but by examples and experience.

I. Let us first consider the case of wild tribes, who are, as nearly as we can judge, in what is called a state of nature. We have whole families, and even races, in Europe in a condition very little removed from that of the wild beasts; but they are generally a degraded and neglected form of mankind who have lapsed from a better state of civilization, and are hardly such good subjects for illustrating our argument as the wild tribes of India, who, so far as historical records show, have been from very early ages in a state at least as barbarous as that in which we have found them of late years. What I am now about to tell you applies to nearly one-fifth of the people of India. Some of them are not much removed above the condition of the aboriginal tribes in Australia. In the Andaman Islands there are remnants of a Negrillo race, who, though far better formed and well developed physically and mentally than the Australian race, have quite as little of artificial civilization about them. In the jungles of Central and Southern India are to be found tribes whose habits seem to approach much more nearly to those of apes than of men. A few of them are said to be absolutely without clothing, and to live habitually in trees; others have no better substitute for clothing than bunches of leaves, while with all of them the use of clothing is limited to the slightest imaginable amount of covering. A little more civilized than these are the jungle tribes, Bhils and Katkurees, and other races who live mainly by the chase. The great body of the tribes on our eastern frontier, the Sontalls and Koles, and many of the clans of Goandwana in Central India, and the Koolies and Thakoors of the west, are one step higher in civilization. They have huts and fowls and cattle, and some of them, especially on the eastern frontier, have slaves : all have some rude cultivation on spots cleared by burning the jungle. Again, one step higher, are tribes known as the Pariah or outcast tribes of Western and Southern India, apparently the remnants of aboriginal tribes conquered by the earlier invaders of Hindostan, and reduced to the condition of serfs or helots. The term "outcasts" hardly describes their condition, because they have never formed any integral part of the purely Hindoo communities; but they are "outsiders" in every sense of the word —forced to live outside the village walls—forbidden to touch or draw water from the wells of the Hindoo community; and though often—in the Maharatta Country always—occupying recognized positions in the village economy as settled cultivators and artizans, they are strictly confined to those services which, however necessary, are associated in all countries with a certain sense of pollution ; they are scavengers, skinners of dead animals, and the like.

The more settled tribes frequently approach very

nearly in civilization to the simpler classes of Hindoo agriculturists and artizans. But they have this in common with their wilder neighbours, that they are all more or less Fetish or devil-worshippers—a fact which distinguishes them broadly from the great body of genuine Hindoos. Altogether of these races I have been describing there are, according to the latest estimates, not fewer than forty millions of souls within the British Empire in India and Ceylon, a population almost as great as that of France or Germany.

Their physical qualities resemble those of savages in every part of the world. All are great observers; they have that peculiar quickness of eye and ear, and of all physical senses, which characterizes wild men, and which you see in any civilized man who, like the backwoodsman or remote colonist, has lived much among the solitudes of nature. But it is not only their external senses of sight and hearing and smelling which are wonderfully quickened by the necessities of the life they lead. Any one who lives much among them will be often astonished at the minute accuracy of observation evinced by them when they come first among the distracting sights and sounds of civilization. In the English official's tent or cutcherry they may appear perfectly dazed and confounded, watching every novelty of the scene around them, and with difficulty made to understand the business which brought them there—though it may be a capital charge, perhaps, of robbery and murder; and yet these same savages, when by themselves afterwards, will imitate with the most unmistakable fidelity—and with infinite humour—every peculiarity of voice and manner in the foreigners with whom for perhaps the first time in their lives they had been brought in contact.

Their only wisdom is that of experience in all matters of daily life; they have, of course, no book-learning, no philosophical systems—nothing of what some of our modern philosophers would call the shams or trammels of civilization. Careless of human life, they suffer little from the physical evils attendant on civilization. Their diseases are generally such as are the consequences of deficient or unwholesome food, or of want, or of malaria. Such of them as have fixed habitations, when they begin to find the spot where they live becoming unhealthy— when their fowls or their children die, or their grown folk suffer from fever—generally conclude that some evil spirits have entered the village, which they forthwith abandon, and move to a spot a short distance off. Every evil in life is attributed to some demoniacal or malicious agency. Their priests are generally little more than witch-finders or exorcists of evil spirits. The marriage-tie is lax among the ruder tribes, but invariably becomes stronger as the tribes become more civilized. They are generally far more truthful than their civilized neighbours, sometimes apparently from innate honesty, at other times from simplicity; but few of them appear to have that abstract regard for truth which we associate with the highest form of civilization. They are all, as a rule, kind and indulgent to their children; but the death of a child is not generally a matter which affects them more than the death of their young cattle, and when hard pressed for means of subsistence there is little trace among the men of that self-sacrifice for the sake of children which is so common in many more civilized communities. There is, as a general rule, little veneration for age, when the old people become burdensome through inability to provide for themselves. A few tribes are still clearly addicted to human sacrifices as the most potent form of propitiating the powers of evil; and most tribes have traditions which indicate that such practices were formerly more common.

One universal feature of all savage life is that everything goes to the strongest. It is not easy to convey to civilized men any definite notion of all that this peculiarity implies; still less to show how prone we are to relapse into—

"The good old rule, the simple plan,
That they should take who have the power,
And they should keep who can"—

when the checks imposed by a civilized organization of society are removed.

I will endeavour to illustrate both the tendency and its results by an instance which was related to me by an old friend, and which struck me as showing how this natural tendency comes out whenever there is a real struggle for existence. My friend was a very intellectual, shrewd Scotchman, who was cured of his youthful fancies in favour of savage life by being shipwrecked half-a-century ago in one of the great old East Indiamen upon the island called Inaccessible, in the Southern Ocean. It so happened that the whole of the crew—with the exception of the captain—and all the passengers, including a large detachment of troops, and numbering several hundred souls of various ages and professions, got safely to the rocky shores of the island, where they lived for some months, supported by the provisions they saved from the ship, and by the vast quantities of eggs of wild-fowl which were found on the rocky ledges of the island. One of the most prominent characters on board the ship previous to the shipwreck had been the surgeon—a man of weak physical powers, but of great and varied intellectual attainments, and of most popular manners and charming disposition. He had possessed during the voyage an unbounded influence over both officers and men—was invaluable to the captain as a supporter of discipline, and to the chaplain as aiding his moral teaching. He had induced all the young men on board to prosecute their studies regularly under his direction, and was a leading authority with regard to all the amusements by which the monotony of the voyage was relieved. He was, in fact, a type of what high intelligence in a civilized community can achieve in the way of legitimate and useful influence. For some days after the shipwreck his old power continued, and was always exercised for the public benefit; but after a while the pressing necessity felt by every soul of the shipwrecked community was the provision of water, which had to be procured from distant scanty springs, and the collection of a sufficient supply of birds' eggs to satisfy the calls of hunger. They had got, in fact, down to that stage of civilization at which the satisfaction of the first wants of nature in the way of food was of pressing daily importance. From that moment all the authority of the man of intellect vanished. He had not the physical strength to carry water or climb for birds' eggs, and the boatswain's mate—an illiterate man, of great physical power and energy, with other qualities fitted to shine in savage life—took the lead and kept it; exercising despotic sway over the whole community as long as they remained on the island.

Possibly some of us might say, "this is all perfectly natural and proper; the result must be a process of natural selection by which the most powerful physical natures will take the lead, and the consequence a gradual improvement of the race." But Indian experience of savage life does not at all confirm this view. The savage races are invariably smaller, weaker, and worse developed than the civilized. Many of the half-civilized are fine men, because they retain their habits of eating animal food, and thrive better than those neighbouring civilized races whose diet is exclusively vegetable; but in such cases their mode of living and kind of diet combines many of the advantages of both civilized and uncivilized life. The results of purely uncivilized existence, so far as I have seen them, are invariably a decreasing population, decreasing size and health, a general tendency to degenerate and to assimilate more nearly to the habits of beasts of the forest. I should doubt if mankind would ever become extinct in the jungles of India, because the smallest remnant of human intelligence gives them such an advantage over the other creatures of the forest, that the extinction of the race seems a very remote contingency. But a gradual dwindling of mind, body, and soul is universally apparent wherever civilization does not intervene to counteract the tendency.

Our experience of the races I have been describing does not agree with the theories of philosophers who maintain that the perfect condition of human nature is to be found among people who live a purely material life, thinking only of matter and its properties, and obeying with unquestioning fidelity all the instincts of their material nature. Such a life *is* led by the most uncivilized and savage of the tribes I have been describing. If the theories of modern materialist philosophers were true, it seems to me these tribes ought to swallow up civilization and all its shams; but practice and experience prove that civilization swallow up them and their materialistic mode of life, and unless they become civilized they are invariably extinguished when they come in contact with civilized communities —not necessarily by war or violence, but by the certain operation of civilization.

This brings us to the question of their religion. What is it, and how is it modified by contact with Christianity?

First, let us observe that not one of them, as far as I am aware, is destitute of some form of religion. As to what may be the case in other parts of the world I cannot tell, but as regards the wild tribes of India—and some of them are probably quite as wild as any in the world—I know of none who do not possess a religion of some kind. It is true, I have been told by some of them in so many words, that "gods are for English gentlemen, respectable Brahmans, and Muhammedans, and that the poor children of the jungle do not pretend to or venture to possess any such luxuries as the gods of the people around them." But in so speaking they thought only of the gods whose shrines they saw whenever they visited the haunts of civilized men; and I never could hear of any tribe, however wild, the members of which did not possess a religion of some kind—a belief in the existence of beings of superhuman power, whose active agency modifies the conditions and objects of life of all mankind. The religion of all the various tribes and classes I am speaking of is more or less Fetish worship; that is they have some form of religion, which consists not always in the worship of evil, but in a practice of deprecatory sacrifice, and petition to malevolent beings with a view to avert evil results to the worshipper or his friends. It is also an invariable feature of Fetish worship that the worshipper is able, by influencing the powers of evil, to effect mischief to his enemies, as well as to obtain good for himself. Time does not admit of more than a brief reference to a few of the commonest forms of Indian Fetish worship. Among the jungle tribes, beasts of prey, and notably the tiger, a common symbol of the spirit of evil, "Wagia," (the tiger-god,) is worshipped by widely distant and unconnected communities. Next in popularity and universal acceptance is the worship of such epidemic diseases as are known among savages. "Matajee," the goddess of small-pox, "Mahamurree," the great death, or cholera, take a prominent place whenever these scourges of savage as of civilized life make their appearance. The sacrifice of a fowl, or even a goat, which is a suitable propitiation of the tiger-god, is rarely efficacious when the goddess of epidemic disease makes her appearance. A rude procession is then organized; a figure dressed up in female garments, and ornamented as well as the means of the community allow, is worshipped and propitiated with sacrifices, conveyed to the limits of the village, or tribe, and there handed over to a neighbouring community, to be carried on or left in the jungle, in the hope that the figure has conveyed with it the seeds of disease, which will thus be passed on to the place of her new residence. I have known this system very efficacious in propagating instead of allaying the disease, in consequence of the terror inspired in the untutored inhabitants of the jungle at finding within their boundary the hideous figure which had been deposited there by their neighbours. If the community which has expelled the figure continues to suffer from the disease, they have no remedy but to disperse and fly.

For such people, I have heard it said in this Hall, "you must have a Fetish of some sort, and a stock or a stone is a better help to devotion than a priest or his sermon." * Let us consider how far this assertion is true—how far it accords with the facts we know.

Let us suppose for a moment the possibility of such a thing as a "Christian Fetish." I am using the words of those from whose opinions I entirely differ,

---

* " Fetishism is a natural concomitant of this stage of our "mental development"(*i.e.*, a stage of crass, savage ignorance); " * * * The only religion possible at this stage is the religion of "sense. * * * Christianity * * has far less chance of success "here than a religion which is purely Fetishistic. * * * If sen- "suous accessories are at all requisite, stocks and stones, idols "and oracles, are far better helps to devotion than the pulpit or ' the priest—the surplice or the sermon."—*Lecture of Jairam Row, in St. George's Hall, November* 12*th*, 1871.

simply for the sake of argument. I would ask any candid opponent who chooses to describe the objects of worship which we place before our poorer and more ignorant brethren as "Fetishes," whether he really thinks such "Fetishes" as are habitually placed before their hearers, as objects of worship, by St. Peter, St. Paul, St. John, or by the priests of our own Church, have anything in common with such Fetishes as form the objects worshipped by the people I have been describing? All Christians agree at least in this, that the religion they profess is applicable alike to learned and unlearned men, to the untutored savage and to the civilized philosopher. Hence the Christian Fetish, if such a Fetish there can be, must be alike the Fetish of the poorest and most ignorant peasant or savage, and of Newton, Bacon, or Locke, of Wilberforce, Las Casas, or Henry Marten.

But can such a thing as a "Christian Fetish" exist? or be preached from any Christian pulpit? As I understand a Fetish, it is a being of evil, worshipped with a view to deprecate its wrath, rather than to propitiate its justice or mercy. Such a worship is opposed to the very fundamental notions of Christianity. Whatever nicknames may be given to partial or distorted statements of our doctrines, this, at least, is certain—that nothing like Fetish worship is consistent with the plainest teaching of any single book of the New Testament. There is scarcely a discourse or a parable of our Lord, or an epistle of His apostles, which does not teach that God is a God of love and mercy, and inculcate love towards all mankind as the foundation of Christian morality. This is the very opposite of Fetish worship, and it is simple misuse of language to talk of a Fetish as a possible part of any real Christian teaching.

But how does Christianity fare when it is brought in contact with Fetishism pure and real, such as is the religion of the wild tribes we have been speaking of? Is it found inoperative? ill-adapted to and inefficacious with an uncivilized and uneducated people? unimpressive upon those whose whole life is a struggle for material existence? or is it found to be mischievous in its effects, and inferior, either in power to affect at all, or to affect for good, in comparison with Fetishism?

To all these questions Indian experience during the last half-century must answer in the negative. Christianity has now been preached to Fetish-worshipping tribes in every stage of civilization, from naked savages of the wildest forests to the semi-civilized Fetish worshippers who are mixed up with the settled inhabitants of the cultivated country; and the invariable result has been to show that Christianity has power to prevail against Fetish worship, and that the results of the acceptance of Christianity by the Fetish worshipper are invariably to raise him in the moral and social scale, and to make him a civilized being. I believe there is no part of

India in which the power of Christian preaching to attract the attention of Fetish worshippers, to win them from the worship of evil and impure deities to the pure religion of Christ, and to raise them in the scale of humanity, has not been thus abundantly manifested. Most prominently are these results visible amongst the Shanars and other devil-worshipping races of Southern India; the Kols and Goands of Central India; the Bhils and Koolies, Mhars, Mangs, and Chumars of Western and Central India. Of all these races it may be truly said that Christianity, as far as its effects have been tried, has proved its possession of the promises of this life as well as of the next. In some parts of the country, as in Tinnevelly and Chota Nagpore, the number of actual baptized converts may be reckoned by tens of thousands, and all exhibit a marked improvement in the habits of social life. They are, as a rule, more temperate and chaste, more cleanly, more honest, and more industrious than they were before conversion.

In other parts of India, as in the Deccan, though actual conversions have not been numerous, the effect upon the whole community of outcasts has been marked and general. Scattered as they are, a few in every village in the country, there is no part of the province which has not more or less felt the influence of Christian teaching, and the result is not only a general inclination to turn from the gods of terror and uncleanness to the God of love, purity, and truth, but a remarkable social change which may hereafter bear political fruit, of which time does not now permit me to speak more in detail.

It is worthy of remark that these results are not confined to Christianity as taught in India by any single Church or sect of Christians. I have seen them abundantly follow the teaching of missionaries of our own Church, and of the Churches of Rome and Scotland—both Free and Established, of various Nonconformist bodies, and, in the most remarkable degree, of missionaries from various Churches of Germany, Switzerland, and America. There is comparatively little difference in the power and extent of the result, except what is obviously due to the number and earnestness of Christian missionaries employed, to their more or less perfect organization, and to the period during which their efforts have been directed to the conversion of Fetish-worshipping races and communities. Nor can it be said that the most learned, the wisest, the most accomplished or best endowed of the missionaries are always the most successful. On the contrary, the most wonderful results are sometimes effected by simple and unlearned men. From all these things we are led to the conclusion that such efforts owe their success to something which all the preachers of Christianity hold in common—the great, simple doctrines of Christianity which all believe—the plain, broad precepts of Christian morality which all teach.

What, then, generally speaking, may be summed up as the results of Christian teaching when brought to bear on the low form of civilization exemplified in the classes of which I have been speaking? It is everywhere a rising in the social scale—a civilizing and humanizing influence, tending to make the believer in Christianity a better man and a better subject. I would ask whether the same evidence of the power and effect of Christianity is not to be found in all we read regarding other parts of Asia, of America, of Africa, and of Polynesia—aye, in all we see around us of the effects of simple, earnest Christian teaching on London Arab life?

I have endeavoured thus briefly to describe the effects of Christianity acting on the wild Fetish-worshipping tribes of India as their own religion. But we have also to consider its effects as acting on them externally—as the religion of those in contact with them as neighbours or rulers. How, as compared with other religions, does Christianity suit them, when it is the religion of their more civilized neighbours or conquerors?

Now in India we can in this aspect compare the action of Christianity with that of various forms of Brahmanism, of Buddhism, and of Muhammedanism. Neither of the former in theory make any call on their votaries to propagate their own faith. The devout Brahman and Buddhist are both separatists in theory—seeking perfection through works and aspirations, among which the conversion of the ignorant and the civilization of the brutal find no place. It is true that both religions are more apt to spread among neighbouring communities of a different creed than is generally supposed, especially when those communities happen to be inferior in the scale of civilization; but the process is one rather of annexation and imitation than of assimilation or conversion; and the result is never more than the production of very spurious forms of Hindooism or Buddhism, the professors of which are never, even after the lapse of generations, accepted as true brethren by the genuine Brahman or Buddhist. Texts might doubtless be quoted from the dogmas of either, which would favour the work of the missionary or civilizer; but personal purification and salvation is the main object of both, and any effort to save the souls or bodies of the savage tribes of the forest from death or disease, whether temporal or spiritual, is attended with a risk of pollution which would prevent almost any zealous Brahman or Buddhist from making the attempt.

Nor is the practice of the professors of these religions much better than their theory—coercion, expulsion, and destruction are the only modes of dealing with savages which find much favour with Hindu statesmen. When effectually coerced, a certain degree of toleration may be extended to them, and they may be protected as useful hewers of wood and drawers of water; but that they have any inherent rights as members of the great human family, or that any obligation rests on the Government to protect or improve them, is a doctrine which never could reach the Hindu administrator through the teaching of his own religion.

The same may be said of the Muhammedan—though his religion, like our own, is essentially one of propagandism. If the savage is willing to be converted, he may, as a member of the great family of Islam, rise in the scale of civilization; but there is little hope for the unconverted savage from any Muhammedan ruler, save in the most abject and unconditional submission; and if Muhammedan practice is sometimes better than its theory in treatment of subject races of another faith, it is often far worse. As a general rule, unpersecuting neglect is the utmost the heathen savage or Fetish worshipper can hope for from his Muhammedan lord.

Vigorous government, in any native state in India, before the overshadowing advent of the great Christian power, generally meant more or less severity towards the jungle tribes. I will give you one of many instances I could quote. In my early life in the Deccan of India, I was engaged one day in trying one of these wild men for some depredation on the property of his civilized neighbours, when a Brahman, who had been high in office under the former Maharatta Government, came in to draw his pension. After listening attentively to the trial, he fell into talk on the subject of how Government should deal with such classes, and expressed as the result of his own large experience that nothing but the most severe modes of coercive treatment were of any real avail. He illustrated his argument by an anecdote of one of the great Soubadars of the Maharatta Peishwa, with whom he had served, and in whose province tribes of wild Bhils had been numerous and troublesome. Coercion and bribery had been tried, with equally little effect in mitigating their depredations. At last the Soubadar got wearied, and having invited all the principal chiefs to a feast, under pretence of largely increasing their subsidies, he set upon and slew them, whilst most of them were helplessly intoxicated, and "then the country," my visitor said, "had rest." He related the details of the tragedy not only without any symptom of horror or reprobation, but much as we might speak of the destruction of a family of wolves or tigers; with a strongly expressed opinion that this mode of—what it is now the fashion to call "stamping out"—was the only sensible way of dealing with such vermin.

This, as I have said, was not a solitary instance of the spirit in which Hindu administrators of the old school would have dealt and did deal with the wild tribes. The case is far different now; and I have no doubt all my young Indian friends would indignantly repudiate any such doctrines of extermination. But I would ask them where they learnt the principles on which they would now act? Was it from their own Shasters, or from the writings and teachings of Christian priests, economists, and moralists? And whence did these latter derive their principles, if not from the storehouse of the Christian Scriptures?

From the days when Warren Hastings encouraged Cleveland to civilize the wild tribes of Eastern Bengal, as so graphically described by Heber, down to our own time, the administration of India has, as a rule, acted towards the less civilized of our subjects and neighbours on principles which the Christian religion alone inculcates, and the result has in every way justified the system, as not only the most humane, but the most efficacious from a political and social point of view. I know in fact of no other system which can pretend to have reclaimed and raised to the position of useful members of civilized society whole tribes and communities of wild and uncivilized men; and the most successful measures adopted for this purpose have been distinctly founded on the precepts of Christianity; sometimes adopted knowingly and avowedly—more frequently, perhaps, unwittingly borrowed—through the medium of that code of Christian chivalry, which however adversely affected, at times, by ambition or cupidity, has never wholly ceased to actuate those Englishmen who, for centuries past, have been most energetic in extending British domination to every region of the habitable earth.

If any one requires proof of the literal truth of what I have said, let him consult the works in which it is recorded how Captain Hall and Colonel Dixon civilized the Mairs of Mairwarra in Rajpotana, or how General John Jacob and his lieutenants reclaimed the wild tribes of Northern Sind. A remarkable instance will be found in the records of Bhil civilization, from the first efforts directed by Mr. Mountstewart Elphinstone and Sir John Malcolm, in which Sir James Outram, Colonels Ovans and French, Keatinge, Douglas Graham, and Morris took part ; and instances more or less striking might be quoted from every province in India. The agents in these and similar civilizing proceedings have been frequently, but not always, men of deep and earnest religious convictions. But even in the case of those who made least pretension to a consistent profession of Christianity, it may be fairly asked whence did the actors get the principles on which they acted ? Not from the precepts of Greek or Roman, of Brahman, Buddhist, or Muhammedan. Still less from the social or economical theories of modern materialists or positivists. The principles on which the wild tribes of India have been, and are being, civilized, are identical with those which guide the teachers of our ragged and Sunday schools for the poor neglected children of this great metropolis. They are Christian principles, and are, as far as I know, to be found formulated nowhere save in the Christian Scriptures, wherein they are laid down as imperative rules of action in our dealings with our weaker and less civilized fellow men.

II. But let us now briefly consider the case of a second great class consisting of civilized men, broadly distinguished from the semi-savages of whom we have hitherto been speaking—men in the stage of civilization which has been reached by the great mass of the populations which we see around us here in Europe. They are living in organized communities, as artizans, traders, agriculturalists, professional men, following all the callings known to modern civilization. How does Christianity affect them? How far is it suited to them?

We shall find it next to impossible to answer this question conclusively, if we confine our attention to Europe and America, because the great majority of our people are, and have been for ages, professed Christians. We may, indeed, compare the Europe of Augustus' time with the Europe of our own, and draw our own deductions as to the effect of Christianity on our civilization. But we shall hardly escape debatable ground, as to how much is due to Christianity, and how much to other causes; or as to whether we might not have been better or worse, had the prevailing religion of modern Europe been other than it is.

Here, again, India may help us. You have there a great civilized population, four times as numerous as that of Christian America, as numerous as all the populations of Europe, excluding Russia. They are quite as advanced in all the arts of social life—I may say they are more advanced—than were the populations of Europe in the time of our grandfathers, before the great French Revolution and the outburst of modern mechanical invention. They have practically had nothing to do with Christianity till within the last half century. But every other religion in the world is there and has been long represented on the grandest scale—idolatries more varied than the popular superstitions of Greece or Rome; a full third of all the Muhammedans in the world, and every form of esoteric religion, philosophies, mysterious and secret creeds without end.

How does Christianity fare in the face of all these powers of the air? Is it forced to give way? Is it silent? inoperative? Is it powerless, or put to shame?

I speak simply as to matters of experience and observation, and not of opinion; just as a Roman prefect might have reported to Trajan or the Antonines; and I assure you that, whatever you may be told to the contrary, the teaching of Christianity among 160 millions of civilized, industrious Hindoos and Muhammedans in India is effecting changes, moral, social, and political, which for extent and rapidity of effect are far more extraordinary than anything you or your fathers have witnessed in modern Europe. Presented for the first time to most of the teeming Indian communities, within the memory of men yet alive,—preached by only a few scores of Europeans, who, with rare exceptions, had not previously been remarkable among their own people in Europe for intellectual power or cultivation, who had little of worldly power or sagacity, and none of the worldly motives which usually carry men onward to success, —Christianity has nevertheless, in the course of fifty years, made its way to every part of the vast mass of Indian civilized humanity, and is now an active, operative, aggressive power in every branch of social and political life on that continent.

Of the external action of Christianity, as the religion of the conquering race, I will say but little ; other races, who were not Christians, in other ages, could and did conquer and civilize ; and if a mere handful of Christianized Europeans have succeeded in subduing scores of potentates, and people counted by scores of millions, they have only done on a very large and successful scale, what Greeks and Romans, Phœnicians and Assyrians, Egyptians, Teutons, Arabs, and other non-Christian races, have done before them, in all time past.

But let me note, as very noteworthy in itself, and as bearing especially on our subject, the spirit and the motives in which the conquerors of our own nation and time have acted ; because they are very different from anything you will find in the spirit or motives of action of any non-Christian race of conquerors I ever heard of. We have had, it is true, in our Indian conquests, enough of ambition, lust of conquest, cupidity, and all the meaner motives which actuate mankind in aggressive wars on their neighbours; but I would ask you what has been the general national sentiment in approving each successive acquisition? I do not speak of the motives of individual actors, but of the English nation at large, in ratifying and retaining the conquests from time to time achieved.

I answer, without hesitation, that it has been a feeling of duty towards the conquered—a conviction that we could not recede without abdicating the power of doing good to great masses of mankind, and thus permitting the existence of much preventable evil. No lower motive would, I feel sure, have sufficed to make the English nation at large approve the action of her children in India in time past, or would now induce Englishmen at large to continue to sustain the burdens and responsibilities of such a charge. It may be a mistaken view—that is matter of argument; but it exists —that is matter of fact, and it is distinctly traceable to the system of morality founded on Christianity— the duty of doing good to your neighbour—which the nation at large recognizes as its rule of action, and it has a very important bearing on the value of Christianity as a civilizing agent. You will find nothing of the kind in the motives, as far as we know them, of any non-Christian nation. But it is singular that you do find them most distinctly marked among the most potent moving causes which have impelled other Christian nations to the conquest of non-Christians. I do not speak now of crusaders, or of the religious element which was traceable among the motives of the Spanish and Portuguese conquerors of past ages, though you know how potent and how elevating, as far as it went, that element was; and how, as the religious motive became fainter, all that gave force as well as dignity to the action of the conquering nation seemed to disappear;—but I would ask you to note how largely the desire to use power for the good of subject races actuates another nation which is perhaps even more than ourselves a conquering power in Asia.

We hear continually of the ambition and rapacity of Russia; but we are apt to forget that there is a power urging Russia on to subjugate and civilize her barbarous neighbours, which is more potent and more persistent than worldly ambition or cupidity, and that is, the religious duty of Christianizing and civilizing: any one who, in estimating the forces of Russian aggressive movement, left out of view the impulse derived from religious convictions among the leaders of national thought—that it was a national religious duty to extend to all barbarians around them the blessings of being within the pale of the Russian Church—would leave out of calculation the most energetic element of the motive power.

This notion of doing good to the conquered is, moreover, an element not traceable among the motives of Assyrians, Romans, Saracans, or other conquering non-Christian nations.

We are not now arguing an abstract question of right or wrong. The desire of conquest is probably one of the most powerful and universal of human instincts. What we are now considering is how this universal instinct is modified by peculiarities of religion; and what I wish you to note is, that in the case of our own nation and of the Russian—two of the great conquering Christian nations of modern days —considerations of which we can distinctly trace the origin to Christian morality add greatly to the effective force of the natural instinct, whilst they elevate and humanize it in a manner of which no trace is to be found in the action of the great conquering nations of other ages and creeds.

We have spoken hitherto of the external action of Christianity on non-Christian communities, such as we find in India. But what are its internal effects when it is received as their religion by the members of those communities who are at about the same level of general civilization as the mass of Europeans in the middle of the last century? Does Christianity act at all on them? and how?

Let us look first at their social life—and here alone the subject is so vast, that one can, in the compass of such a lecture as this, barely touch on one or two characteristic points. Let us, for instance, consider the action of Christian teaching on Indian caste.

I need hardly remind you that all Indian civilized communities have one general characteristic which distinguishes them from similar communities in other parts of the world and in other ages—they are all bound by the traditions and practices of Hindoo caste. Volumes would not suffice to describe Hindoo caste and its effects, social, religious, and political. But there is an aspect in which it may be presented which may give you some faint idea of its nature and power, though it represents only one of the peculiarities of the great caste system. The peculiarity to which I allude is that it is a great system of trades' unions, more universal and better organized than any of the unions with which we are acquainted in Europe. Their origin in India is lost in antiquity. The earliest histories we possess recognize the system as one which had already grown up, and it appears more or less to have swallowed up and assimilated the foreign elements and nationalities which at different times have been imported into India. As far as experience goes, Christianity alone appears to have the power of resisting the absorbing influences of Hindoo caste.

It must not be supposed that the results of caste are altogether evil. How much mischief caste does I have not time to describe, but I will briefly refer to some of its good effects. It maintains a high standard of skill in all the arts of life. Even in a country which for the great part of a century has been the theatre of incessant desolating war, artizans, and even artists of the highest skill, are still to be found, owing their existence, or the possession of their arts, mainly to the system of caste, which binds every man to the profession of his forefathers. More than this: caste has a great immediate effect in maintaining a moral standard. I do not say that in the long run, and in remoter results, the institution of caste is not one of very immoral tendency. It is, I believe, infinitely inferior in point of morality to the system of Christian morals; but speaking with regard to immediate results, there can be no doubt that one of the primary effects of a strict system of caste is to maintain a very considerable strictness of morals.

Of its evils I will only select two. It prevents anything like national union, and it ensures a more or less rigid form of social slavery.

It is, I need hardly tell you, diametrically opposed to all the principles of Christianity. A religion which teaches, as fundamental doctrines, the essential unity of the human race—the brotherhood of every member of that race—and the potential possession by every such member of every blessing of this world, and of a boundless future;—such a religion can have nothing in common with a great system whose essence is divisions innumerable, impassable here and hereafter, and practically annihilating the brotherhood of man. Christianity is, as you all know, perfectly compatible with a strict observance of gradations in social life, but of anything approaching the Hindoo system of caste it is the declared enemy. What then, as matter of experience, is its effect on the great mass of the civilized Hindoo communities, which are, with such rare exceptions, devoted adherents of caste?

I answer shortly that intimate contact with Christianized Europe and a general diffusion of some slight knowledge of Christianity have been the death-knell of caste as the social bond of Hindoos. Such a system—the growth of thousands of years, among hundreds of millions of people—does not die in a day. It may be that only the first blow has been struck, but that blow has been a fatal one. It may take ages to work out the result, but the result can no longer be doubtful. It is not I alone who think so. You cannot gain the confidence of any thoughtful, honest, educated Hindoo, without finding out that this is his conviction. He may put many subsidiary causes in the foreground. Our superior military strength, and our freedom of political and social thought and action—our railways and other means of rapid intercommunication—our free press—our all-embracing literature and open education—our uniform laws,—these and many other agencies will occur to him as the most efficient solvents of his ancient social system. But he instinctively feels, what we ourselves are sometimes slow to perceive, that all these institutions and agencies are somehow the products and offshoots of our religion—that Christianity is logically and legitimately the foundation, the wellspring of influences, under a hundred shapes, moral and material, which, while they constitute our national life and strength, are destructive of things as they have hitherto been in Hindoo social life. He feels that the system of caste is doomed, and can never more reign, as it reigned but one generation ago, over the millions of Hindostan. Moreover, most thoughtful Hindoos are ready to confess that caste would have little chance of a reprieve even if we were turned out of India to-morrow. The strange truths which sink so deep into the hearts of people, and influence all their thoughts and actions, have not been taught by any State agency, and form no part of the apparatus which the English rulers have consciously employed. Indeed, it is apt to be charged as a reproach against our Government, that it has been too indifferent to missionary work,—and the charge is well founded, as far as general abstinence from all active co-operation can make it; but I believe such abstinence to have been necessary and right, and in the result conducive to the spread of Christianity. Experience shows that a temporary withdrawal of the protection of the English Government, such as occurred in some parts during the Mutiny years of 1857-8, so far from extinguishing Christianity, helps to spread it; and candid and thoughtful Hindoos are not slow to perceive that even if the English were now to leave India and were not succeeded by any other Christian power, it would still be impossible to counteract the destructive influences already at work, and that caste, as a system of impassable social divisions, must, ultimately, give way before the ideas which have taken root during a few generations of close contact with Christian Europe.

It would be impossible to contemplate without a shudder such results as the solution of all the ancient bonds of society, among so many myriads of people, were it not that the new influences have shown themselves at least as potent in binding mankind into new social combinations as in dissolving old social ties.

It is a curious fact that Christianity—whilst, as one of its fundamental principles, abjuring all claim to interfere authoritatively in matters of social or political organization, whilst inculcating the paramount duty of acquiescence and obedience to all lawful social arrangements and political institutions—has proved capable, beyond all other systems, of inspiring successful attempts at political and at social organization. Since the Roman society and polity began to decay, men enthusiastically imbued with the spirit of Christianity have ever been foremost in the task of building up that great fabric of European civilization which now dominates over the world. Whether in the wilds of Scandinavia, or among idolatrous Teuton hordes, in the cloister, in the camp, in the parliament, or in the guild of mediæval Europe—or, in later ages, asserting by speech, by pen, or by sword, the rights and obligations of mankind—the strongest and most successful organizers and constructors, social as well as political, have ever been men of the strongest, deepest, most earnest religious Christian convictions; differing, it may be, most widely as to particular doctrines of their common faith or particular practical applications of their theories, but all deriving their inspiration from one common source, and referring, as the ultimate authority for all they do, to one book, briefer than the scriptures of any other faith, and which inculcates all its moral precepts with a clearness and simplicity which an intelligent child can comprehend as perfectly as the most advanced philosopher.

We may learn something of the comparative power of Christianity, as a civilizing and constructive agency, by comparing the great ecclesiastics who advised Charlemagne, and Alfred, the Conqueror, Edward the First, and our Tudor sovereigns, or the religious men who in later days have worked out our present political system, with the Roman philosopher, the Hindoo recluse, or the Muhammedan fakeer, to whom the conquerors of other nations might have had recourse for advice in organizing their dominions. We shall do well to remember that the great organizers of our own nation were generally typical examples of the Christianity of their own day; when they were assured that mankind needed the devotion of their lives and labours, the argument was all-powerful to draw them to the service of the State. Is there any other religious system which thus makes public duty a religious obligation? I cannot find it in Greek or Roman philosophy, absorbed in the search for truth; still less in the Hindoo or Muhammedan systems, where the highest merit is attributed to ascetic observances which are utterly incompatible with attention to worldly affairs.

I mentioned as two prominent evils of the Hindoo system of caste, that it prevents anything like national union, and reduces the bulk of mankind to social slavery.

How effectual a cure Christianity supplies to the latter tendency needs no argument or illustration from me ; but a word on its civilizing effect as a bond of national union. I can speak from experience, that the want of such a bond is most keenly felt by educated natives of India, of every class and creed, who desire to see their own countrymen rising in the scale of civilized nations. It is possible that at one time, under native sovereigns, caste, after a fashion, supplied such a bond. Its iron rules bound together all ranks and classes, and the political edifice was stable as long as all external influences were excluded; but all depended on the strictness of such exclusion, and it is possible, that even without the foreign invasion to which Hindoo caste owes its destruction, the edifice must in time have been sapped by influences which, like Christianity, do not necessarily require foreign agency for their introduction. However that may be, many educated Indians are convinced that the bond of caste can no longer be relied on; and even those who have no leaning to Christianity feel that whatever else may be proposed in the shape of new philosophies or systems of education, all lack the essential element of including the lowest as well as the highest classes in its grasp. Caste did this by including all in one bondage—Christianity does it by embracing all in one brotherhood. What else can be relied on, in these days of vast nationalities, which render feudal subordination so impotent, I know not.

For the present, patriotic Indians are generally content to acquiesce in foreign dominion, as the sole alternative to internecine civil discord. The time, I believe, must come when they will see that the influences which form the real bond of union between their foreign rulers are equally capable of uniting the scattered elements of their own social and national existence, and they will accept Christianity as that civilizing element which alone can render their own independent national existence possible.

But the time when this truth can obtain general acceptance is probably still distant, and educated Indians generally hold that some reform of their own system is still possible, and far superior to anything which Christianity can offer them. Their arguments are naturally powerful with those who are living entirely for the present—for the enjoyment of the things of this world, and who have no object but to make the most of this present life. For all such it must be confessed that the attractions of Christianity are less marked, when it is compared with any great worldly system, which, like the Hindooism or Muhammedanism of the trading, mercantile, and agricultural classes, places its *summum bonum* in a well regulated enjoyment of the things of this life. The lofty aims and self-denying precepts of Christianity have comparatively small attractions to those who are devoted to the pleasures of sense, to the accumulation of wealth, or even to many forms of intellectual luxury. For all such, the worship of Aphrodite or Mammon, whether in an abstract form, or in the form so commonly seen in India—the actual material worship of the creature—presents superior attractions. It is when the world and the things of the world, its pleasures and ambitions, cease to be the first objects of desire, that Christianity offers, to those who have been absorbed in the pursuits of the world, that which is not to be found in any other religion. To the prosperous trader, artizan, or agriculturalist, thriving in his own business, and wishing only to enjoy the good things it obtains for him, almost any religion, or no religion except the worship of himself, may suffice. He cannot be capable of the happiness which a Christian philanthropist, or a devoted Christian, can attain even in this life; but he can at least enjoy things as they are, and, if he can keep out of sight the future, and his obligations to those around him, he may live in great enjoyment. But it is otherwise when suffering or adversity overtake him, when he becomes anxious regarding the world beyond the grave, or seeks to know his duty to his fellow-men. In all these respects there is no comparison between the teachings of Christianity and those of any other form of religion. In adversity or in suffering, or when the conscience is aroused to ask what is our duty with regard to our fellowmen—no religion can give a perfectly satisfactory answer except Christianity; and the results of experience in India do not in any respect contradict what we should *a priori* expect in this respect. Missionaries tell us that they make small way among the prosperous traders or farmers, except when grief has softened the heart, or adversity has shown a necessity of some support other than that which can be derived from worldly enjoyments.

III. But we have still to consider the action of Christianity as a civilizing element on a third class of men,—infinitely smaller in number than either of the great classes we have been considering,—but most important as directors of the opinions of the world. I allude, of course, to those who are raised above the sordid material wants of the first class we have described, whose main object is not, like the great majority of the second class, how to exist, or enjoy life, but rather to teach mankind the end and objects of life and the best mode of living. These are the educated few who are the great teachers of mankind. How does Christianity affect or act on them?

I might dwell on habits of mind which are most congenial to Christianity, and which are distinctly fostered by it, and which are also peculiarly characteristic of some of the greatest teachers of mankind; such are love of truth, and teachableness of disposition. It might, however, be truly said that such habits of mind are not peculiar to Christianity, and that they are to be found in the greatest teachers of all ages and creeds.

It is difficult in Europe to imagine what would be the condition of things apart from that Christianity in the midst of which every member of every class has been brought up, and which must unconsciously, by its influence or traditions, have more or less modified every opinion he holds.

But in India we have, in their unaltered original form, the prototypes of every system of philosophy which has ever existed in Europe, and we may learn something of the relations between those systems and Christianity, as a civilizing element, by observing the attitude of Oriental teachers of philosophy in all its branches towards our religion when it is presented to them.

Time, of course, does not admit of even the barest enumeration of the various schools of philosophy, still less of an examination of their tenets. But there are a few broad characteristics of the grander divisions of Oriental teaching which it may be well to notice, however briefly, with reference to their general bearing on civilization.

There is this common to them all—their philosophies are all for philosophers. They aim to teach the teachers of mankind, and so indirectly act on mankind at large; but the notion of a teaching which, like that of our Lord and His apostles, was to be received, wholly and completely, by all the body of disciples, and which, as far as it is necessary to happiness in this world or the next, was to be learned as perfectly by the poor and needy as by the rich—this notion, which pervades all Christianity, is utterly opposed to all Oriental philosophies. It is to be found more or less perfectly expressed, and not unfrequently obviously borrowed from Christianity, in several of the eclectic religions, which, from time to time, spring up in the east, and have, from this cause mainly, acquired great, and often permanent, popularity; Sikhism and its derivatives, like the Kuka schism, owe much of their popular acceptance to this feature in their teaching; so do the precepts of Kubeer Punt, and of Tukaram, the popular Maharatta poet; but to the higher Oriental philosophies it is unknown, and its absence gives to Christianity, which possesses it in the fullest degree, an immense practical advantage over them, as a civilizing element.

Something of the kind may be found in the brief formula of the Muhammedan Creed, the repetition of which constitutes almost the sole intellectual passport for admission to Islam; but the whole genius of the philosophies which have received any bias from

Muhammedanism is exclusion of the vulgar. Poverty is inculcated as almost necessary to a high tone of sanctity, but the ruling idea is the exaltation of self—the exact opposite to that denial of self, which is the first step in Christian practice, and which makes Christianity essentially a religion for all mankind, and not for any one sect or nation.

This is the most important element in what, for want of a better word, I would term the "aggressiveness" of Christianity. The earnest Christian is irresistibly impelled by the spirit of his religion to communicate its benefits to others. He may not rest whilst any remain in misery or darkness. This aggressive spirit is of wonderful power as a civilizing agency. There is nothing like it in the spirit of Brahmanism or of Buddhism; and the aggressiveness of Muhammedanism is as infinitely inferior, in power and in endurance, as fear is inferior to love, as a motive of human action.

And this suggests a word on Christian toleration, which seems to me an equally distinctive feature of Christianity, and a most potent element of civilizing energy. There is nothing of it in pure Muhammedanism. It is not to be found in the Koran, with its more than Mosaic exclusiveness, and its energy in exterminating all difference of opinion. Great civilizing Muhammedan sovereigns like Akbar were compelled to import from Christianity, or its derivatives, that toleration which was their glory, and the secret of their success as benefactors of mankind. It seems to me that it is the absence of this element which causes the sterility of Muhammedanism, and its want of power as a civilizing agency; and as this feature is the essence of Muhammedanism, we cannot hope for anything of a real permanent civilizing influence from any modifition of that creed.

This is of more importance to us here in Europe than we might at first suppose, because, if there can be such a thing as Muhammedanism without a genuine faith in Muhammed, we have amongst us very popular creeds which have strong affinities to that religion. Next to self-worship, which is common in many other creeds, the most striking and usual aberration of Muhammedanism is towards the worship of the God of forces, or of success; towards a belief that all the enjoyments of sense are the rightful heritage of the faithful who dare to seize them, and towards uncompromising and unarguing hostility to all who differ from the true believer's creed. The same spirit is manifest in all these respects in many of the anti-Christian schools of modern European philosophy and literature. Many grave treatises, and many more romances, of the present generation among ourselves have more of the inspiration of the Koran than of the New Testament, and if the rules and proceedings of the Fenian organization or the Parisian Commune were studied without a knowledge of the time and place where they were enacted, they would be more likely to be attributed to the camps of Omar or

Tamerlane than to the heart of Christian society in this century.

But to turn to the spirit of toleration to be found in other creeds. The toleration of the Brahman or Buddhist philosopher, striking as it appears at first sight, proves when examined to be simple indifference or neglect.

The absence of all active spirit of persecution, as long as the opponent is quiescent and submissive, which makes both Brahman and Buddhist practically so tolerant, is the offspring of contempt, and has nothing in common with the toleration which springs from the desire to do by all men as we would that they should do by us.

Time is wanting for any detailed comparison of the civilizing tendencies of either class of creeds with those of Christianity. I will mention but one obvious tendency of the teaching of each, which seems to me to place it, as compared with Christianity, in a position of decided inferiority.

Of the innumerable schools of Brahmanism, none is more popular in India than that of materialists, who teach that we can know nothing, certainly, save of matter and its properties; and that belief in what we call life or spirit, save as functions and properties of matter, —and by consequence any belief in a spiritual deity, —is a hopeless error and delusion. Something of the same kind is sometimes taught among ourselves, and into its truth or falsehood we will not now enter. But of its value as a civilizing agency we may form some idea, if we consider that there is hardly one of the practices which the English Government has been engaged in putting down, in the interests as we believed of all humanity and civilization, which is not clearly defensible under any moral code which can be deduced from such a creed.

For instance, infanticide, or at least the slaying of all children for whose nurture ample provision cannot be assured, is clearly defensible upon materialistic principles. So is the practice of Suttee, and the slaughter of all who have an incurable disease, or who from age or infirmity are unable to provide for their own subsistence. The great community of Thugs have excellent materialistic reasons for their mode of possessing themselves of the property of others, nor do I see how any form of rapine or appropriation, which practically enunciates the right of the strongest, can be objected to by any strict materialistic philosopher. Clearly there is no form of vice, so long as it is not directly prejudicial to health, from which a thorough-going materialist need be restrained. He is himself the sole judge of right or wrong, nor need he regard anything except in its relation to his own physical enjoyment.

Pressed with considerations of this kind, the Brahman materialist generally evades all obligation to construct any theory of moral duty. The only obligation he acknowledges is to find out the true nature and laws of matter, and how he can best live in accordance with those laws. The search is a long one, and while it is in progress the whole world may go on its way—unenlightened, unless it will follow the researches of the philosopher.

Surely there is nothing in such systems which can compare to the work, past or possible, of Christianity as a civilizing agency.

Nor is the case much better if we turn to Buddhism, the worship of pure reason, of which also one could find examples under other names among ourselves. No doubt it has achieved, in times past, triumphs of civilization of which there is scarcely any parallel in history. But it is equally clear that there is some defect which causes it now to give way, as a practical civilizing element, before Christianity. As a religion for all mankind (apart of course from all question of its truth) Buddhism is proved, by the inexorable logic of facts, to be weaker than Christianity.

It seems to me, the cause is not far to seek—Buddhism places its *summum bonum* in escape from passion, and from all connection with matter, from life and from existence, as involving passion. Such a system may evolve a high morality, or construct a great fabric of political wisdom; but it has nothing to offer mankind, nothing which comes so home to the instincts of all humanity as the Christian doctrines of the resurrection of the body and life everlasting in union with a glorified body. We may debate for ever over the proof of either doctrine; but as matter of fact and experience, there can be no doubt that they appeal to the hearts and instincts of mankind in a manner which the atheistic annihilation taught by the Buddhist philosopher never can.

Something of the feeling which I have endeavoured to express, of the paramount power of Christianity as a civilizing agency, and a bond of political union, is apt to show itself instinctively where it might least be suspected.

If a despot in Christendom is anxious for his throne, or if politicians find that the people long neglected are getting loose from all social and political ties, they are apt to call in the Christian teacher, as though he possessed some spell, the utterance of which could calm the wild passions of unrestrained and untaught humanity. Such men forget that Christianity is no charm or magical device, and that its power rests in the hearts of believers. Let them be wise in time, and before they put away from them the teachings of Christianity, and deliberately abjure its obligations as their rule of political and social life, let them remember that such gifts are not often twice offered to men or nations; and that to nations, as to men, it may happen, after once rejecting them, to find no place for repentance, "though they seek it carefully with tears."

THE CONTRAST

BETWEEN

PAGAN AND CHRISTIAN SOCIETY.

BY

THE VERY REV. CHARLES MERIVALE, D.D.

THE CONTRAST BETWEEN PAGAN AND CHRISTIAN SOCIETY.

THE use of Sacrifice, it is admitted, has been very general, or we may perhaps say universal, throughout the world. Wherever at least there has been an idea of God, and a belief in His existence as an efficient agent in the world around us, there has been the use of Sacrifice. As far as we can trace, the practice or rite has reached back to the remotest antiquity. It has been enjoined in religious systems which claim to be even more ancient than that of Moses and of the Bible. We find it in the Vedas no less clearly than in the Hebrew Scriptures. In Persia and Phœnicia and Egypt and Arabia, it dates probably as far back in the night of ages as any that can be alleged from the Divine records with regard to the children of Israel, or of the patriarchs before them. We must either ascribe its origin to a primitive, or so-called patriarchal revelation—a Divine command delivered through unknown channels, ages before

Moses, to a race far earlier than the Jewish, and suppose it to have been propagated by this race throughout the nations of the earth, and the Jewish nation among the rest—or we must conceive the idea to have grown up instinctively in the heart of man, and spread by natural diffusion from clime to clime, from religion to religion ; to have been embraced, under the teaching of the Hebrew lawgiver and under the special sanction of the Mosaic revelation, by the children of Israel from this common human original. The belief in a Divine revelation to the Jews and Christians seems to me to be in nowise concerned with the solution of this question. The elder and the later Scriptures are equally silent as to the origin of Sacrifice ; they nowhere declare or presume that the idea was Divinely revealed, or the practice authoritatively enjoined by God. In the earliest of our Scriptures Sacrifice is always spoken of as a thing in common use, but no hint is given of its having been originally commanded. And, accordingly, different views have been held upon the subject. The ancient Fathers, it may be observed, generally held that the practice was purely natural in its origin ; and the ancient Fathers, familiar as they were with the heathen world, had a wider sympathy with it, and believed better things, and hoped better things of it, and of the hold it had, however imperfectly, upon Divine truth, than the theological schools of later and less liberal ages.

But, setting aside this question as of little practical

moment, I would impress upon you the remarkable fact that Sacrifice, after having been so universally used through all previous ages, in all heathen countries, so far as we know, the most civilized as well as the rudest, and not in heathen countries only, but in all non-Christian countries, including the Jewish, has, in fact, entirely ceased throughout Christendom ever since the first promulgation of the Christian doctrine. The practice has ceased ; the idea is abandoned ; its religious significance is utterly repudiated. The Gospel has abolished Sacrifice. The Sacrifice, as a Christian believer would say, of Christ has been accepted by the Christian world as the consummation of the idea, which has been from that moment superseded in the minds of all Christian believers, and can never be revived among them. The fact, I suppose, is undoubted. It seems to me a very remarkable one. I have been invited to set forth in some sort the Contrast between Christian and Pagan society. The moral, social, and political contrast is indeed manifold and intricate. The more I think of it the more I feel my inability to do justice to it, to represent to you its history or its philosophy, in the compass of a lecture. All I can do is to lay before you in this one great fact a fundamental ground of contrast between the Pagan world and the Christian, and thence proceed to indicate, rather than to sketch, much less to develop, its moral and spiritual result. Even so I may hope to suggest important conclusions as to the claim which the Christian religion makes on our intelligent and earnest belief.

Now if we supposed the idea of Sacrifice to have originated in a special revelation, we might easily invent a theory to account for its extinction by a special revelation also. The notion, it might be said, of the religious efficacy of Sacrifice was first suggested to man by Divine grace, and afterwards kept alive supernaturally, for the express purpose of fixing men's minds upon the Great Sacrifice that was to be performed in the fulness of time, in the person of the Divine Saviour. The whole subject would then be a mystery, referred to God and His dealings with mankind, and removed altogether from the category of natural causes and developments.

But if we take the other alternative, that which is more likely to approve itself to the theological views of the present age, and suppose that Sacrifice sprang in the first instance from some natural instinct of man, some universal sentiment, some want or aspiration of the human race, how extraordinary must it appear, that this natural and universal instinct should be suddenly, universally, and for ever extinguished by the final Sacrifice of Jesus Christ, wherever that Sacrifice is accepted as an historical and theological truth!

If we look for the source of religious emotion, we seem to find it in the sense, so common, so universal among us, of the existence of some superior Being, some higher life, some greater power, with whom we are inexplicably connected, on whom we are mysteriously dependent. The child first acquires this idea from its experience, perhaps, of its own natural dependence on the superior strength of its elders—the savage from his consciousness of the great powers of Nature, by which he lives and has his being, while he is controlled at the same time and educated by them. This, it would seem, whencesoever derived, is the first idea of God, as a Being of power, mysterious and undefined, but ever real and present with us. The idea of Divine power in the abstract soon passes into its special manifestations. Hence the idea of God as Creator of the world and all that is therein—the Creator of the world as it first sprang into existence, then of the world continuing and advancing, ever varying yet ever the same; of life and the laws of life; of body and the laws of body; of mind and the laws of mind. Hence the idea of God as a moral Being with a moral design—a Providence adapting means to ends through an infinite series of purposes, constantly attracting and as constantly eluding our investigation. Hence, once more, the idea of God as a Being of infinite goodness as well as of infinite power, of infinite holiness as well as of goodness; as a Being, therefore, of infinite justice as well as of love—as the awful abstraction of eternal and immutable Right. If man began, then, with a mere blind awe of God, such as has been compared to that of a dog for his master, he advances, step by step, to amazement, fear, and reverence; if he began with a sense of his own littleness, he grows to a feeling of humiliation and self-abandonment. He must be utterly abased and overwhelmed at the conception of the infinite distance between himself and all that he can call his own, and the great God, the Creator, the Sustainer, the Ruler, and the Avenger. Surely he must sink in despair unless he can discover some means of putting himself in communion, in sympathy, with this infinite Being, of securing a share in His regard and interest, of obtaining the assurance of His grace and favour.

A modern poet has asked us why we should shrink from living alone, reminding us in solemn tones that we are all born alone into the world, and must all die alone, and leave it, and that even while we are performing our pilgrimage on earth, in the company of our fellow millions, yet we are for the most part solitary in our thoughts and conscience, and that

> "Not even the dearest heart and next our own
> Knows half the reasons why we smile or sigh."

But it is this very consciousness of spiritual solitude that enforces the higher and deeper conviction that we are never left actually and entirely to ourselves. We must acknowledge that our existence is, after all, bound up with another existence, our soul with another soul, our personality with another personality. There is, we are assured, a Being ever near us, ever about our path and about our bed, and that spieth out all our ways, with whom we enjoy spiritual relations even beyond the scope of our limited imaginations. The religious sentiment of man declares that there is such a Being;

that we do hold communion with Him; nay, more, that this communion or sympathy may be indefinitely enhanced by efforts of our own. We call Him God; we confess His presence within us, though we cannot see or feel Him; we recognise the fact of our spiritual relation to Him, after the analogy of those electric sympathies of which we have sensible experience, though we cannot trace them to the action of the senses. We feel ourselves not absolutely, not essentially, alone in the world, but rather in the presence of a Stranger, whom we are inclined to admire the more for the imperfectness of our knowledge of Him; and we yearn towards Him from our lone personality as the patriarchs of old towards the stranger who approached their solitary dwellings, and allowed them to open their hearts, and make question and reply about the things of the outer world, and exchange the greetings of human sympathy and interest.

"Be not forgetful to entertain strangers," says the writer to the Hebrews, "for thereby some have entertained angels unawares." The expression is apparently proverbial. We might be glad to trace its derivation, and learn through how many generations the idea it embodies has been familiar to man. Is it simply a devout reflection of the Jewish mind upon the Scriptural legend of Lot's reception of the angels at Sodom, or of the "three men" under whose likeness God is said to have appeared to Abraham in the plain of Mamre? Or is it a reminiscence of traditions more widely spread throughout the ancient world, and still faintly repeated to us in the records of Pagan mythology, of the descent of the deities on earth to partake of human hospitalities, and leave a blessing or a curse, according to the reception they met with from their creatures? Undoubtedly the human mind, meditating anxiously and fervently on the mystery of its communion with the Divine, has imagined to itself the visible occurrence of such blessed intercourse on many occasions, and gathered strength for its struggle with its own spiritual solitude from the conviction it has then acquired of the actual presence and companionship of God. It has been under Divine guidance—it has been, we may well believe, through special revelation—that men have been led to conceive of a time when He was wont to reveal Himself sensibly to His favoured creatures, and to converse with them familiarly, even as friend with friend.

Such is the tradition conveyed to us in the earliest records of the Hebrew Scriptures—that is, in the earliest consistent records of human history and human imagination. Such is the tradition of God visiting the first parents of our race in Eden, when Adam and Eve "heard the voice of the Lord God walking in the garden in the cool of the day:" when "the Lord said unto Cain, Where is thy brother?" and Cain said unto the Lord, "My punishment is greater than I can bear;" and Cain "went and hid himself from the presence of the Lord:" and again when "God said unto Noah, The end of all flesh is come before me." However frequent are God's communications with His chosen people through messengers and prophets in the later ages, the manner of His intercourse with them is never again represented as so direct and familiar as in the earliest chapters of the book of Genesis. Whatever men may think of the composition of the first book of the Hebrew Scriptures, the primitive simplicity of its subject-matter reflects beyond all controversy the earliest known condition of the religious sentiment among men.

But the most ancient of Heathen traditions declare a similar belief in the personal revelation of God to man. The Hindoo mythology represents the Deity as descending periodically to earth in a series of personal incarnations. The legends of Greece may be traced no further than to the date of the Iliad and the Odyssey; but there can be no doubt that ages before the composition of those most ancient of poems the idea was rife, throughout the Hellenic and Pelasgian world, that the Divine Existences might mingle occasionally with human society, and reveal themselves as friends and benefactors to their favourites among mortals. Such intercourse all mankind regarded as the supreme felicity. The stories of such blessed visitations were repeated with awe and gladness from mouth to mouth, and all men rejoiced in the possibility of becoming so favoured and blessed themselves. All believed, and all imagined how such visits might be solicited and obtained; how, if obtained, the blessing might be improved to the utmost. Men, it was conceived, might be admitted to banquet with the Immortals; to sit at meat with them by invitation to their heavenly entertainments; to receive them as guests under their own humble roofs, and gratify them with the modest repast they tendered with hospitable sincerity. But thus to enjoy the society of the Divine Powers was a special grace reserved for a few only, the tradition of which alone survived in the grosser ages of human corruption. Such marvels could hardly be again experienced until men, corrupt and abominable, should have recovered something of their primeval purity. Meanwhile let them cherish the tradition of the past by a symbolic ritual; let their pious faith engage the Powers above to actual renewal of the lost communion, at least invisibly and spiritually. The act of Commemoration and the act of Communion would thus become blended together in their minds, and would never, perhaps, be clearly distinguished the one from the other.

Such, it would seem, was the first origin of the practice of Sacrifice and Oblation—the offering up to the Deity of such things as man felt to be agreeable to his own carnal appetite—fruits for the taste, flowers for the smell,—whatever was rich and rare and beautiful in his own apprehension; and therewith the flesh and blood and fat of animals, the noblest and most enlivening banquets among his fellows. In the smoke of the sacrifice which mounted up to heaven men beheld the elemental food ascending to the abode of the Deity, and most nearly corresponding with the lightness and delicacy of the ethereal natures — the nearest approach which material conception could make to a purely spiritual essence. The intimations vouchsafed to us of the state of men by our primitive records give us no other idea of Sacrifice than this— that it is simply the offering of faith and thankfulness in memory of a past communion with God, with the hope of bringing Him again into communion with His worshippers.

I have thus far described what may be called the eucharistic idea of Sacrifice, the idea of a blessed communion of man with God, set forth under the token of offerings of thanksgiving. It seems tolerably clear that this is the earliest idea of Sacrifice conveyed both by the Hebrew and the Greek records of primitive antiquity. But I am not concerned to insist upon it as the true origin of the world-wide practice of which we are speaking. It conceives of the Deity as primarily a God of love; but it must be determined by the temperament of the individual man, or the genius and character of a nation, whether God shall be regarded primarily as a Being to love, or a Being to fear; which of these is the first and fundamental conception it is presumptuous to decide and idle to speculate. We find the two conceptions blending one with the other as far back, perhaps, as history can carry us. If the earliest Greek religions were brightened with a general hue of cheerfulness and sweetness, it is not less true that they were partly founded upon traditions of gloom and terror also. The primitive rites of Phœnicia and Arabia were orgies of blood and fire, and the Levitical law of Sacrifice—strong and vigorous as a protest against the abominations of Baal and Moloch, as became the first religious reformation in history—was fearfully marked with a sense of the wrath of God, and the necessity of appeasing it. If we take the eucharistic as the earliest idea of Sacrifice, it is impossible to say when the idea of propitiation became first blended with it. As far as historical records can trace them, the one was as widely spread and as fully developed as the other. The favour of the Divine Being was to be engaged, and His anger to be averted. Some sacrifice was required on the part of man to prove his sense of subjection to God. He must confess his own nothingness in the sight of God, and prove the sincerity of his confession by submitting to some loss in token of it. Sacrifice became no longer the mere spontaneous offering of what was pleasant to man; it was the surrender of something that involved an actual loss and damage to him. The slaughter of beasts was an actual loss to the worshipper, and the sincerity of his religious feeling was tested, and perhaps rudely measured, by the amount of loss he thus incurred. But more subtle ideas soon intervened, if, indeed, we can pretend that more subtle ideas were ever absent from the imagination, intently busy about the means of bridging over the chasm between the human worshipper and the divinity he worshipped. It was not by the loss to the worshipper only that the god was to be propitiated and delighted. The feelings of the victim itself came into consideration. The sufferings of the beast seemed to reflect a vicarious merit upon the man who offered him. The worthier the victim, for his size, his strength, his beauty, his innocence, the greater the merit of the offerer, the more effective the propitiation of the inscrutable Power who accepted it. When this fearful conception had once entered into the mind of man there was humanly no limit to be assigned to it. Very early indeed in the career of history did it become accepted; we can hardly trace the time when it was not so; and very early indeed—and here again we can hardly limit the antiquity of its introduction—did it culminate in the most fearful of its inevitable results. I refer, as an illustration of my meaning only, to the early chapters of Genesis. The sacrifice of animal life is recorded in the same context with the offering of fruits. The sacrifice of Isaac, proposed, but not accepted, by the God of Abraham, reveals to us, if we needed the revelation, that four thousand years ago the offering of human life in propitiation was a common and recognised form of Divine worship. We Christians shrink with horror from all shedding of blood, even of animals, in the service of God. There may be nothing cruel in it. Beasts must die, and must die by the hands of man. It might be fantastic to denounce the sacrifice of the living animal on the score of cruelty and inhumanity. But we may and must denounce it, as the source from which must logically spring, and from which has sprung, in all countries, in all times, under the sanction of all religions, except those which we claim to come direct from Divine teaching, the sacrifice of the human victim, the shedding of the blood which is the life of man.

This, then, is the *ultima ratio* to which the idea of sacrifice tends. I have spoken of the universal acceptance of this idea among all human creatures who recognise at least the being of a personal God, a Creator, a Ruler, and a Judge. Let us now look more closely into this fact. I do not pretend, indeed, to follow up so wide a subject exhaustively. My object in this lecture is to point out a marked contrast between the actual development of the Christian religion, and of the most illustrious and most refined among the heathens.

The deltas of the Nile, of the Euphrates, of the Ganges, or the Indus, are the earliest known settlements of human civilization. Here are the cradles of the most ancient of heathen religions; here were the sources, the farthest that we can trace of the most common and most widespread sentiments of mankind. In all these nurseries of our race we find the same constant idea taking fast hold of the imagination, and dominating the devout affections of man. The Mosaic records make no reference to the usage of sacrifice among the Pharaohs in Egypt; but Herodotus, the father of secular history, affords us ample evidence that in his time, and, as we may infer, for uncounted ages before him, the Egyptians made the sacrifice of animal life a marked feature in their religious ritual. The bull, the swine, and the ram are severally mentioned as the offerings most grateful to Isis, Osiris, and Ammon; and these were accompanied by many unbloody sacrifices, the offering of milk and fruits, and cakes and spices. Authors of a later date than Herodotus make special reference to the very ancient sacrifice of human victims, for which, it is asserted, that of animals was only a later substitute. Thus it is particularly declared by Plutarch, that in the town of Ilithyia, Typhonic—that is, *red-haired* men—used to be burnt to the goddess there inhabiting, and their ashes thrown into the air. But these, it was suggested, were primitive and barbarous rites, and in a more enlightened age waxen figures were actually substituted for men of flesh and blood, and these again were ultimately replaced by animals. Sacrifice, however, in some shape or other, was the last resource—the *dernier mot*—of Egyptian civilization in its most flourishing period, when it attained the art and science required for the building of the pyramids; when it offered a storehouse of ethical wisdom, to which the sages of the Grecian world, at the summit of its intelligence, might resort.

The antiquity of civilization on the Euphrates may probably equal that on the Nile; but both the records and the traces we retain of it are less distinct. Here, too, the idea of Sacrifice seems to have been immemorially prevalent, and was reported by the Fathers of the Christian Church to have been indigenous in Chaldæa and Babylonia. Nor was the practice less rife throughout the neighbouring regions, the progress of which was not less marked than that of Babylonia, such as Syria, and Persia, and Phœnicia. Our first conception of the religious systems of all these countries bespeaks the prevalence of sacrifices of all kinds, from the offering of the fruits of the earth to the massacre of human beings, to the slaughter of the purest and most innocent victims as the most meritorious and efficacious, to the passing of children through the fire to Moloch. The Syrians, the Persians, the Phœnicians, and the Carthaginians were each in their time and place the highest exponents of heathen culture. Each in their time, each in their place, advanced mankind to the highest pitch of moral and æsthetic refinement of which it might then and there seem capable.

Among the worshippers of Brahma, on the Indus and the Ganges, there seems to have been possibly an earlier, certainly a more durable, and we may believe a more polished, phase of culture than any that we have hitherto noticed. We have ampler knowledge of the eligious systems of the Hindoos, through the existing records of the Vedas, than of any other primitive people. Throughout the ritual of the Vedas the use of Sacrifice is paramount. Sacrifice is the one great idea which imbues the whole of their religious teaching. "The gods," they declare, "killed a man for their sacrifice. But that part of him which was fit for being made an offering went out, and entered into a horse. Thence the horse became an animal fit to be sacrificed.

"The gods killed the horse ; but the part fit for being sacrificed went out of it, and entered into the ox : thence the ox became an animal fit for being sacrificed.

"The gods killed the ox; the part entered into the sheep, and the sheep became fit.

"The gods killed the sheep, and the same happened to the goat.

"The gods killed the goat ; but the part entered into the earth : thence the earth became fit for being offered.

"The earth turned into rice : hence the simple rice-cake represents the animal sacrifice. The rice-cake is called Purodâsa ; he who offers Purodâsa offers the sacrificial part of all animals."

According to this scientific development of the first principle of sacrifice—the devotion, namely, of man to God—the rice, the simplest and most universal fruit of the earth, becomes a comprehensive representative of all other sacrificial objects. But the offering of rice does not really supersede the other offerings. The sacrifice of man has been from all historical times, and is still, in manifold forms, a general practice of Hindooism. The sacrifice of children, of widows, of old men—the drownings in the Ganges—the prostrations under the wheels of Juggernaut—all bespeak the perpetuity as well as the universality of human sacrifice throughout the most polished nations of ancient and modern India. The offering of animals of all kinds, as well as of fruits of all kinds, is still a practical commentary on the pretended comprehension of all sacrifice in the offering of the simple rice-cake.

The world of India is a microcosm in itself, and almost every ethical conception which has presented itself to the imagination of our Western peoples has passed through the mind of these Orientals also. But the intellectual masters of the modern world are eminently the Greeks and the Romans. From them we have inherited or learnt the process of intellectual reasoning, which still makes their thoughts as our thoughts. We can follow out their ideas and appreciate them in every point. The mass of literary remains which they have left us puts us in actual possession at this day of the stores which they have been accumulating so many ages before us. Accordingly their civilization is essentially our own; there is no chasm of intellectual discontinuity placed between us and them, as there is between us and the Egyptians and the Assyrians of old, and the Hindoos both ancient and modern. There is, however, no fact with which we are more familiar from our early studies than that of the universal use of sacrifice among the Greeks and Romans. From Homer to Juvenal every volume of classical antiquity teems with sacrifice. Throughout the Hellenic world its origin is concealed in the deepest obscurity. The eucharistic, the propitiatory, the expiatory,—all these ideas prevail among the Grecian worshippers, and seem to be intimately blended one with another. What were the primitive objects of sacrifice seems to be no less indeterminable. Aristotle, indeed, hazarded the assertion that the first-fruits of the field were the oldest kind of offering, whilst that of animals belonged to a later usage. But high as this sage's authority ought to be on such a subject, there seems reason to believe that he is speaking rather from vague conjecture than from any scientific deduction from the facts of history accessible to him. The earliest records we possess point to much earlier traditions of human sacrifice; there is said to be no Grecian city or people on whom the guilt of human sacrifices is not fastened; and a usage so widespread among them may fairly be reckoned to have had some primitive origin handed down from their common progenitors. The Greeks seem, indeed, from the first to have most fully embraced the common conviction that blood is the seat of the soul and of life, and hence especially acceptable to the Deity, as the highest and best of natural things—

the prime and bloom of the whole natural world—fit therefore for a gift to Him, and a token of gratitude for benefits received, if not rather for the propitiation of His favour, or in deprecation of His wrath and judgment. For blood, again, from its close connexion with human passions, might be regarded as the seat and root of sin, and by blood the guilt of sin might seem most naturally to be capable of redemption. Whether the sacrifice of human blood was an enhancement of the price paid by the blood of animals, or whether the blood of animals was regarded as a substitute, accepted by the indulgence of the gods for the extreme penalty of human life, is a question which must ever remain historically undetermined.

What has been here said of the Hellenic use of Sacrifice may be advanced equally of the Roman. The diversities of ritual among these two peoples, whose religious ideas sprang generally from some common origin, can be of little importance on the present occasion. But the point to which I would lead you is the effect of Greek and Roman civilization, at its highest point of progress, upon the primitive idea which we have had placed before us. The advance of culture and refinement, the progress of the arts, the dissemination of general intelligence, the growth of humanity, seem clearly to have had no effect in weakening this primary idea of the necessity of sacrifice for communion with the Deity, for propitiation, or expiation of sin. What these were at the first, obscurely indicated as they are by the earliest dawn of historical light, the same they seem to have remained. Take, for instance, the period of the upper Roman empire, the period when the refinements of the Hellenic world were most widely and most fully developed. We do not find that the practice of sacrifice was in any degree abated. On the contrary: the accumulation of wealth, the profusion of expense, the enhancement of luxury and self-indulgence, all contributed to make sacrifice more universal and more extravagant than ever. Thus Julius Cæsar, on the morning of his assassination, slaughtered one hundred victims—so runs an almost contemporary story—in the desperate endeavour to obtain the genuine tokens of an atonement, which the entrails of the victim were required to present. It was calculated that on the death of Tiberius, when all the world was madly rejoicing at the accession of Caligula, a hundred and sixty thousand victims were offered throughout the empire in token of the universal joy. Augustus and Marcus Aurelius required so great a number of beasts for their fanatical services, that it was said first of the one, and the saying was afterwards applied to the other, that all the calves and oxen prayed that they might never return from their campaigns, for if Cæsar conquered the cattle must be exterminated. When the Emperor Nerva reduced by a decree the number of the sacrifices publicly appointed, it was for the special purpose of relieving the state finances, the burden upon which had become intolerable.

Many other such instances might be produced to show that the amount of offering increased with the wealth—increased, that is, with the civilization of Rome. It was never materially checked by any higher and more philosophic views of the futility, or even the impiety, of the common idea of Sacrifice, as generally embraced by all the heathen peoples. But we must not suppose that even among the heathens the doctrine itself had no intelligent and devoted impugners: the philosophers of the Hellenic world were not untrue to their high calling, and did not scruple to denounce the usage as a sin and an absurdity. We have unfortunately lost the mass of Greek ethical literature between Aristotle and Epictetus, which contained probably a more valuable contribution to the history of the human mind than any that we have had preserved to us; but a faint reflection of it at least is preserved in some scattered and desultory fragments of the Roman, and from these we learn that a few intelligent thinkers at least, and some intelligent schools of thought, maintained a gallant though most unsuccessful battle against the idea which we have seen to have been so generally prevalent.

Ceremonial religion has its Nemesis; the human conscience at last rises up and rebels against it; the doctrine that by ritual observances the favour of the gods may be secured,—that by vows, and lustrations, and sacrifices, of whatsoever kind, this favour, once lost, may be recovered and satisfaction made for all failings and transgressions,—the fond fancy that the finite may be brought into communion with the Infinite by the mediatory effect of a solemn ceremonial,—this revolts the truly penitent, devout, God-fearing conscience. The reaction against the idea of Sacrifice which we can show to have taken place among the leaders of thought at Rome,—which we may believe, though we have lost the means of tracing it, to have occurred at an earlier period in Greece,—to which I shall presently refer as it manifested itself among the Jews,—was the result and the token of advancing humanity. It was the result of a kindlier culture, a wider observation of man, and a deeper apprehension of the Deity : it was the effect of the later Greek philosophy, of the school of the Academy, and still more of the Porch. But it was quickened and vivified, I believe, by the urgency of public affairs. A period of public affliction is always a season of much personal searching of heart. We can see very plainly how the individual conscience of the Roman was probed to the quick by the trials and sufferings of the civil wars : how his eye was turned inward upon himself by external disaster, and he was driven to the confession of his own weakness and sinfulness in the sight of Heaven. The ethics of Cicero are utterly inconsistent with the idea of the efficacy of Ritual or of Sacrifice. For politic reasons, the philosophic statesman may consent in words to uphold them ; but the inconsistency of his argument, in his book on Laws, for instance, and his book on Moral Duties, is palpable. In the remains of Varro the inconsistency of the position of the political reasoner is even more apparent. Varro does not throw even the decent veil of Cicero over his conclusions, but openly urges his countrymen to maintain the ceremonies and culture of the State religion, while they acknowledge to themselves that such beliefs are false, and such practices futile. But these were the prophets of the Pagan religion of their day—men far in advance of the popular sentiments—leaders with no doubt a scanty train of followers : men who have left a mark in literature, but failed of any deep recognition from the social history of their age. If their wiser appreciation of the worthlessness of sacrifice was due to the progress of culture in minds of the highest order, we must not fail to notice how superficial and transient was the effect it generally produced.

While Cicero was elevating morality above dogma, and Varro was upholding the forms of religion as a matter of form only, a more vulgar politician, and a man who was no philosopher at all, the upstart Emperor Augustus, was recalling the people of Rome to the revival of all the ceremonies of their fathers, and rehabilitating the traditions of a blind superstition along with her temples and her sacrifices. All Rome at his instance, and after his example, rushed headlong upon the ancient ways. The philosopher and sage reformers were left to their sneers and protests; the people clutched again at the cherished ideas which an age of unbelief had almost torn from them—and the old world-wide superstition of sacrifice was again diffused with more boundless extravagance than ever. We read the remains of a few enlightened politicians, we compare them with the timid questionings of popular poets or the fitful declamations of rhetoricians fresh from the sceptical schools of Athens, and we fancy that light was beginning to dawn at last athwart the thick gloom of the used-up Hellenic religions; but however these may have become rotten at the core—and in fact they were always rotten—they continued to parade and vaunt themselves in their outward forms and services; and the use of sacrifice continued to be practised, even more and more, throughout the remaining centuries of heathen Rome. When once and again these outward forms seemed for a moment to be falling, they were revived by fanatical enthusiasts, by a Domitian among tyrants, by an Apollonius, an Aurelius, and a Julian among ideologists. The effect of culture and civilization among the Romans—the heirs of the culture and civilization of the Greeks—was, on the whole, to extend rather than to limit the primitive and universal idea of the moral significance of Sacrifice. The history of the later Roman civilization is notably a record of religious revivals, and is in this respect one of the most curious subjects of intellectual study at all times, and perhaps especially so at the present. All these revivals were marked in succession by a more and more vehement recurrence to this great first principle of all heathen religion—the moral significance of Sacrifice.

There is something painful to contemplate in the mere fact of bloodshed on so large a scale as that which was of not unfrequent recurrence among these polished peoples of antiquity, when hundreds—thousands—nay, tens of thousands—of animals of various kinds, the noblest as well as the meanest, were thus done to death on stated and regular occasions. Possibly it is a mere sentiment that is shocked at the death, the painful death, of such multitudes of living creatures; but it is something more than a sentiment that is outraged by the spectacle of multitudes of human beings brought together to witness these horrors, to rejoice over them, to regard them as a gratification to the all-good and the all-just God, and even a satisfaction to Him for their own sins and transgressions. But this is not all. We must never forget, nor suffer ourselves to put out of sight, the fact that the use of bloody sacrifices has always, with one or two signal exceptions, of which I have presently to speak, been preceded, or accompanied, or followed by its most shocking and terrible outgrowth—the slaying of the human victim. The slaughter of bulls and goats in sacrifice is, of course, innocence itself—innocent in itself, innocent in its consequences and effects—compared with the slaughter of men, women, and infants. Yet all heathen religions reek with human blood thus shed; and the most refined of the nations of antiquity are little more free from it than the rudest. The civilizations of antiquity generally looked backward rather than forward. Their golden age was a past, and not a future. They expected no improvement from progressive development, but rather regarded all progress as a decline from a primitive perfection. And accordingly they were always loth to part with any ancient usage, and rather yearned on all occasions for recurrence to the ancient principles. Athens in the age of Pericles or Socrates would hardly have invented or drifted into the sacrifice of human victims; nor would Rome have done so under Augustus or Hadrian. Even under the commonwealth at Rome there are faint and ambiguous traces of legislation against it; but this was rather a precaution against the use of human blood in magic, than a protest against it as a principle of religion. Undoubtedly the Grecian mind, even while allowing of the rite, and celebrating it in its most hallowed legends, felt a certain aversion from it, and spoke of it with horror; while the Phœnician peoples seem to have gloated over it with a frantic delight. The Greeks, and particularly the Athenians, devised various means of evading the practice, even while regarding it as a duty, by the substitution for the human victim of animals, or of mere lifeless images. Yet in spite of the disgust thus indicated, we are said to find traces of it throughout almost the whole Hellenic world, in the cultus of almost every god, and in all periods of their independent history. There is no nation, we are assured, of which more numerous or more various human sacrifices are recorded; and it may be inferred, from the language of Plato, that in the highest stage of Hellenic culture such offerings were still in use among many Grecian peoples.

There is, however, evidence which cannot be rebutted, that the use of human sacrifice was never entirely extinct in Rome during the continuance of the Pagan empire. Deities there were, to whom on certain occasions such sacrifices had been offered from the earliest times; and we cannot set aside the indications we receive from various quarters, crowned as they are by express assertions as late as the fourth century, that they were still not unfrequently resorted to, and especially in times of public emergency. Both in Greece and Rome such rites were used for the expiation of public rather than of private sins, and the conciliation of the gods to the interests not of the individual, but of the nation. The numerous stories of human sacrifices, some of them of the most wholesale description, by Julius Cæsar, and Augustus and Sextus Pompeius, may be exaggerated, but must not be set aside. "The Greek and the Gaul" were buried in the Roman Forum as late as the age of Pliny. The living death of the unchaste Vestal, repeated for the last time by Domitian, was a religious sacrifice rather than a criminal execution. Hadrian deemed it necessary to legislate against human sacrifices, as in use in the middle of the second century. Yet this edict did not prevent the sacrifices of Commodus, Didius, Caracalla, Valerian, Aurelian, and other later emperors, down to the time of Julian the Apostate. These rites were, indeed, in many cases connected with magical practices rather than the public service of the temples; but even so they testify not the less to the prevailing and, as it might seem, the ineradicable conviction of the human heart, that Divine favour may be obtained, and Divine wrath averted, by the shedding of human blood as the choicest of all offerings. One striking instance of this prevalent feeling shall be mentioned, as standing distinctly apart from all public ceremonial or political significance. In the time of Marcus Aurelius, Aristides, the rhetorician, on a transient relief from an incurable malady, believed himself to be divinely informed by the god Æsculapius, whose priest he was, that he owed his amendment to the self-devotion of his brother Hermias; but he was further assured that the cure could not be complete unless his sister Philumena laid down her life for him also. This sacrifice was accordingly accomplished, and Aristides lived, it seems, to record it with pious gratitude to the god of medicine.

These notices give a very slight and meagre sketch of the well-attested prevalence of sacrifice, and even of human sacrifice, throughout the most polished ages of ancient heathen civilization. I have drawn your attention to ages of civilization only, and passed by the multitudinous records of a similar kind, extending over almost all the heathen countries with which we are acquainted in modern times, as well as in ancient. No doubt there are traces of an awakening of the human conscience to the folly and enormity of these practices, under the growing influence of humanity and culture; but we see how ineffectual any such reaction has been to eradicate the profound original instinct, and to fortify the heart and judgment against the stress of extraordinary temptation. There is, however, strong evidence that the progress of humanity in the Roman Empire was powerfully assisted by the impulse of Christian feeling, even while Christianity itself was despised and persecuted. The light shed by the true religion upon the idea of Sacrifice could not fail to represent the practices of the heathen world in colours odious and intolerable. To trace the Christian idea of Sacrifice we must go far back into history, and revert to the sacrificial system of the Jews disclosed to us in the Levitical law, and patriarchal usage. I need only point out to you the religious significance of all the Jewish sacrifices, admitted by all Christian interpreters as a prefiguring of the future Sacrifice of the Redeemer. This is what we, as Christians, hold; to us the ritual of the Levitical law, bloody as it is, painful and even revolting as it must be to the conscience purified and refined by the softening influences of the Gospel, is explained by the reference we believe it to bear to the one great Sacrifice of Christ, offered once for all for the sins of the world. For us, as Christians, even the offering of Isaac by his father, commanded as a trial of faith, but Divinely averted, is humanized and sanctioned to the conscience by the Divine Antitype in which it is ultimately consummated. And this inchoate human sacrifice, be it observed, is the one single instance throughout the revealed history of God's dealings with His people in which any appearance of a Divine sanction is given to the offering of man by man in thanksgiving, in expiation, or in propitiation. Patriarchal usage and the Mosaic law are both wholly free from the taint of human sacrifices. Whether with the general concurrence of our Christian theologians, we regard the sacrifices of the Jews as a preparation for the offering of Christ—a prefiguration of the Divine design conceived from the beginning of the world—or whether we proceed further to give them a more secular interpretation, and admit them as a Divine economy, making use of existing human ideas for Divine purposes, and winking in Divine omniscience at the times of man's ignorance,—this great fact, this singular fact remains, that of all the great mass of ancient religions, Judaism seems to stand alone in its entire rejection of the most cruel and odious of human enormities. Derived themselves from the Semitic stock, of which all other off-shoots have been prolific of these bloody horrors—placed in the midst of the man-slaying tribes of Canaan—drawing their luxuries and refinements from the child-burning votaries of Moloch, the flower of the Phœnician civilization—the Jews kept themselves untainted throughout with the slightest trace of devotion to the unhallowed offering of man by man. The Sacrifice of Jesus Christ, in as far as it can be compared with the human sacrifice of which we have been speaking, stands alone in Jewish history. The idea which it represents is the consummation of the idea of Sacrifice as realized in the offerings of fruits and flowers and and the life of animals; but it does not represent, and no secular interpretation can allege that it was developed out of, the practice of human bloodshedding.

One word more about the persistency of the idea of Sacrifice, and the instinctive origin which it seems so strongly to indicate. As with the Greek and Roman civilizations, so with the Jewish. In each case, at a certain corresponding era of culture and refinement, the conscience of the votary was smitten with the suspicion, ripening into conviction, that the practice of sacrifice could have no real power with God. The prophets among the Jews preached the same doctrine, regarding it as the philosophers among the Greeks and Romans. "For thou desirest not sacrifice," says the Psalmist, "else would I give it Thee: Thou delightest not in burnt-offerings. The sacrifice of God is a troubled spirit; a broken and a contrite heart, O God, shalt Thou not despise." "And Samuel said, Hath the Lord as great delight in burnt-offerings and sacrifices as in obeying the voice of the Lord?" "To what purpose," says Isaiah, "is the multitude of thy sacrifices unto Me? saith the Lord. I am full of the burnt-offerings of rams, and the fat of fed beasts, and I delight not in the blood of bullocks or of lambs." Many more such passages may be cited, but none, perhaps, so strong as that of the prophet Jeremiah, which seems in words actually to deny the Divine institution of sacrifice at all: "For I spake not unto your fathers, nor commanded them in the day that I brought them out of the land of Egypt, concerning burnt-offerings or sacrifices. But this thing commanded I them, saying, Obey My voice, and I will be your God, and ye shall be My people." It was on the strength, perhaps, of this stout assertion that Chrysostom, among the Christian Fathers, declared that sacrifices were not ordained by God; while Tertullian represents them as an economy whereby the God of Israel withheld His chosen people from the idolatry of the surrounding Heathens; and Irenæus argues that they served simply as figures of the one Christian sacrifice, and had no force in themselves.

Even among the devouter Jews these denunciations were held to indicate that the Levitical sacrifices might relieve men from legal impurities and temporal punishments, but had no reference to the future and the spiritual. But, under whatever excuse, the fact remains the same, that the glosses of the prophets continued to be generally a dead letter only. As with the Greeks and Romans, so with the Jews, the exposure of the futility of sacrifice had no real effect in checking the practice, or diverting the incurable propensity of mankind towards it. With the stirring language of Isaiah and Jeremiah and all the rest in their ears, the Jews still brought their bulls and lambs to the altar, year by year continually. Down to the period of our Lord's ministry there was no cessation of the stream of sacrificial blood in the Temple. Our Lord Himself did not scruple to accede to the usage of the people, and allowed His Apostles to prepare for Him the Paschal Supper. As long as the Temple of Jerusalem remained standing, the sacrifices of the Holy Place bore witness to the solemn observance of the law of Moses, and to the one great predominant idea of Sacrifice, common to the Jews with all the Heathen nations.

A scholar of deep and various learning, but of more learning than penetration, and more penetration perhaps than candour,—I mean the great historian Gibbon, —has pointedly remarked of the religion of Mahomet, that it demands neither a priesthood nor sacrifice. He aims, of course, a double back-handed blow at the Christian religion and the Jewish. Of the first of these covert sneers it is not my business now to speak, though, sneer though it be, it might not be difficult to refute it. But the other admits of a double reply. In the first place, the religion of Mahomet is in some important features a very ape of the Jewish and the Christian, and embraces no small portion of the traditions and the usages of the earlier systems, on the outskirts of which it was conceived and brought into being. As with the fall of the Temple and the cessation of the cultus of the Temple, the sacrificial ritual of the Jews came to a sudden end, or continued to be but faintly and fitfully observed; as with the sacrifice of the death of Christ—itself a mere figure of a sacrifice—the use of sacrifice ceased for the Christian Church, except in figures, entirely and for ever; so we might well expect that the Mahometan religion should form an exception to the rule which we have seen to have been hitherto universal, and that among the Mahometans the idea of Sacrifice should be fully and permanently abolished. But it is not so. The remark of Gibbon is far too sweeping. Mahometanism has its sacrifices, although it may have no regular priesthood. The Koran itself is said to contain no specific injunction of the rite; the outward cultus of Islam is limited to prayer and fasting, and ablution and pilgrimage. But the Koran does undoubtedly assume the existence of sacrifice as an ancient and pious usage, and attaches to it a grace and a blessing. And again, though the Prophet may have abstained from distinctly enjoining it, there is no question of the prevalence and strict obligation, even to this day, of the actual practice. Sacrifice is universally acknowledged by Mussulmans as a duty and a meritorious act, with an expiatory virtue attaching to it. The Grand Caliph sacrifices a camel annually at Ispahan as an act of national expiation. The descendant of the Great Mogul at Delhi has made in our day a similar offering. The popular ceremony of the Buckra Eed takes place at a great Mahometan festival in the autumn of every year, when a goat is sacrificed, like the scapegoat of the Israelites, to bear the sins of the people. We may remember the anxiety with which the recurrence of this festival was regarded during the Mutiny in India, lest it should prove the occasion of a fanatical outbreak among the Mahometan population. Dean Stanley reminds us, in his lectures on the Eastern Church, how the traveller Burkhardt could only enter Petra in Arabia under the pretext of sacrificing on the tomb of Aaron. The railroad from the Danube to the Black Sea was inaugurated within the last few years by the sacrifice of two sheep. But, finally, "the vast slaughter of victims at Mecca is the only scene now existing in the world"—so Dean Stanley continues—"that recalls the ancient sacrifices of the Jew and the Pagan," that is, I would say in its extent; but the religion of the Hindoos still retains, as we have seen, and devoutly cherishes the principle. I will only add that, faithful as the outcast child of Hagar to its affiliation to the religion of the Hebrews, Islamism has never, I believe, given countenance to the idea, so prevalent as we have found it elsewhere, of Human Sacrifice.

It is enough for my present purpose to point out the universality, as I venture to call it, of the idea of Sacrifice among the nations of the heathen world, with whom I must also comprehend the Jewish and the Mahometan; among all nations, I should, perhaps, strictly say, whose religion embraces the idea of thanksgiving, of propitiation, and of expiation ; among all nations actually, with whose blood and lineage Christianity has come in contact. I deal with the bare fact ; I am not concerned now, at least, with the causes or results of this world-wide practice, with the spiritual wants which may be supposed to have suggested it, or the effects upon the spiritual life which it may be supposed to have produced. I need not say another word about the horror even of human sacrifice, which we have seen to have been almost always attendant upon it. I simply point to the historical fact—and I ask the philosophers and the psychologists to account for it—that the idea of Sacrifice has been co-extensive with the heathen religions, and still continues to be spread far and wide among heathen peoples; that the progress of civilization and refinement and sensibility has had no substantial effect in checking it ; that human wit and human wisdom have utterly failed in permanently discrediting it ; so that we seem compelled to regard it as something natural to man—something inherent in his constitution, innate in his very being. Yet from the day that the Gospel of Jesus Christ was preached with power this idea has received a mortal blow. Wherever the religion of Christ has penetrated the sacrificial altars have fallen to the ground—blood has ceased to flow, whether of man or of beast; even the innocent offerings of fruits and flowers have lost all interest and reputed obligation, and no Christian worshipper has ever dreamt of making such offerings in thanksgiving, or in propitiation, or for the expiation of sin. This is a simple historical fact, and, letting alone all its spiritual significancy, it may well arrest our attention as such, and demand our reverential admiration. It is evident that a new power has come into the world—a new force has been introduced to contend with the original instincts and impulses of universal manhood. Man has found a new Master; human nature has come under the influence of the Divine. The Great Being who first placed man upon the earth, with certain instincts and aptitudes, and gave him a disposition for the attainment of certain ends by certain means allotted to him, has suddenly, all at once, in a moment's time, refashioned His handiwork, and made this same man amenable to other influences, while he learns to abominate and trample upon the old.

Strong as such language is, it will not, I feel sure, be found too strong, upon a candid review of the facts which have been alleged. Is there anything parallel in human history to the revolution which has been thus set before you? Has any religion or any philosophy, has any moral teaching, effected such a victory over human nature? Has any political training created a new spirit in the heart of man, and relieved it from any one of its innate propensities? Compare this triumph of Christianity—for such I may surely call it—with the bent which from time to time has been given to human disposition, to thought and practice, by the ethics of Plato or Zeno—by the politics of the Spartans and the Romans—by the religious training of a Mahomet, or, if you please, of a Loyola—by the shrewd logic of a Luther—by the burning fanaticism of a Peter the Hermit. Over and over again have great effects, even some lasting effects, been produced upon the temper of a people, of an age, of a series of generations, by great truths or great falsehoods struck out by the force of human genius. We seem to recognize in them, sometimes, an inspiration from God Himself; sometimes, perhaps, we interpret them as a delusion of the devil. But in the great moral revolution which has been effected by the Gospel in the suppression of the practice of Sacrifice, in the eradication of the principle of Sacrifice, we discover a work of another type altogether from any of these—an effect reaching far wider—an influence permanent, and, we may well believe, eternal.

And it is upon the extent and permanence of this revolution that I insist, before I would lead you to the consideration of its intrinsic value—immense as that too may be shown to be—in reply to the question so often advanced by the impugners of Divine revelation,

—the question which, I suppose, all of us, in these days of free discussion and precipitate speculation, have often heard : What great effect has Christianity, after all, produced ? What title does her history give her to the Divine authority and origin which she claims? Here, I say, is an answer to our hand—one, I think, not the least striking among the many that may be adduced. Here is an effect produced by Christianity, to which I challenge all human history to produce a parallel, in demonstration of her *power*, and, for the present, of her *power* only. I maintain that there is no evidence of human power elsewhere to be compared with it. It seems to my mind to approach to a new moral creation —a reconstruction of Man's moral nature—which I can account for only by a Divine impulse specially imparted to him. The material Creation, indeed, is now asserted by many to be a mere process of natural evolution—an assertion they have not hitherto substantiated. For myself I am bold to deny that even this moral creation, as I have termed it, can be shown to have been naturally evolved—that there is anything in history parallel, anything in moral reasoning analogous, to the sudden and complete extinction of the human idea of Sacrifice from the moment when Jesus Christ, the one real sacrifice for Man, was offered to God upon the cross at Calvary.

But this evidence of power is not all ; far from it. There remain yet to be traced the evidences of moral effect and moral purpose, in the extinction of this idea, which must combine with it in testimony to a Divine revelation.

The heading which has been given me for the lecture I have ventured to offer is this :—" What has Christianity done for man individually and socially ? The contrast between Pagan and Christian society." —Now the course I have taken may fairly require some apology, for the license which was accorded to me, of treating my subject in my own way, may seem to have been exceeded by remarks extending only to the abolition of Sacrifice. But I have been really running more nearly within the lines assigned to me than may at first sight appear. So wide and manifold a subject can, you will easily see, be treated here in its fundamental principles only. To follow it out in detail would demand a volume, or several volumes. I look, therefore, for some fundamental principle which shall most strikingly mark the external contrast between Paganism and Christianity, and I seem to find none more striking than that which I have now set before you. But I require, further, that this principle shall indicate a moral as well as an outward or social revolution ; and this I find in it also. The Gospel extinguishes the idea of outward Sacrifice—of the offering to God, in thanksgiving, in propitiation, in expiation of sin, the outward objects of man's love and interest, flowers and fruits, and the life of animals, and, above all, the life of man. But the blood of Christ once offered, the Gospel demands self-sacrifice

—the sacrifice of patience, resignation, mortification, and even martyrdom. "The Christian esteems it the highest evidence of God's favour that he is counted worthy to suffer for faith, truth, and righteousness." "All sufferings have a general relation to sin, and are so far chastisements, but purifying chastisements, which God sends now as a Father, that He may not inflict them hereafter as a Judge." "Trials are a means of perfection, and pledge of Divine grace." Such are among the commonplaces of Christian morality; but I have a pleasure in quoting the words of the illustrious Döllinger, himself an eminent example of patience under trial, himself, if not a martyr, a confessor at least for high and solemn principles of Christian revelation.

Such, I say, is the fundamental idea substituted for sacrifice by the Gospel. What then, starting from this idea, has Christianity done for man, individually and socially? Individually it has taught him the virtue of patience and endurance, enforced by sanctions unknown to the heathen world—sanctions no less strong than those on which the heathen reposed his idea of outward sacrifices. Socially, it has taught him, suffering himself, to sympathise with suffering in others; it has taught the simple rule, which no force of words can more forcibly express, to do as we would be done by. Mark at a glance the wealth of the new ideas which this simple rule brings, and has brought into operation. Hence the prevailing notion of the unity of mankind—a notion fondly guessed by some sages of antiquity, feebly recommended by poets and rhetoricians—a notion which, under the pressure of circumstances, much more than of conviction, slowly and tentatively introduced itself into the jurisprudence of a world-welding empire. Hence the abolition—partial even as yet—of deep national distinctions: the extinction — incomplete even yet, but marching on inevitably under the banner of Christianity—of the great social crime of slavery. Hence the elevation of woman, and the respect paid universally in words, imperfectly, indeed, but far beyond the highest heathen example, to personal purity, to temperance, soberness, and chastity among Christians. And hence, once more, the progress among us of philanthropy generally, in ever-widening circles—the principle that no man lives for himself, but every man for the benefit of his neighbour—that it is the duty of every Christian, in his sphere, to teach and to preach, to spend and to be spent, as a minister, layman though he be, of one common religion ;—the principle, I repeat, of self-sacrifice, which is the Christian counterpart to sacrifice among the heathen. The sage of early Grecian culture—a Thales, a Pythagoras, a Plato,—went about the world learning, as best he might, truth and wisdom; and therein he recognised a duty. The sage of the later and completer culture of Rome—a Dion Chrysostom, a Musonius, an Apollonius—went about teaching and preaching such truth and wisdom as he had acquired; and he, too, recognized a duty, and acted according to his light. But none of these, if he believed in deity at all, was exempt from the degrading influence of superstitions which we Christians have exploded. Socrates, the wisest of the heathen, sacrificed a cock to Æsculapius. Aurelius, the most virtuous of the heathen, slaughtered his hecatombs to Jupiter. None of these conceived the example which Jesus Christ first gave, and which I trust a multitude of His followers have humbly tried to follow—the example which forms in itself the one most striking contrast—the one most significant and most fruitful contrast between Pagan and Christian society—of none of these was it said, of no Pagan that I ever heard of has it been said, or could it be said, " He went about doing good."

I believe, then, that the contrast between Pagan and Christian society lies mainly in the development of the principle of Self-sacrifice. To prove and illustrate this position in vindication of our Christian belief would require, as I have said, the space of a volume rather than of a lecture. Whether I may have an opportunity of carrying out the argument, such as I have sketched it, here or elsewhere on future occasions, I will not pretend to anticipate. I have yet to learn whether the foundation we have this day laid is deemed sufficient to bear the noble superstructure, as I venture to call it, which I have indicated only in a feeble outline. I trust at least, that what has been said will not be wholly thrown away, but will have led some here present to views and considerations of no little importance towards maintaining the sacred object we have all, I hope, at heart, the defence of the Truths of Christianity.

THE FORCE IMPARTED

TO THE

EVIDENCE OF CHRISTIANITY,

FROM THE

MANNER IN WHICH A NUMBER OF

DISTINCT LINES OF PROOF CONVERGE IN A COMMON CENTRE.

BY

BENJAMIN SHAW, Esq.,

BARRISTER AT-LAW, M.A., LATE FELLOW OF TRINITY COLLEGE, CAMBRIDGE.

THE FORCE IMPARTED TO THE EVIDENCE OF CHRISTIANITY

FROM THE MANNER IN WHICH

DISTINCT LINES OF PROOF CONVERGE IN A COMMON CENTRE.

IF I had thought that in coming here to-day I should appear to assume the office of a teacher, I should have hesitated long before accepting the invitation of the committee. But I hope I may rather be allowed to consider that we are simply about to spend an hour in inquiring together into the most important subject that can occupy the attention of responsible beings.

Bishop Butler has said "that the speculative difficulties in which the evidence of religion is involved, may make even the principal part of some persons' trial." He explains this by saying that "as the chief temptations of the generality of the world are the ordinary motives to injustice or unrestrained pleasure; or to live in the neglect of religion from that frame of mind which renders many persons almost without feeling as to anything distant, or which is not the object of their senses: so there are other persons without this shallowness of temper, persons of a deeper sense as to what is invisible and future, who not only see, but have a general practical feeling, that what is to come will be present, and that things are not less real for their not being the objects of sense, and who from their external condition may have small temptations to behave ill, small difficulty in behaving well, in the common course of life."

Hence he considers that "what constitutes, what chiefly and peculiarly constitutes the probation in all senses of some persons, may be the difficulties in which the evidence of religion is involved; and their principal and distinguished trial may be, how they will behave under and with respect to those difficulties." *

These words seem to me not less true now than when they were first written. It may be they are even more so. As there are individuals, so also there are generations for whom peculiar trials are appointed. Possibly what Butler speaks of may be a special trial of this generation. If so, it may not be useless for us to notice how considerately and gently he speaks in this passage of those who are subject to such difficulties. His own experience had, no doubt, taught him the difference between honest perplexity and wilful

* "Analogy," part II., chap. 6

unbelief. It is surely very desirable that Christian apologists in our own day should be equally careful to recognize this distinction.

Our subject to-day is, "The force imparted to the evidence of Christianity from the manner in which a number of distinct lines of proof converge in a common centre."

It has been usual to treat this subject by showing that the final result of various great lines of argument is the same—that by whichever of several great roads we travel we arrive ultimately at the same destination. I shall have something to say presently on this view of the subject, but I desire, in the first place, to draw attention to the fact, that what is true of the grand result is true also of the successive minor stages on the road to that result. I shall seek to show that in very many cases the arguments which converge to the same final conclusion are themselves made up of applications of the same principle of convergent proof on a smaller scale.

To begin at the beginning : the first point may be said to be the trustworthiness of the records on which Christianity is based.

This trustworthiness obviously depends on *two* things :—

1. Were they a trustworthy account of events when first written?

2. Have they been handed down to us in their original condition without substantial alteration?

We will begin with the second, because, though historically later, it is logically prior. If the records as we have them are not in a trustworthy condition, we can derive no benefit from what they may have been in their original state.

I say, then, that the Christian Records have been handed down under such circumstances as afford a guarantee for the substantial genuineness of the text, greater in some respects than can be produced for any other writings of ancient times.

The copies of the New Testament (says Mr. Scrivener) "yet existing in manuscript, and dating from the fourth century of our era downwards, are far more numerous than those of the most celebrated writers of Greece or Rome. Such as have been already discovered and set down in catalogues are hardly fewer than two thousand. . . . . On the other hand, manuscripts of the most illustrious classic poets and philosophers are far rarer, and comparatively modern. We have no complete copy of Homer himself prior to the thirteenth century, though some considerable fragments have been recently brought to light, which may plausibly be assigned to the fifth century; while more than one work of high and deserved repute has been preserved to our times only in a single copy.

"Now the experience we gain from a critical examination of the few celebrated MSS. that survive, should make us thankful for the quality and abundance of those of the New Testament. These last present us with a vast and almost inexhaustible supply of materials for tracing the history, and upholding (at least within certain limits) the purity of the sacred text: every copy, if used diligently and with judgment, will contribute somewhat to these ends. So far is the copiousness of our stores from causing doubt or perplexity to the genuine student of Holy Scripture, that it leads him to recognize the more fully its general integrity in the midst of partial variation. What would the thoughtful reader of Æschylus give for the like guidance through the obscurities which vex his patience and mar his enjoyment of that sublime poet?" *

Here then at once we find an illustration of our principle. We have the double advantage both of *older* MSS. and of a *greater number* of MSS. than in the case of profane authors. You will observe that these two advantages are by no means identical, nor does the one imply the other. We might have possessed a very limited number of MSS. of great antiquity, or a very large number of MSS. of recent date. As a fact, we have both, and our text is the result of careful deductions founded *both* on the antiquity *and* on the number of our copies.

Again: in taking the latter point alone, viz., the number of our copies, we have a striking example of

---

* Scrivener's "Introduction to the Criticism of the New Testament," p. 3. Camb., 1861.

convergent proof. So far as it is founded on the multiplicity of MSS. which uphold it, our text is clearly the result of a proof derived from a number of witnesses all speaking the same, or nearly the same, thing.

Again: for the authentication of the correctness of our received text (I am speaking of course of its broad and substantial features) we have another and a wholly independent class of witnesses.

The Fathers of the Church were in the habit of making frequent quotations from Scripture in their works. These works are in our hands in great numbers, and it is obvious that had it been possible to falsify the texts of our Bibles, the most industrious corrupter could not have tracked out all the citations that lie scattered up and down in the writings of Christian antiquity. These, therefore, form an additional security, and a security possessed by the Christian Records in a degree far beyond that of other writings. There have never been writings which have been so copiously quoted, by so many persons, and under such different conditions. This line of proof, then, is strictly independent of that afforded by biblical MSS., and the two converge in support of our present Scriptures.

But it may be said that the Fathers were partisans, and that their citations are not to be relied on.

This argument is somewhat unreasonable. It really cannot avail to shake the great outlines of Scripture to which the Fathers give their attestation, whatever force may be assigned to it as to smaller points.

But assuming it to be reasonable, I desire to point out that we have other and completely independent sets of witnesses to check and balance the former.

We have good evidence that our present Scriptures were referred to not only by the orthodox, but by heretics, and we cannot but see that each party must have acted as a spy on the other, to detect error and fraud.

Nay, more, we know that not only Christians but heathens dealt with the documents on which Christianity is founded. Celsus Porphyry, and Julian (as may be seen in Paley's Evidences), in their controversies with Christians attacked the early records of the religion. And from the nature of those attacks there is room to perceive that the Records in question were substantially the same as those which we now have in our hands.*

Once more: versions were made in comparatively early times of the Christian Scriptures. Many such are in our possession, and these also show that the originals from which they were translated were identical with our present sacred books in all main points.

Now you will observe, that it by no means followed that because the Gospels, the Acts, and the Epistles happen to be extant in MSS. unusually ancient and

* See the observations of Norton on one doubtful passage of Celsus. "Genuineness of Gospels," vol. i, p. 63.

unusually numerous, *therefore* they would also be the subject of quotation to a remarkable extent by friends, still less by foes. Nor was it a consequence flowing from any or all of these circumstances that they should have been translated at an early period into various languages.

These then are separate lines of proof, all tending in a greater or less degree to establish the substantial identity of the New Testament, as we have it, with the Books as originally written. And so many, and such forcible lines of proof, do *not* exist for other writings.

One more point still demands notice. The style and language of the New Testament are of themselves evidence of its date and authorship. Bishop Marsh has not hesitated to state this in the most decided terms. He says, "The language of the New Testament is precisely such as we might expect from the persons to whom the several parts of it are ascribed. But we may go further, and assert, not only that the language of the Greek Testament *accords* with the situation of the persons to whom it is ascribed, but that it *could not* have been used by any person or persons who were in a different situation from that of the Apostles and Evangelists. It was necessary to have lived in the first century, and to have been educated in Judea, or in Galilee, or in some adjacent country, to be *enabled* to write such a compound language as that of the Greek Testament. Unless some oriental dialect had been *familiar* to the persons who wrote the several books of the New Testament, they would not have been *able* to write that particular kind of Greek by which those books are distinguished from every classic author. Nor would this kind of language have appeared in the several books of the New Testament even though the writers had lived in Judea, unless they had lived also in the same age with the Apostles and Evangelists. Judea itself could not have produced in the *second* century the compositions which we find in the New Testament. The destruction of Jerusalem, and the total subversion of the Jewish state, introduced new forms and new relations, as well in language as in policy. The language, therefore, of a fabrication attempted in the second century would have borne a different character from that of writings composed in the same country *before* the destruction of Jerusalem."*

And even if any should doubt the possibility of assigning the date quite so peremptorily as is here done by Bishop Marsh from considerations of language alone, they will certainly not dispute that these considerations do at all events determine the time approximately and within certain unmistakable limits.

And the result is, that we have an independent species of evidence that the text of the New Testament, as we have it, indicates an origin, both in place

* Bishop Marsh's Lectures, part v., pp. 88-90.

and time, which is quite in harmony with what is ascribed to it on external grounds.

We come now to the other point—the trustworthiness of the records in respect of what they state.

It has often been observed that in this point of view the force of the argument is weakened by our habit of looking at the Bible as one book. However proper this may be in another aspect, we must for our present purpose look at it as, what it originally was, a collection of pieces by different writers. It is thus alone that we perceive the force imparted to the statements by the fact that they are made by several distinct authorities.

But before going further it may be expedient that we should devote a few moments to ascertain the opinion of competent judges as to the weight which testimony acquires when the facts of a case are deposed to by several independent witnesses. It will be best for this object to take other than theological writers; and none can be better than those whose profession requires them continually to sift and try questions of evidence.

I take then a legal writer of acknowledged authority on the theory of evidence, and I find him putting the force to be derived from coincidence in the testimony of independent witnesses in the strongest form.

He even cites with approbation the proposition that " in a number of concurrent testimonies, where there has been no previous concert, there is a probability distinct from what may be termed the sum of the probabilities resulting from the testimonies of the witnesses; a probability which would remain even though the witnesses were of such a character as to merit no faith at all. This probability arises purely from the concurrence itself. That such a concurrence should spring from chance is as one to infinite; that is, in other words, morally impossible. If therefore concert be excluded, there remains no cause but the reality of the fact."

And he quotes an observation of Lord Mansfield in respect to an old decision reported by two several reporters, neither of whom merited much confidence. Lord Mansfield said, "It is objected that the books are of no authority; but if both the reporters were the worst that ever reported, if substantially they report a case in the same way, it is demonstrative of the truth of what they report, or they could not agree." *

It is needless to remark at any length how much this principle of the weight due to concurrent testimony is intensified when each witness deserves fair credit in himself. In such a case the resulting probability of truth is not the *sum* of the separate probabilities that the witnesses taken separately are speaking the truth, but the *product* of these probabilities; a principle of calculation which shows how vastly the addi-

* Taylor on Evidence, vol. i., p. 75 (5th edition).

tion of each fresh witness increases the credibility of what is deposed to.*

And Paley is, no doubt, right in the observation that the corroboration derived from the concurrence of witnesses goes beyond the mere particulars in which they actually coincide.

"A principal witness in a cause," he says, "delivers his account: his narration, in certain parts of it, is confirmed by witnesses who are called afterwards. The credit derived from their testimony belongs not only to the particular circumstances in which the auxiliary witnesses agree with the principal witness, but in some measure to the whole of his evidence; because it is improbable that accident or fiction should draw a line which touched upon truth at so many points."†

But it will be said that in the evidence for the Christian Religion we are dealing, not with legal evidence, such as is treated of by jurists, but to some extent at least with second-hand evidence.‡ It becomes therefore necessary to see whether any qualifications ought in fairness to be introduced on this account.

The point is of importance, because a person of sceptical mind will often ask you whether you think

* See Best on "The Principles of the Law of Evidence," p. 405 (4th edition).
† "Horæ Paulinæ," chap. v.
‡ See, for instance, Luke i. 1—4.

such evidence as you are relying on in support of Christianity would ever prevail in a court of law.

In legal proceedings (it may be urged) we usually admit only the evidence of eye-witnesses. We cannot restrict ourselves to such evidence in the history of Christianity.

Again, we apply in trials at law the test of cross-examination, to ascertain whether the witnesses are really independent or are confederates. This also is beyond our power when we deal with witnesses who are no longer living.

The objection, I may observe, is a very thorough-going one. It tells against history in general, for there are few histories that have not very extensively to rely on evidence at second-hand. But in truth there is something a little misleading in the contrast thus sharply drawn between history and law. The distinction ought rather to be made between inquiries into contemporary matters and inquiries into past ages. On the one hand, there is such a thing as contemporary history; and such history has in some cases been written by persons who were themselves eye-witnesses of what they narrate. On the other hand, law has frequently to deal with past days, as in cases of pedigrees extending over several generations, or in the trial of ancient customs. And in these cases law, like history, can but take the best evidence in its power. Accordingly entries in Family Bibles, inscriptions on tombstones, the declarations of deceased persons, statements found in old deeds and documents, become of necessity (within certain limits) admissible evidence.

The objection to derivative or second-hand evidence in connection with recent events is not so much that it is necessarily untrustworthy, as that in such cases evidence at first hand is ordinarily procurable. Hence, when a litigant keeps it back, and tenders only what is derivative, he raises a presumption against himself that he is suppressing the testimony of the original witnesses from a fraudulent motive.

This presumption disappears when the primary evidence is no longer to be obtained.

History, in fact, when dealing with past ages has securities of its own.

"The tribunal of posterity" (says a philosophical writer) "differs immensely from all others; for it is one of unlimited jurisdiction, both judicial and inquisitorial; it is ever sitting, ever investigating, ever judging: barred by no prescription, bound by no estoppel, and responsible to no human authority. The securities for the truth of the records and traditions of the past which time has brought down to us, consist in the multitude of sources to which they can be traced, the large number of persons whose interest it has been to preserve them from oblivion and corruption; above all, the *permanent effects* of events, visible in the shape of monuments and other pieces of real evidence, customs, ceremonies, and the like; and finally, the actors in the scene having passed away, there is rarely either opportunity or interest to fabricate evidence in furtherance of their views or justification of their conduct."

This writer therefore treats it as a fallacy to suppose that historical evidence, because of a derivative or second-hand nature, is necessarily weaker than legal evidence.

"The fallacy," he says, "consists in treating each generation as one single person, by whom a bare relation of the fact has been handed down to the next, and not as consisting of a number of persons interested in ascertaining its truth; besides wholly overlooking the corroborative proofs supplied by permanent memorials and the acts of men." *

And he cites the words of Mr. Hallam, who says: "The presumption of history, to whose mirror the scattered rays of moral evidence converge, may be irresistible, when the legal inference from insulated actions is not only technically, but substantially, inconclusive." †

It is impossible to state more strongly the principle which we are to-day engaged in discussing.

But it will still be asked, how shall we ascertain

---

* Best's "Principles of the Law of Evidence," pp. 56-58.
† Hallam's "Constitutional History of England," vol. ii., p. 106 (7th edition). See further, as to Historical Evidence, chap. vii. of Sir G. C. Lewis's work, "Methods of Observation and Reasoning in Politics" (London, 1852), and notice his distinction between secondary evidence when contemporary and when non-contemporary.

that the witnesses on whom we rely are independent? For this, as we have seen, is the first requisite, otherwise there is no real concurrence, but mere repetition. Now, in historical evidence we must draw our conclusions on this point (amongst other things) from a careful analysis of the narratives themselves. This analysis must be so conducted as to ascertain whether one narrative is a mere echo of another, or whether there are those minor variances between them which tend to show that they are derived from different sources, in short, from the reports of different witnesses.

It is at this point that the differences which exist in the accounts of what is manifestly the same event by the respective Evangelists are of so much importance. I need not go into them at length, nor does it belong to our special subject to-day to consider how they may be reconciled.

The strange fact is that it apparently escapes the attention of some persons, that did no such differences exist we should lose our principal means of proving that we have several distinct lines of testimony, and should consequently be disabled from using with effect the argument from their concurrence.

But it may perhaps be said that, after all, the facts only amount to this, that we have considerable identity in the different Gospels, accompanied by considerable variety; and it may be objected that this does not necessarily lead to the conclusion that we are dealing with accounts derived from independent witnesses. The facts of the case (it will be urged) may be explained with equal probability by the hypothesis that there was but one original witness, and that the variations are due to the one story having been handed down through different channels, and to its having received legendary corruptions and additions in its course, varying in each case according to the particular channel through which it came down.

Now there are various observations which may be made in reply to this objection.*

The early era at which we know the Gospels to have been promulgated and received does not appear to leave time for legendary interpolations to have been made to such an extent as the argument requires.† Again, the variations between the Gospels often consist of additions which are wholly contrary to what the legendary spirit would have framed. Thus, for instance, the additional passages given in one Gospel and not in another are frequently found to place the Apostles in a discreditable light in regard to want of faith, or in other respects, and as the object of legends is generally to magnify the leaders of the movement, it is obvious that there could be little temptation to add episodes of such a character to the original story.

* Besides the observations here offered, the arguments in Norton's "Genuineness of the Gospels," part i., should by all means be studied.

† See Tischendorf's "When were our Gospels Written?" English edition. Religious Tract Society, London, 1867.

Then, again, they frequently introduce gratuitous difficulties (I mean, gratuitous if they had not actually occurred), which sometimes necessitate explanations in the passage itself. As an example I may refer to the last chapter of St. John (which narrates what is not found elsewhere), where the words, " If I will that he tarry till I come, what is that to thee?" are stated to have given rise to a tradition, which the writer felt bound to go out of his way to correct. In fictitious writings men are not wont gratuitously to create stumbling-blocks for the sake of afterwards removing them.

Or again, they contain admissions *primâ facie* unfavourable to the cause, which a legendary spirit would hardly have inserted. As, for instance, the statement that on several occasions after the Resurrection our Saviour was not at first recognized by His disciples.

Lastly, there is a remark which seems to me deserving of careful consideration.

Legendary additions made by different classes of persons in different places, and represented by the variations of the several Gospels respectively, would obviously have no connection with each other. Derived from different minds, and due to distinct causes, they would stand in no mutual relation ; there would be no clue by which to bring them together, because they would be fictitious, and would rest on no common basis of truth.

On the other hand, in the case of merely incidental differences in accounts derived from various sources, each of which sources afforded a veracious but independent narrative, there may be usually found points of reunion, so to speak, indications that there is a common ground of reality. Now let us apply this to some of the statements found in one Gospel and not in another.

St. John gives the raising of Lazarus, which is not told in the other Gospels, but in the course of the story we find traits in the characters of the actors in the scene which are similar to other traits of these characters as depicted elsewhere. Martha, when she hears that Jesus is come, hastily goes forth to meet Him; while Mary, the more quiescent character, sits still in the house; but Mary, when at length she is brought out by her energetic sister, falls reverently at His feet weeping—an action which is not recorded of Martha. Even in the solemn scene at the grave, the busy, managing, and (if we may venture so to say) interfering character of the good Martha breaks forth. When the command is given to remove the stone she interposes with the well-meant objection, "Lord, by this time he stinketh, for he hath been dead four days."

Do we not feel intuitively that these characters are drawn from the life? and are they not identical with the Mary of St. Luke, who sits in reverent stillness at Jesus' feet, listening to His words, and the active, practical Martha, cumbered about much serving, and interrupting the discourse to beg that her sister may be commanded to help her in her work?

It is scarcely necessary to observe that the raising of Lazarus has been represented as an event of such importance that it could not have been omitted by other historians had they known of it; and that as they must have known of it if true, it can only be a subsequent invention. In short, it is treated as a positive discrepancy. Now, it is just in this point of view that the minute evidence of consistency in the delineation of the finer traits of character is valuable, as indicating that the narrative has just those points of relation with what is told us elsewhere of the family of Bethany which a true story would have, but which, from their delicate nature, would probably be beyond the appreciation of the composer of a mere legendary accretion.

Again, take the converse, viz., a point stated by St. Luke, omitted by St. John, *i.e.*, the Ascension.

Suspicion, it may be said, is cast on the statement of St. Luke by the circumstance that this cardinal fact is not narrated by St. John, who must have known it had it happened. True, St. John does not *narrate* it, but he *assumes* it. He reports our Saviour as saying, "What and if ye shall see the Son of man ascend up where He was before?" (ἐὰν θεωρῆτε τὸν υἱὸν τοῦ ἀνθρώπου ἀναβαίνοντα), words which point to a visible ascent in the presence of spectators, and are quite inapplicable to a mere inference that our Saviour had ascended to heaven, simply because He had disappeared from among men.

Once more, St. John gives the account of our Saviour's washing the Apostles' feet, which is not given elsewhere. But St. Luke, in his account of the Last Supper, makes our Lord say, " I am among you as one that serveth," which is hardly intelligible except in relation to His having laid aside His garments, and girded Himself with a towel, like a menial slave, as described by St. John. Moreover, St. Luke, by telling us that there was a strife for pre-eminence among the Apostles (which is not mentioned by St. John), probably gives us the circumstance which occasioned our Lord's practical lesson in humility.

We have been dealing with apparent variations, and have been seeking to show that they do not necessarily indicate subsequent unauthentic accretions, but that they may rather perhaps point to that very species of minor diversity which shows the existence of independent original testimony, and thus entitles us to insist on the argument that we have really distinct lines of proof.

From this we pass almost insensibly to the coincidences which show affirmatively that those lines of proof converge, and this not only in the main topics, but in minor points where coincidence seems beyond the reach of fraud, and cannot be due to chance.

Thus in St. Mark we have the charge brought against Jesus at his trial that he had said, " I will destroy this temple made with hands, and in three days I will build another, made without hands." St. John does not mention this charge, but he does mention (what is not given by Mark) the language which gave rise to it. "What sign shewest thou us, that thou doest these things? Jesus answered and said unto them, Destroy this temple, and in three days I will raise it up." Neither historian gives the whole of the information required. Each gives a piece, and the pieces *dovetail*, and that with such exactness as to indicate to us in what the false witness consisted, viz., in turning "Destroy this temple" into "I will destroy."

Again, in Matthew xxvi. 67, we find the soldiers saying to Christ, "Prophesy who is it that smote thee." What wit or meaning was there in this piece of profanity? Why should there be any difficulty in fixing on the smiter? St. Matthew leaves us without explanation, but we gather the solution from Luke xxii. 64, where it is mentioned that they had blindfolded the Saviour.

Such coincidences surely belong to truth. On this head I would earnestly recommend the careful study of Paley's "Horæ Paulinæ," Blunt's "Undesigned Coincidences," and Birks' "Horæ Apostolicæ."

The object is to show that the coincidences are real and important, while yet they relate to points so subtle that they could hardly have been invented, and so remote from the apprehension of any ordinary reader that it would never have been worth while to invent what not one in a million would perceive.

It is of course impossible to display in a single lecture the force of such an argument. It depends wholly on a comparison of many small particulars in a large number of instances. But to show the power which it exerts on practical minds, I may venture to mention an anecdote. I was recently speaking on the subject of perjury in courts of law with a friend who holds a judicial office, and he expressed his conviction that the evidence on which most dependence was often to be placed was not that of hardy and direct assertion, but that which received incidental confirmation from the putting together of independent circumstances; "In short," he said, "the sort of coincidences in Paley's 'Horæ Paulinæ.'" It is only necessary to add that he referred to Paley merely from its appropriateness to the subject. Paley had not been mentioned in the conversation, nor had we been speaking in the remotest degree of theology. The book was cited simply as an example of the kind of evidence which my friend's practical experience had led him to consider as the most convincing. And the mention of Paley's work leads me to observe that the coincidences in question exist not merely between the Gospel narratives, but between the Acts and the Epistles, and this in the most recondite and, at the same time, inartificial manner. Such coincidences are very forcible, because the Epistles are not professedly historical. They deal with doctrine; facts and events only come in incidentally. Yet in many instances the agreement is of the most remarkable kind.

I can now, however, only deal with some broad features in which the Epistles support the Gospel history.

It, perhaps, has not occurred to everyone that, chronologically speaking, the *earliest* record of the appearances of Christ after the Resurrection appears to be that given by St. Paul in 1 Corinthians xv. The Epistle in question is prior in date to any of the Gospels. And it is in substantial harmony with what the Gospels tell us. Yet it is obviously improbable in the highest degree to suppose that the writer of a Gospel had recourse to an Epistle of St. Paul to a church in Greece, in order either to draw his materials thence, or for the purpose of taking care that his own statements were not at variance with those which St. Paul had previously made.

In fact, the early date at which the Epistles to the Corinthians must have been written show us that the fact of the Resurrection must have formed the substance of the teaching of the first preachers of the new religion from the very first.

Supposing for a moment that the Gospels and the Acts could be found to have been written at so late a date that unauthentic miraculous stories might have been inserted in them, still, the Resurrection could have been one of them; for we have proof that St. Paul preached it from the first, as the fundamental fact of Christianity, the very kernel of the whole system. It could not have been a fiction, invented to give credit to the Gospel which he preached; for without it there was no Gospel for him to preach. "If Christ be not raised, then is our faith vain."

So again, the First Epistle of Peter speaks of the Resurrection in a way quite in harmony with that apostle's sermons as reported in the Acts. And of the facts of the Resurrection he, if any man, must have been an original witness. Supposing therefore, for the sake of argument, that certain apparent diversities (whether real or not) in the narrative of the Resurrection, as given in the respective Gospels, could be shown to detract from the confidence to be placed in these narratives, there would still remain the direct statements of St. Paul and St. Peter, not to mention the clear implications to be found in the Epistle of James.

Nor must I omit here to mention the support which the statements of miraculous works contained in the Gospel, receive from the testimony of the Acts and Epistles in relation to the performance of such works. Not only do the Acts and Epistles everywhere assume the miracles of our Saviour, but they show by their own testimony that miracles were still wrought. Take for example the remarkable collection of miracles of healing stated to have been wrought by Paul at Melita. These miracles are said to have been performed by a man, of whom all that was known by the population of the island probably was that he was a prisoner being conveyed in legal custody to Rome on some criminal charge, and the fact of the miracles is deposed to by the writer, himself evidently an eye-witness. The unexceptionable nature of the evidence, and the absence of predisposing causes for credulity or enthusiasm on the part of the persons healed, are extremely noticeable, and render this case worthy of much attention.

Again, in St. Paul's letters we have his own statement that he wrought miracles. This statement seems to render nugatory the attempt to explain away the narratives, and tends to resolve the question into the single issue of St. Paul's own veracity, or conscious fraud. The words are found in an Epistle which the most sceptical of modern critics admit to be genuine, viz. 2 Cor. xii. 12, and they seem to be sufficiently explicit. "Truly the signs of an apostle were wrought among you in all patience, in signs, and wonders, and mighty deeds." Similar language occurs in another letter of undoubted genuinenesss. In Romans xv. 18, St. Paul says, " I will not dare to speak of any of those things which Christ hath not wrought by me, to make the Gentiles obedient by word and deed, through mighty signs and wonders, by the power of the Spirit of God, so that from Jerusalem and round about unto Illyricum I have fully preached the gospel of Christ."

The importance of these statements may be seen from the observation of Gibbon as to later miraculous narratives.

"It may seem somewhat remarkable" (he says) "that Bernard of Clairvaux, who records so many miracles of his friend St. Malachi, never takes any notice of his own, which in their turn however are carefully related by his companions and disciples. In the long series of ecclesiastical history, does there exist a single instance of a saint asserting that he himself possessed the gift of miracles?" *

If "ecclesiastical history" is here meant to be distinguished from apostolic history, this challenge may possibly be unanswerable; but if it includes the earliest age of Christianity, it seems expressly met by the passages just quoted.

These passages then we are entitled to rely on as affording a confirmation of the statement of the Gospels that the religion was founded under miraculous agency. It is a confirmation found in the letters of a man, who in these letters pours out his whole heart to the persons to whom he writes, and in so doing exhibits a character which the discerning reader will scarcely judge capable of conscious fraud. It is a confirmation afforded, not of set purpose, but incidentally, and is therefore the more free from sus-

* "Decline and Fall," chap. xv.

picion; and the nature of the confirmation is this, that if St. Paul wrought miracles, there can be little reason to doubt the accounts of those who say that his Great Master did so. His evidence converges to the same point with that of the Evangelists to this extent, that Christianity had a miraculous origin.

Before leaving the subject of Testimony it may be well to advert to a remarkable letter from a wholly distinct quarter, that of the heathen Pliny, a witness not to be suspected of partiality. His evidence is confirmatory, at all events, to this extent, that it proves the early faith and habits of the Christians to have been precisely such as would be accounted for on the supposition that the story in the Gospels is true. Pliny, in his famous letter to Trajan, says that the Christians were wont to meet together on a stated day, before it was light, and sing among themselves, alternately, a hymn to Christ as a God.

This letter introduces another point of convergent evidence. It indicates that acts were done and ceremonies observed in honour of the Author of Christianity; and this too within a very limited space of time after the events narrated in the Gospels are said to have taken place. And I think it difficult for a candid mind to doubt that what Pliny refers to is the same as that worship of the Christians described by Justin in his Apology, a few years later, as taking place on the first day of the week, and that it to some extent confirms Justin's account. At all events, Justin himself bears witness to the fact that the first day was observed, and that its observation was in memory of the Resurrection. This being so, it falls within the principle laid down in the passage which I quoted just now as to historical evidence. It comes within "the permanent effects of events visible in the shape of monuments and other pieces of real evidence, customs, ceremonies, and the like," which were there spoken of, as you no doubt remember, as a peculiar security for the truth of the records of the past.*

Thus far we have been travelling along the great highway of historical evidence. In so doing we have found that from time to time along the route junctions took place with other paths, which, starting from distant and unconnected points, were found after awhile to fall into the same line.

We are now to leave the main road, which we have been hitherto pursuing, and to trace the course of other main roads, which, though never coinciding with the one we have just followed, during their course lead ultimately to the same great goal.

Instead of considering the coincidence of testimony, we shall deal with the *consilience of inductions*. As before, I shall venture to premise a few words on the recognized force and value in secular investigations of the principle of which we are to speak. It is thus

* See further on this point Leslie's "Short and Easy Method with the Deists."

described by Dr. Whewell, in reference to the inductive reasonings of physical science.

"The evidence in favour of our induction is of a much higher and more forcible character when it enables us to explain and determine cases of a *kind different* from those which were contemplated in the formation of our hypothesis. The instances in which this has occurred, indeed, impress us with a conviction that the truth of our hypothesis is certain. No accident could give rise to such an extraordinary coincidence. No false supposition could, after being adjusted to one class of phenomena, so exactly represent a different class when the agreement was unforeseen and uncontemplated. That rules springing from remote and unconnected quarters should thus leap to the same point* can only arise from *that* being the point where truth resides."†

He gives as an instance the fact that the force of universal gravitation, which had been inferred from the *perturbations* of the moon and planets by the sun and by each other, also accounted for the fact, apparently altogether dissimilar and remote, of the *procession of the equinoxes*.

"Here," he says, "was a most striking and surprising coincidence, which gave to the theory a stamp of truth beyond the power of ingenuity to counterfeit."

In other words, if a theory which we are led to

---

* Hence he applies the name "consilience of inductions."
† "Philos. of Induct. Sciences," vol. ii., p. 230 (edit. 1840).

adopt as the only satisfactory solution of an important class of phenomena, turns out subsequently to be also the only adequate interpretation of another important but wholly distinct class of phenomena, we gain one of the strongest possible proofs that our explanation is *the true one*.

It need scarcely be added that if our hypothesis, instead of being found to explain *two* distinct series of phenomena, should turn out to be the means of reducing under the same great principle three, four, five, or more such independent series, the conviction of its truth would rise indefinitely, till it gained a height which would be practically infinite, that is to say, which no longer admitted of the slightest doubt.

So much, then, for the principle as applied to physical philosophy. Applying it to the question now before us, we find it to stand thus :—

The historical facts connected with the origin of Christianity, as brought before us on the faith of testimony, are of such a character as apparently to require for their explanation the theory that the Religion so originated is a Divine Revelation.

Our next step is to examine other classes of phenomena distinct from those we have just considered, though lying within the same great sphere of investigation.

Let us take, for instance, the leading phenomena presented by the system of Judaism, out of which, historically speaking, Christianity arose.

And here it might, no doubt, be appropriate to enter on the great subject of prophecy. But time does not admit, nor do I feel myself competent for so vast a task. It can be treated in detail only by means of a separate lecture. All that I can do is to present a brief outline of general facts. Well, then, we must start with the fact that the Old Testament system was probably the only ancient religion which developed a conscious personal relation to God in the mind of the worshipper, and brought about a sense of communion between the creature and his Creator.

Other systems may have inculcated with more or less force the maxim, "Thou shalt love thy neighbour as thyself;"* but can we find any that pretended practically, and as a duty of general application, to proclaim, "Thou shalt love the Lord thy God with all thy heart, and with all thy soul, and with all thy might." † For the relationship inculcated in the Old Testament was not of a mere mercenary, but of a moral kind. It was not merely one of fear, but of gratitude and affection.

Again, was there any other religion which effectually impressed its adherents with a deep or practical sense of the holiness of God, and of the evil of their own sinfulness? If this must be answered in the negative we must admit that this religion had moral and spiritual elements which, as compared with other ancient

* Levit. xix. 18. † Deut. vi. 5.

religious systems, rendered it something not only superior in degree, but distinct in kind.

But this religion, thus entitled to our deepest attention from the lofty moral and spiritual principles contained in it, involved also a complex sacrificial system, avowedly intended to teach the doctrine of atonement for sin. Such a system, when standing in connection with such principles, deserves a respectful consideration which it might not otherwise receive. It is, to say the least, a remarkable fact, not to be overlooked.

Now, this system continues with partial interruptions down to the coming of Christ, and Christ adopts and applies it to Himself in a remarkable way. He claims to give His life as a ransom for many, to shed His blood as the blood of the new covenant shed for many for the remission of sins. These words can hardly be divested of sacrificial allusion. He is the victim of the new covenant; the word *new* indicating that the old covenant is passing away.

It is scarcely straining the words to infer that it is implied in them that the old system is drawing to an end because it has accomplished its object, because a greater sacrifice is at hand. But how do events correspond with this language? Christ is put to death, and that (contrary as we learn to the original intention of His enemies) at the very time of the great passover sacrifice. Forgiveness through His atonement is offered to the Jewish people in the preaching of His Apostles for a few years—just time sufficient for that people to hear and reject the proffered terms. And then by the fall of Jerusalem, and the annihilation of the Holy Place, their sacrifices are for ever made impossible.

If we add to this that our records declare that Jesus Christ expressly predicted this event, have we not on the whole a series of facts, pointing in no ordinary manner to one hypothesis for their solution, viz., that the relations of the Mosaic system with Christianity are such as to indicate that Christ was really the antitype of a divinely appointed system of typical ordinances, and to confirm the position that He was sent of God as the Saviour of the world?

Will it be said that this is not in reality an independent line of proof, because Christ and His followers were Jews, and of course adopted and fell into Jewish habits of thought? The answer is that the thoughts we have been expressing were *not* Jewish thoughts at the time of Christ's appearing. Though it is true that they were then expecting their Messiah, and thus confessing that the time for His coming had arrived, yet their thoughts were of triumph and conquest, and they rejected Christ because He went contrary to them.

I submit therefore that we have here a really independent series of phenomena, calling for the same explanation as is demanded by the historical facts of the Gospels, and therefore confirming the truth of that explanation. And I would add that we are bound to carry on the series of phenomena one step further, and to include the remarkable position which this Jewish nation has held ever since their rejection of Christianity. They have been a people without a country, a race which never falls into and fuses with the other races of the world, yet which is a homeless wanderer among them. To this must be added that a doom of this very nature was laid down for them in the original records of their law, in case they persisted in disobedience.*

We have next to consider what became of this religion of Jesus, what have been its fortunes in succeeding ages, and what position it occupies at this day. On this head I shall avail myself of the eloquent words of a modern writer: "What Jesus did, what He taught, and what He suffered, during those three brief years, became instantly a spring of spiritual life to the world. Dreamy, distorted, grotesque views of God and His purposes, of man and his destiny, give place to clearer, nobler, more consistent, more exalted views. Conscience recovers its sensitiveness, and exerts its all-conquering power. Society feels its heart throb with new life. There has evidently been infused into it an element of nervous vitality, to which it has long been a stranger. The spiritual in man's nature, obedient to some invisible law, struggles with the

* See Deut. xxviii. 62—65.

material, and proves its title to supremacy and its competence to maintain it. Life gains upon death. Sensibility, power, enjoyment, in respect to Divine things, to truth, to righteousness, to communion with the Highest, widen their domain, and the limits within which healthy action goes on are rapidly enlarged. There is resistance—but to no purpose. A religious life has been evoked, and cannot be stifled by coarse and violent methods. Nor scoffs, nor threats, nor sword, nor fire, nor philosophy, can put out that which, but a few years before, it seemed impossible to kindle. Rome smiles incredulously at first, then feels in its own veins the tingle of spiritual vitality, strives to expel the strange invasion, and is itself subdued. Much perhaps of what meets the eye is symptomatic only; but beneath it, and perceptible to unprejudiced observation, there is a substantial reality, a faith that can remove mountains, a full assurance of hope, the hope of immortality, a constraining and victorious love."*

I need not trace at length the subsequent progress of Christianity. It is as well known as it is remarkable as a fact of history. But it must always be borne in mind that it is not the simple progress of *a religion* that is insisted on as an argument in its favour. It is the progress of *this particular religion*, being, what it is, a religion inculcating maxims of purity and self-denial, opposed to the natural impulses and habits of

* Miall's "Bases of Belief," p. 52. London, 1853.

mankind, and demanding the inward as well as outward subjection of the whole man. Gibbon attributes its success in a great degree to its promises of a speedy and happy immortality. But he should have remembered that the Christian heaven could hardly have been a tempting object to any but Christians. The desire for it, if intelligent and founded on the promises of Scripture, presupposed a moral progress and an identification of happiness with holiness, which, to say the least, was not the characteristic of the Gentile world in the days of the Roman Empire.

At this point I cannot omit to notice a passage in one of Professor Tyndal's works. He is commenting on an argument of Mr. Mozley's, that the extraordinary spread of Christianity indicates a miraculous origin, and he says: "As regards the function of miracles in the founding of a religion, Mr. Mozley institutes a comparison between the religion of Christ and that of Mahomet, and he derides the latter as 'irrational,' because it does not profess to adduce miracles in proof of its supernatural origin. But the religion of Mahomet, notwithstanding this drawback, has thriven in the world, and at one time it held sway over larger populations than Christianity itself. The spread and influence of Christianity are, however, brought forward by Mr. Mozley as a 'permanent, enormous, and incalculable practical result' of Christian miracles, and he actually makes use of this result to strengthen his plea for the miraculous. His logical warrant for this proceeding is not clear. It is the method of science, when a phenomenon presents itself, to the production of which several elements may contribute, to exclude them one by one, so as to arrive at length at the truly effective cause. Heat, for example, is associated with a phenomenon; we exclude heat, but the phenomenon remains; hence, heat is not its cause. Magnetism is associated with a phenomenon; we exclude magnetism, but the phenomenon remains; hence, magnetism is not its cause. Thus, also, when we seek the cause of the diffusion of a religion, whether it be due to miracles or to the spiritual force of its founders, we exclude the miracles, and, finding the result unchanged, we infer that miracles are not the effective cause. This important experiment Mahometanism has made for us. It has lived and spread without miracles; and to assert, in the face of this, that Christianity has spread *because* of miracles, is not more opposed to the spirit of science than to the common sense of mankind." *

It savours of presumption to utter a criticism upon any reasoning of Professor Tyndal founded, even by analogy, upon a physical experiment—ἀλλ' ὁμῶς εἰρήσεται.

I venture to submit that in order to the conclusiveness of an experiment such as is described, it is indispensable that all the other conditions and elements of the phenomenon, with the single exception of the one intentionally excluded, should be

* "Fragments of Science," p. 51.

the same in both cases—neither more nor less.
If, when we exclude magnetism, in order to ascertain whether the phenomenon remains the same in its
absence, we have unadvisedly permitted some other
potent cause to enter, our experiment is inconclusive.
The movement of a needle may be due to magnetism, or it may be due to accidental impact or
concussion. If when we remove the former element
we are not careful to guard against the introduction
of the latter, the needle may be equally put in motion,
though no magnet be near; and yet it may be
perfectly true that its movement was really due to
magnetism in the case when no impact or concussion
took place, but when the magnet was present. So in
the case before us. It is surely erroneous to speak of
Mahometanism as having made *the* experiment in
which alone we have any interest, viz., whether *such*
a religion as Christianity could have been successfully
founded without miraculous agency. Mahometanism
had no miracles, but it had two potent influences
which were absent in early Christianity—the physical power of the sword, and the sensual hopes and
promises which it held out to its disciples. These
may account for its diffusion. Magnetism then truly
may be wanting, but impact has introduced itself
instead. The conditions of the question have ceased
to be identical, and I respectfully contend that the
experiment is inexact and proves nothing.

It is not therefore the mere progress of Christianity that is relied on, but the fact that its progress, marvellous in itself, has been made in opposition to some of the most deeply seated tendencies of human nature.

To which must be added, that wherever it has been received in its primitive purity it has exercised the most beneficial effects alike upon individual and national character.

Nor can these phenomena be explained by attributing them merely to the excellence of Christianity as a code of ethics, and by disjoining its moral system from its historical origin.

The same author, from whose argument for Christianity I have already quoted, shows with great power that the Christian system is inseparably associated with an individual personal history.

"So far," he says, "as the world has been moved by Jesus Christ, it has been by faith in, not so much what He said, as what He was, what He did, what He suffered. All the doctrines of this system have, from the beginning, been regarded—whether properly or improperly is not now the question—as springing out of, associated with, and coloured by, the life of the Nazarene. Strictly speaking, *He* is the spirit of Gospel testimony. His relationship to God, His mission to man, His mediatorial office, the tenour of His life, the purpose of His death, the triumph of His resurrection, the unlimited extent of His authority, these are the ideas, all personal in their reference, which have mainly wrought the revolution we have just glanced at. *He*, as pictured to us in the Gospel narratives, and illustrated in the apostolic writings, constitutes the one source of this spiritual power, the mainspring of the whole movement. The hopes, the fears, the joys, the sorrows, the sympathies, the resolutions of His followers cluster round Him as their sole and sufficient object. Their penitence is elicited by His trials and agonies. Their peace is peace in Him. About Him their tenderest and strongest affections twine themselves. His word is their law, His love their motive, His example their stimulus, His sympathy their solace. It was His name which inspired with courage and fortitude "the noble army of martyrs"; it is the story of His life and death which still is most effectual to subdue man's heart." *

Now it seems indisputable that the original documents of Christianity might have put forth fair claims to be held authentic and genuine, and the Christian system might have stood in the connection with Judaism which I have indicated; and yet the religion might never have become generally diffused, or, if diffused, might never have succeeded in effecting those moral revolutions which we know it has in fact produced for the benefit of mankind. It might have been an unimpeachable code of ethics, but not a living force in human nature.

* Miall's "Bases of Belief," p. 57.

Or it might have exerted a certain force on mankind by the mere intrinsic excellence of its morality, but this force might have been quite apart from any special personal regard for Him who promulgated its maxims.

I would add an observation not to be lost sight of, in relation to the kind of evidence with which we have just been dealing.

The evidence of miracles may, or may not, be weakened in proportion as the number of ages increases through which that evidence has to be handed down. But the evidence derived from the spread of Christianity, from its beneficial effects, is of necessity founded upon experience, and is clearer and stronger now than it was for the early Christians.

Here, then, we have independent phenomena, each of which might exist without the other, but all of which do in fact co-exist together. And if we find that the hypothesis which explains some of them is also applicable to solve the others, can we forbear from drawing a very strong inference that we have got the right solution? And is that solution any other than the view that Christianity is Divine?

Before concluding, I would mention one other point.

Sir John Herschel says that "the surest and best characteristic of a well founded and extensive induction is when verifications of it spring up, as it were, spontaneously into notice, from quarters where they might be least expected, or even among instances of that very kind which were at first considered hostile to them. Evidence of this kind is irresistible, and compels assent with a weight which scarcely any other possesses."

I do not in the least desire to underrate the existing difficulties of biblical criticism, but I think in relation to the veracity of the Bible narrative there are some cases, at least, which are of a kind analogous to what Herschel here speaks of. I mean where apparent difficulties of a formidable kind have on further examination been found actually to yield confirmation to the veracity of the Scriptures.

Daniel relates that King Belshazzar was slain in the city of Babylon when that city was taken by the Persians. Profane historians say that the capture of Babylon took place in the reign of a Babylonian king called Nabonnedus, or Labynetus, and that this king was absent from the city at the time of its fall. Moreover, instead of being slain he was made prisoner, and kindly treated.

The discrepancy appeared for many years extremely formidable. But we now find that in an inscription, discovered only about twenty years ago, Nabonnedus, the last native king of Babylon, is introduced as stating that his eldest son bore the name of Belsharezar, and he speaks of him in a way which suggests that he had associated him with himself in

* "Discourse on the Study of Natural Philosophy," chap. vi., p. 180.

the government. Hence there is no difficulty in supposing that while Nabonnedus was absent his son was entrusted with the command of the city.

But not only is this view probable in itself, it is, in fact, incidentally confirmed by the very text of the Book of Daniel. When Belshazzar promotes Daniel he makes him "the *third* ruler in the kingdom." But why the *third*? In every other case in the Old Testament the favourite is advanced to the *second* place in the kingdom, the place next to the king.* The answer obviously is that Belshazzar himself occupied the *second* place, and that in placing Daniel in the *third* he did as much as under the circumstances was possible.†

So again, on the authority of Herodotus, who speaks as if the vine did not grow in Egypt, doubts have been cast on the veracity of Genesis, because Pharaoh's butler speaks of pressing the grapes into the king's cup. But it is now clear from representations on the Egyptian monuments that the cultivation of the grape, the art of making wine, and the practice of drinking it, were well known in Egypt, at least from the time of the Pyramids. It is therefore Herodotus who must either have been imperfectly informed, or must have been speaking of a particular part of Egypt only.‡

* Gen. xli. 40-45; Esther x. 3; Dan. ii., 48, 49.
† See Prof. Rawlinson's "Historical Illustrations of the Old Testament," printed for the Society for Promoting Christian Knowledge. London, 1871. p. 170.
‡ *Ibid.*, p. 49.

My time is exhausted, but my task is still unperformed. Instead of exploring the whole field, I have but shown you here and there a few spots, where, if you dig patiently for yourselves, you may find hidden treasure. I am very sensible that I have left much untouched. It must not be inferred that I am disposed to neglect or underrate it, because time compelled me to omit it.

On the whole, I must be satisfied—indeed I shall be more than satisfied, deeply thankful—if, in this day when the tides of modern thought seem to some to be obliterating many of our old landmarks, I shall have succeeded in pointing to some ancient footprints uneffaced by those restless currents—

> Footprints which perchance another
> Sailing o'er life's solemn main,
> Some forlorn and shipwrecked brother
> Seeing, may take heart again.

MAN: A WITNESS FOR CHRISTIANITY.

BY THE

REV. JOSEPH ANGUS, M.A., D.D.

MAN: A WITNESS FOR CHRISTIANITY.

IT is natural for a lecturer to magnify his office, and to claim special honour for the subject he has undertaken to discuss. What has deepened his own convictions, he cannot but believe will impress others.

While aware of this tendency, and making full allowance for it, I must still think that the theme I have to present to-day is remarkably weighty and clear. Under both Testaments there were long ages in which the argument from prophecy and miracle, from the authority of a living teacher or the charm of an inspired presence, had small force; and yet under both Testaments there has never ceased to be intelligent faith. Even in the age of miracles, the preaching of the Gospel produced readier conviction than miracle itself. The plain man or the unbeliever, on entering the Christian assembly and hearing the Divine message, was convinced by what he heard, and had to acknowledge that God was among them of a truth. It was always blessed to have seen and to believe. It is still more blessed not to have seen and yet to believe : more blessed—not surely because the evidence is defective and the faith credulous, but because the evidence is more spiritual and the faith more holy. In Richard Baxter's younger days, the evidence that most impressed him, he tells us, was the miraculous; later, it was the prophetic and the historical; and, last of all, the internal—the fitness of the Gospel to produce peace and holiness. This is the "self-evidencing power of Christianity," the "portable evidence," praised by writers of all schools of thought from Hooker and Pascal and Owen to Coleridge and Vinet.

I. Christianity is a theistic system. It teaches that there is a God, a first cause of all things; a God who combines in Himself whatever we love in a father or revere in a judge. He is, as Plato calls Him, the great cause of all, the ideal of whatever is fair and just. The evidence that supports this view of God—based as it is on human nature and on observation—modern science, with all its discoveries and changes, only confirms.

That science busies itself, as we know, with distances and forces that are immense. It busies itself also with molecules so small that, when multiplied a hundred thousand times, no eye has seen them or can see.* These molecules have qualities of their own when apart; and they have other qualities when com-

* Tyndall, "Fragments of Science," p. 151, etc.

bined; nor is it easy to put any limit to the properties that may be supposed to inhere in them. The telescope and the higher mathematics reveal distances of stellar space which are bewildering in their vastness. The microscope and facts of chemistry—which compel us to believe in the existence of molecules compared with which the test-objects of the microscope are immense—reveal magnitudes which are equally bewildering in their smallness; while each molecule has properties of its own as undoubted as the properties of the stars.

To take an illustration—

Water has long been a favourite theme with natural theologians. Dr. Whewell has treated of its laws as proofs of the wisdom and goodness of the Creator. Ancient philosophy deemed it an element; modern science tells us it is a compound. The hydrogen and oxygen that form it have very different properties— different when they are separate, and different when they combine. At the freezing-point of water, and far below that temperature, their particles rush away from one another with great force. Send through the two a flash of electricity, and they chemically combine. Subject them now to cold, and the result is a hard, brittle solid, whose particles closely cohere, forming geometric figures, facets of crystal, leaflets of hoar-frost, each with a beauty surpassing our most cunning workmanship. Put into this water living vegetable matter, and the water will give up, under chemical action, an equivalent increase of life. Let it now be imbibed by an intelligent living agent, and it will be used, in part at least, in sustaining thought and quickening feeling. That life or thought are themselves qualities of water or of its molecules, no scientific student of nature will affirm. But it may be readily conceded that there is no life or thought on earth without waste or change of the fluid substance which helps to make up the living, thinking being.

If an inquirer can conceive of these molecules as possessing a tendency to become gases, and in these gases a tendency to become water, and in water a tendency to become a transparent solid—nay, possibly, to become life and thought and feeling—he will have some conception of the theory of evolution : a theory which some are applying to the explanation of the entire system of Nature.

These discoveries of science in relation to water are typical. They have been repeated in many other substances. Nor is it possible to say what further discoveries of a similar kind are before us. But none of these discoveries affect the doctrine of causation. Every material thing is a force, or a collection of forces, and each has its properties, or property. That what seem simple forces are many, that what seem many properties are possibly one, are conclusions that do not change the questions which science seeks to settle, viz., What is the nature of the force at work, and under what conditions does it act? Water may be gas, and gas molecules. Life, thought, and volition may be properties of molecules as are weight and attraction. The question still arises, whence comes this force, which is at once material, vital, and moral? Either it is God, or it comes from Him.

Now the one point upon which my theme leads me to insist is, that this argument is based on human nature, on the very laws of thought, and on experience. The only two possible theories of human nature in relation to such questions as we are now considering are (briefly) Platonism and Aristotelianism. From Plato to Hamilton on the one side, from Aristotle to Comte on the other, all philosophy may be grouped, with slight characteristic differences, around one or other of these two. No third centre is possible.* Plato maintains that from the very ideas that are inseparable from the thinking substance, we believe in causation and in a first cause. Aristotle maintains that the search for causes is an attempt of the understanding to put into a simple form the facts of the senses. There is truth in both theories. There are things we cannot but believe, feeling the opposite to be unthinkable or self-contradictory. So far we are Platonists. And among these things may be reckoned the impossibility of the self-creation of a universe, and the existence of a first cause of all. But besides, the doctrine of a first cause is as complete a generali-

* Coleridge, "Notes on English Divines," p. 15.

zation as any we can form, and is forced upon us by the understanding, that is, by experience itself.

Let us mark the argument. Phenomena imply a force competent to produce them. When active, that force shows itself in motion; when quiescent, it still exists, only dynamically or potentially. We believe in force, for we see results that imply it. So in Natural Theology. There are energies in nature; there is thought, and feeling, and volition in man. If these can be proved to be properties inherent in matter, either matter is God, endowed with all His attributes —self-subsisting life among them,—or there is a God who gives to matter, or to spirit, or to a mysterious combination of the two, the properties which are seen or are implied in the phenomena. Whichever of these generalizations is the sounder, the method of each is as scientific as any generalization in physics.

But it is said the force we call God is unseen, and perhaps spiritual. So far it differs from the forces of the material world. Can we reason from the visible to the invisible, from the material to the spiritual? Here, again, the answer is plain. Biologists, who make the microscope and the scalpel their teacher, are prone to think that force must exist in a visible shape. But Professor Tyndall warns them that chemistry holds very different language. Between the limit of the microscope and the molecule there are forces, probably numberless, of which no instrument can take note. We have not seen them or touched them; but still we believe in them. And, he adds with his usual frankness, after we have reached, if we ever reach, the primordial atoms, each endowed with its own property, the property itself will probably remain unseen; and men will still ask whence it came, and how it was produced.

No doubt the force we are seeking in our science is spiritual. But this creates no new difficulty. Is galvanism, the force which sends a message in a few seconds round the world, material—that is, has it extension and resistance? Is light material, or has any one seen even the fluid medium whose waves are said to produce it? None can tell what these forces are; yet we reason about them both as realities without misgiving. Besides, the connexion of phenomena with what is unseen and spiritual is one of the widest and commonest of generalizations. Every child becomes aware of himself as a source of action and thought and feeling. The acts that follow from his own volitions are among the most familiar phenomena he has to observe. The acts and looks of others—mother, father, nurse—are all traced by a process of deduction to the volitions of the agents, and the deduction is regularly verified by questionings more or less reverent. As the child grows in years he grows in this wisdom, and at length he observes millions of phenomena which he connects, not with dead force, but with the feelings and thoughts of other beings. The belief therefore in mind and in volition as the origin of the changes of force, and (in the common meaning of the word) of force itself, is at once an instinct of human nature, and one of the widest generalizations of human experience.

This reasoning may seem abstruse; but it is practised every day, and by all classes. To ascribe the phenomena of the world to a force competent to produce them is in accordance with common sense and with common observation. To ascribe them ultimately to one who is spiritual, himself endowed with intelligence, and capable of acting upon matter, is a generalization, sustained by the nature of many of the phenomena we have to explain, and by the consciousness and the daily life of us all. The existence of God is as clearly proved, even "His eternal power and divineness," as the existence of any force or of any volition or thought or thinking substance. As clearly, I repeat. And if this seem a poor conclusion, let me say that we have none clearer or stronger for the existence of the material world, or for the existence of our own spirit. All we really know of either is that in the one case we have sensations, and in the other feelings and thoughts which we ascribe to a supposed cause—a world (a Not-I or Non-Ego) without us, and a Spirit (an I or an Ego) within.

"Two things," said Kant, "fill me with awe: the starry heavens and the sense of the moral responsibility of man."

We have all a sense of right and wrong. If any

man whom I have never injured wish me ill, or try to inflict ill, I feel that he treats me unjustly, and I may give expression to my disapprobation. If under like circumstances I wish ill to another, I feel that I do him injustice, and I am not surprised if he express disapprobation of me. My feeling of injustice is my sense of wrong; my expression of disapprobation is of the nature of punishment. It may not be my business to express disapprobation, or to punish; but the feeling is as becoming as is the approval of a virtuous act; and indeed the one is only another form of the other. The hatred of iniquity is inseparable from the love of holiness. And these feelings are found among all nations. There are no doubt very different judgments passed by different nations on the same acts; but on the mental states which produce acts most agree; and whether they agree or not, there is what we call a sense of right and wrong among them all.

Or the fact may be put in another form. Looking at human nature, and adopting Butler's analysis of it: we have each particular affections; we have each a tendency to seek happiness—self-love, as it is called; and we have besides a conscience, whose office it is to control the whole man. From our very make it may be affirmed that particular propensities are meant to be subject to self-love, and self-love to conscience. In this sense men are made for virtue, and virtue is natural to them.

Or the fact may be put in another form. We are created under law, not only under a law of unvariable sequences, but "a law laid down for the guidance of an intelligent being, by an intelligent being having power over him."* Such is Austin's definition of all law, in the proper sense of the word. That law implies sanctions, and suggests irresistibly the idea of a lawgiver. In all climes, and in every tongue, this recognition of the quality of moral acts, this sense of right and wrong, this feeling of "oughtness" and of moral obligation is found. And though it may be difficult to prove logically in the first instance that therefore there must be a Creator whose authority sustains the law and vindicates it, for the conviction of oughtness is at first a sentiment rather than a syllogism; yet when once the truth is surmised or announced we accept it in morals as readily at least as we accept the doctrine of causation in the science of nature. Nothing depends, it will be noted, on the question whether conscience is an inherent or an acquired principle, whether it is a simple property or a compound. If it be inherent, as Plato held, that fact will be with most men a sufficient title to veneration. If it is itself a result of processes like those which produce other acquired sentiments—patriotism or friendship, for example—still its universality, its immutability and independence, caring as it does for nothing but the rightness of acts, and its direct action on the will, all

* Jurisprudence, i., pp. 88—94, 3rd. ed.

show that it is the result of a tendency in man, a force that bespeaks wisdom and holiness in the Creator. This reasoning may no doubt be questioned, as the whole doctrine of Causation is questioned; but it is sustained by the arguments of the ablest inquirers from Plato to Mackintosh, and by the convictions of almost the entire race. The road by which we ascend in reason from conscience to a moral governor is indeed shorter and clearer, and far oftener trod, than the road from phenomena to a first cause. Both processes are strictly scientific. Both are in accordance with facts and with the tendencies of the mind. Both are forced upon us by the understanding, the faculty which generalizes experience; and by the reason, the faculty which accepts intuitive or essential truth.

Is it I who say these things, or saith not the law the same? "From the creation of the world, the invisible things of God become distinctly visible, when studied in the things He hath made." "When men who have no law do by nature the things of the law, they show the works of the law to be written on their hearts, their consciences accusing them, or it may be defending them;" and they recognize in its decisions more than a human authority.

II. But Christianity is a remedial system. It presupposes guilt and ruin. It announces free forgiveness, provides in its own way for the formation of a holy character, and secures for all who believe happiness and eternal life. These announcements I desire briefly to examine in the light of reason and experience. I do it under the conviction that, as Fenelon puts it, the best way to defend Christianity is simply to state it. It is largely its own evidence. Really to know the truth is to believe; as on the other hand to act out belief is the easiest way to profounder knowledge and assured conviction.

1. I begin with what Christianity presupposes—our guilt and ruin.

The fact of man's sinfulness is clear; the startling thing is what Scripture teaches as to the degree of it and God's feeling towards it. We imagine that sin is in our acts only, and that our hearts are ever better than our lives. Scripture tells us that it is our nature, and that our hearts are ever worse than our lives. We are apt to think that it dishonours God to suppose Him grieved or made angry by our sins. Scripture reserves its strongest expressions to denounce them, and to describe the fierceness of the Divine anger, though blended with tenderest pity, in relation to them.

Theology proceeds to define this sinfulness—as its custom is. It pronounces man to have "fallen very far from his original righteousness." The Latin article of the English Church is even stronger, "quam longissimè distet." The Westminster Confession is stronger still, and speaks of man as "altogether depraved." Popular thought, which delights in clear and vivid utterance, describes this depravity as "total."

I am not anxious to defend all these expressions, nor do I care to repudiate them. Substantially they vindicate themselves, when once they are explained. Let us take the last, the strongest of all. When we speak of *total* depravity, it is not meant of course that all men are alike bad, because totally depraved; for Scripture recognizes all the shades of character that are recognized by common sense. In our Lord's day there were young men whom He loved, as there were scribes and Pharisees, hypocrites, whom He strongly denounced. Nor is it meant that all men are as bad as they can be; for "evil seducers still wax worse and worse." What it means is that sin has tainted *every part* of our nature, changing affections into passions, self-love into selfishness, searing darkening and enfeebling the conscience, and making even our intellectual faculties less vigorous and clear. It means that *every act* and *every feeling*, even in the best of us, is wanting in holiness, through deficiency in its measure, fault in its motives, or through the absence of that general regard for God's will and claims which is essential to all divine virtue. It means, finally, that there is *no hope of salvation* for any of us through the merit of our doings or tears. If saved at all, it must be through free mercy. Salvation in any other way is totally, completely beyond us. Is there anything unreasonable in these statements?

Or is it depravity that startles us—the affirmation, viz., that there is in us all a nature prone to evil?

This depravity is as much a fact of experience as it is of revelation. It is as clearly an induction as any law of science. Gravitation is proved by the fact that all bodies, when free to move, show a tendency to move towards one another; and man's depravity is proved by the fact that when left to himself he always displays a proneness to evil. . . . All our knowledge of the lower animals and of natural objects is gained from their doings in the one case, and from their sensible qualities in the other. We speak of the disposition and properties of each. We talk of the faithfulness of the dog, of the ferocity of the tiger, of the poisonous nature of the foxglove, ascribing to each a prior tendency that accounts for the peculiarities we see. It is just thus we verify the doctrine of human sinfulness. The passions and the selfishness which have prevailed in all nations, and which nothing seems able to subdue,—the nature and the number of the crimes which men commit, in spite of all the restraints put upon them by Providence, by conscience, by law—the fact that every man does commit sin, and the consciousness of us all that we are prone to many sins we do not commit—the seeds of vice which are discovered even in children—the opposition of our inclination to all efforts at improvement felt even by the renewed,— all justify the statement that in man's very make as he now is there is something that leads him astray. To assert depravity is simply to assert the quality of a species. It is to reduce what is true of every single specimen of our nature to a general expression which is applicable to the whole nature; and to ascribe effects to some force adequate to produce them. In short, it is as accurate to talk of human depravity, intending thereby to affirm the existence of a prior universal disposition to sin, as it is to affirm the most certain laws or the soundest generalizations in science. Our nature is not more certainly rational than it is sinful.

And yet there is much in relation to this truth that is matter of faith. That this tendency to sin was not our *primeval* condition, that there was once a golden age of innocence and happiness is a matter of revelation, though poetry and traditional history have preserved some fragments of the truth. The *degree* of our sinfulness, the *guilt* and the *misery* of it, are also largely matters of revelation, and are accepted less from experience in the first instance than from faith.

And this is all natural. The fact of our sinfulness is ascertainable by experience. The degree of it is not. We are not only born with depraved tendencies, themselves unconscious of their depravity, but when we begin the process of self-scrutiny, the depravity which is natural to us has been further confirmed by habit, itself a second nature. The very instruments therefore we use in detecting the quality have lost much of their discriminating power. . . . The whole framework of society, moreover, assists this work of deception. Sin loses its odiousness, and ceases to be felt as sin, when we are surrounded by it; just as the impure air of a room remains unnoticed till having changed it for fresh air outside we attempt to enter it again, or as the enormous weight of the atmosphere becomes imperceptible by being universal.

Nor is the influence of our likes and dislikes to be forgotten. When conscience speaks, men find it more pleasant to silence it than to obey its teaching. The faculty by which men judge of sin is delicate in proportion to the dignity of the office it has to discharge. Its structure is as tender as that of the eye: and both are in our own keeping. A diseased organ may be relieved, as we know, by healing the disease or by paralyzing the nerve; and so there are two ways of escaping an angry conscience. We may cease from the evil that provokes it, or we may resolutely refuse to listen to its voice. In fact, men turn away from what they cannot contemplate without self-censure, till at length the light is put out or the power of vision is *for a time* withdrawn. . . . Need I say, how all these hindrances to the formation of an adequate conception of the degree of our sinfulness are strengthened by the mysterious silence which God preserves in his Providence. Among His judgments, as among His mercies, we walk by faith. For His name's sake He defers his anger; but men fail to understand His forbearance. " Because sentence against an evil work is not speedily executed," men's hearts are set in them to do evil. Here we deem justice perfect

in proportion as punishment follows close upon crime;
and so under God's government, if the punishment is
not seen to follow, we deny or question the guilt.
"These things hast thou done, and I kept silence;
wherefore thou thoughtest that I was altogether
such a one as thyself." The very immutability of God's
laws in nature, proof as it is of God's superintendence,
becomes proof to the imagination that God will not
punish, and therefore there is no reason why He
should. All things, men say, continue as they were
from the beginning of the creation. Stricken or per-
plexed by the admonitions of conscience, men go
forth under the open sky, and all seems peaceful
there. There is no handwriting upon the wall of that
temple to confirm the voice of terror that had spoken
within. The lover of pleasure, the idolator of gain,
the wrong-doer, the prosperous despiser of God, is
not now struck down in our streets; and men are
thence confirmed in their hope that they are not
guilty, or that sin is less of an evil than their fears had
supposed.

And what is the conclusion of all this reasoning?
Simply that Scripture teaching on sin is sustained by
history and by experience; and yet, through the
corrupting influence of depravity, we have no adequate
sense of the completeness of our ruin. These lessons
every thoughtful, earnest man finds impressed on his
own heart the more deeply as he advances in the
divine life. Growth in holiness means growth in

humility. And with such growth comes a deeper conviction of the truth of that record which shows him his true nature alike in the failings of good men and in solemn dogmatic teachings, which are found in marvellous consistency from the third chapter of Genesis to the last of Revelation. There we behold as in a glass our own image, as certainly as the image of our Lord. Nor is it easy to say which is the more impressive or the more true!

2. As a remedial system, the central truth of Christianity is the death and resurrection of Christ. This truth was announced in figurative language to Nicodemus in our Lord's earliest recorded discourse,* It was repeated again and again to His own disciples, with whom He talked "of the decease He was to accomplish at Jerusalem." More than a fourth part of each Gospel is devoted to the story of it. His apostles proclaimed it wherever they went. So mighty did it prove, that the most successful preacher that ever lived resolved to know nothing among men but Jesus Christ, and Jesus Christ as crucified. More than fifty times it is appealed to in the Epistles as a ground of consolation, and as a motive to holiness; while the men who profess to be Christians, and still love and practise sin, are denounced, not as the enemies of the precepts of the Gospel, but as emphatically the enemies of the Cross. The glory of

* John iii.

Christianity is Christ, and the glory of Christ, so far as concerns us men and our salvation, is the Cross. Such is Scripture teaching, and such I believe is human experience.

The most obvious ground that can be taken on this theme is, that the death of Christ is an expression of His own love and of the love of the Father, and a proof of His sincerity; as His resurrection is a proof of the divineness of His mission, and a pledge of our own. "Greater love hath no man than this, that a man lay down his life for his friends." "He that spared not His own Son, but delivered Him up for us all, how shall He not with Him freely give us all things?" He foresaw and foretold His approaching sufferings, and steadfastly set his face to fulfil them. This is not the manner of deceivers. The reality of a future life is now proved not by argument, but by fact. He,—not His teaching but Himself,—is to us the Resurrection and the Life! I have called this the most obvious ground. It is ground defined in the creeds of the early Church, as it is accepted by all classes of Christian people. It may be called low ground. It treats of no mysteries—unless it be of the love that prompted Him to die, and of the mighty power whereby He rose from the dead. It says nothing of the spiritual significance of His dying. And yet what yearnings of human nature are met by these simple announcements—the Divine love, the victory of man over the grave. What would the world be without them, and what evidence of their truthfulness is supplied by their adaptations to the needs of the race!

But the Cross has deeper significance. All Christians are exhorted to consider it and to be conformed to it—to have in them the same mind that was also in Christ Jesus.

To consider it and to be conformed to it! What views it gives of human nature. Men made like you and me have put Him to death. Some have thought that virtue needs but to be seen in order to be worshipped. Here the divinest virtue becomes incarnate, and on the Cross men are doing what they can to extinguish it for ever. . . What views it gives of the evil of sin! All the suffering He sought to alleviate, the leprosy and the death; all the suffering He encountered, the perverseness and cruelty of His persecutors, the desertion and unbelief of His disciples, His tears and agony and cryings, all had their origin in moral causes which it was the work of His life to remove! . . What views it gives of duty! Men murder Him and He prays for them. The Father forsakes Him, and still He trusts Him. Had He been content to blend Sadduceeism and Pharisaism and Heathenism into one religion—to sanction all as meaning the same thing, He need never have suffered. But He assailed them all, and of His faithfulness the Cross was at once the evidence and the result. . . What views it gives of a holy, noble life! How possible it is to conquer the

material by the spiritual, to mortify all that is gross
and earthly, to be in contact with sin and death and
emerge the nobler for suffering. How blessed to
deny ourselves, and by self-sacrifice to leave the
world holier and happier than we found it. How
instructive that even the Son does not His own will,
but the will of the Father that sent Him. . . What
a strange blending was there in His character, and
what a like blending ought there to be in our own,
of nobleness and humility, of heroism and patience,
of pity for sinners and hatred of sin! And how many
millions have been influenced by such thoughts in
every generation, since these scenes were first witnessed.
By the Cross, multitudes have been crucified to the
world, and the world to them. Never has there
been in the history of the race a mightier power than
this moral power of the Cross!

But it has still deeper significance. Many passages
of Scripture speak, as we have seen, of His sufferings as
of something in which we share : many others speak
of them as of something in which we have no share.
" He died, the Just for the unjust." " He Himself bare
our sins in His own body on the tree." His cross
touches our hearts, and strengthens our will, teaching
self-denial and submission; it also pacifies our conscience, doing for us what we could never have done
for ourselves. Some who acquiesce in all that has
been said up to this point pause here, and scruple to
go further. Let us respect their scruples, only re-

membering that what is further to be said on this theme does not weaken in any degree the previous evidence, and has special force of its own.

The feeling of guilt is universal. Men have instinctively the conviction that Law must be vindicated. Sin means guilt, and guilt means punishment. Nor is it possible, as it seems to me, apart from the Gospel, to free the human mind from the misgivings which these terms imply. The provision of the Gospel for meeting these misgivings is in the Cross. "The life" our Lord there gave He gave as a "ransom for many." The "blood" He there shed was shed for "the remission of sins." There God "set Him forth as a propitiation through faith in His blood, that God might be just and the justifier of all that believe." It is in Him therefore that "we have redemption through His blood, even the forgiveness of our sins." I cannot dwell upon this aspect of our Lord's work, or upon the philosophy of it. I can only note the result. Justified by faith, we have peace with God. We believe in the Divine love. We believe no less in the Divine holiness. We accept a free pardon, looking for the mercy of God unto eternal life; and yet we hold that the sanctity of law and the holiness of God are as completely maintained as if the guilty had been condemned! Millions have found in these beliefs both peace and holy affection—what meets at once the demands of their conscience and the yearnings of their heart!

3. The first effect of the Gospel when men believe is forgiveness, the cancelment of the guilt of sin. Its chief design, however, as a remedial system is holiness. The "great and precious promises" it reveals are given that we may become "partakers of a Divine nature." The New Testament knows nothing of a salvation that consists only in pardon. Men are saved in the fullest and truest sense just in proportion as they are holy. This arrangement is surely reasonable; and yet it is so rare in religious systems as to be an evidence wherever it is found of an origin higher than human.

The dependence of forgiveness on faith, and the freeness of forgiveness, coming as it does at the beginning of a Christian life, have often been urged as objections to the Gospel. But if the truth be exactly stated, the objections cease. Justification through faith—a free pardon on believing—is no doubt the Scripture teaching; but the faith which justifies—the belief of the heart—is from its very nature the beginning of a holy character. Let a man believe that Christ is the gift of the Father's love, that His self-denying life is the noblest model, that in dying He did homage to law, that we deserve what He suffered, that the chief evil under the government of God is the sin which He dies to remove; and the belief is inseparable from holiness. The moral quality of the faith is not indeed the meritorious ground of forgiveness, but still it is an essential element of the faith which is required if we are to be forgiven.

The freeness of forgiveness and its place at the beginning of the Christian life is no less striking. To some it may seem as if the arrangement would have been more conducive to holiness had the Gospel bidden men to be holy that they might be forgiven, instead of saying "Be holy, because you are forgiven." But there are grave reasons in human nature against this change; and the holiest men have recognised the wisdom of the Divine order; "Ye are risen with Christ, therefore set your affections upon things above:" "Ye are not your own, ye are bought with a price, therefore glorify God in your bodies and in your spirits which are God's." Most religious systems teach the duty of holiness in some sense, and promise forgiveness. It is the *order* of these blessings that distinguishes the false system from the true. The Gospel proclaims a free pardon, and then supplies motives which influence the will, and impel men to holiness; the motives owing their force to that faith which is at the outset the germ of a holy life. Thus is it that men are not only forgiven—they are *sanctified*, made holy through the faith which is in Christ.

On the nature of this evangelical holiness I cannot now insist. It is essentially the admiration and the practice of whatever is true and righteous and loving; not of the first two only, but of the three combined. It is begun in the soul through the force of motives as various as the instincts of men, the fear of punishment, the desire of happiness, the yearning of the heart after something nobler than anything the world contains ; often by personal attachment to Christ, loving loyalty to Him for what He *has done for us*, a feeling not the highest in the Christian life, though leading to the highest, viz., attachment to Him for *what He is.* It always involves in a world like ours self-denial,--the subjection of the lower principles of our nature to the higher, and of our will to God's. In its highest form it teaches us to use every power and gift in promoting the holiness and the happiness of all around us. This is the exactest definition that can be given of God's glory, the manifestation of His character in the holiness and happiness of intelligent creation ; and in proportion as His glory is our end, we are partakers of His nature, perfect as our Father in heaven is perfect. We tread in the steps and are conformed to the image of His Son.

It is the design of the Gospel not only to teach this holiness, but to produce it in individual character and in national life. With this view it reveals truths that purify the heart, supplies motives that influence the will, and it adds the promise of that *divine help* which the most thoughtful heathen writers, philosophers, dramatists, historians, have affirmed to be essential if man is to attain to Divine virtue.

If we know these things, and have felt them, we need no further evidence of their truth. We have the witness in ourselves, as clear and as strong as the evidence either of reason or of science.

Men taunt us sometimes with our divisions. "If we become Christians," they say "which of your sects are we to join, for you seem endlessly divided?" And I reply, In all that is essential to Christian life true Christians agree. Ask any Christian man what he thinks and feels of the evil and the desert of sin, what of his dependence for forgiveness on the free and righteous mercy of God in Christ, what of his need of renewal and of personal holiness, and I venture to affirm that his answers will commend themselves to the hearts of Christian men of all sects and of every age. No doubt there may be diversities of opinion on the language he employs, and diversities of intensity in the feeling with which particular truths are held. But in all that is essential Christian men substantially agree. And the reason is, that wherever there is true faith there is penitence with loving humble trust, and the earnest desire to be holy. There are, no doubt, parts of Christianity not included in this enumeration, and important parts. Everything indeed that God deems to be worth revealing is worth our knowing. But still the fact remains, that the elements of Christian life, our thoughts and feelings in relation to sin, to God in Christ, and to holiness, are alike in all Christian hearts. They share the immutability of Him who is objectively and subjectively the sum and the centre of them all. They are "The same yesterday, and to-day, and for ever."

4. But, finally, the remedial system of the Gospel would be incomplete if it did not make provision for human happiness. The desire of happiness is an instinct of our nature, none the less that it is strangely misjudged. Some think it too strong; whi'e, in fact, it is too feeble. Too strong, indeed, it is, compared with conscience; too feeble compared with the force of the affections it ought to control. Our propensities—passions—would often be checked if only we had a stronger sense of our real good. Some think it the measure, the motive, the very essence of virtue, and claim to have in it a safer foundation for morals than in conscience itself. They forget that this instinct also is blinded and corrupted by sin, and that men are after all better judges of what is right than of what is best for them. Some think that the desire of happiness is selfishness, and that God does not care to gratify it. But clearly our happiness must be as dear to the Divine benevolence, as our holiness is dear to the Divine purity. It is impossible even to conceive of an infinitely benevolent God ceasing to take delight in the happiness of his children. And certainly in Scripture God appeals to this instinct as often as He appeals to conscience itself. Our happiness is dear to Him!

The first provision of the Gospel for the promotion of human happiness, whether in individuals or in nations, is identified with that great spiritual change which begins the religious life. Under the government of

God sin and misery are indissolubly joined. If men will love sin, if they will be selfish and passionate, they must be miserable. It is probably impossible for the blessed God Himself to make bad men happy. But let their hearts be changed, let them love what God loves, and hate what God hates, and a foundation is laid for happiness that nothing can overthrow.

And when once this foundation is laid, and men agree with God on all the great principles of His government, His acts—the administrative part of it so to speak—need create no fear. The announcement is as true now as it was in the first age: "To them that love God all things work together for good." The inspired reasoning is as conclusive as when the Apostle first used it—"He that spared not His own Son, will He not with Him freely give us all things." The command is still binding, "Be *care-full* for nothing; but in everything by prayer and supplication, with thanksgivings, let your requests be made known unto God." Disappointments and trials will come; but meanwhile a thousand sources of pleasure are open to us. For everything beside, we commit our way unto God, having no anxiety but to do His will and to bear it, knowing that what He does is ever "wisest and kindest and best."

Of course these lessons may have a place in our creeds and exercise no influence; but let them be believed by the heart, become principles of our individual and national life, and misery becomes impossible. We have "days of heaven even upon earth!"

Here then is in brief the argument. My reason and my understanding—intuition and experience—demand a First Cause of all things. My conscience demands a Lawgiver and Judge. My entire nature cries out for forgiveness, for holiness, for happiness. The world "sighs to be renewed." Christianity meets every one of these instincts in a way peculiarly its own, and yet intelligible and complete. It is so true in the descriptions it gives of things which are within the domain of my consciousness that I am ready to believe it when it speaks of things which are beyond it. I am sure of the "earthly things" it describes, and am disposed to believe in the heavenly. Acting upon the measure of faith I have, I get more light and deeper conviction: till in the end I am prepared to maintain, from inward feeling even more than from external evidence, that there is nothing truer than the Gospel, as there is nothing so holy in its tendency when once it is believed, or so blessed in its results!

Perhaps it may be said in reply, This argument requires that men love part of the Gospel and act upon it, even before they are persuaded of the truth of the whole. I concede it: and plead the more earnestly for Christianity on that ground. In common life, the neglect to act on what we know to be true and right in small things makes men incapable of ascertaining what is true and right on a grand scale. So deeply did Grotius feel this consideration, that he regarded the very evidence of Christianity, and the way in which it reveals itself to the loving and obedient, as itself one proof the Divine origin of the Gospel, showing itself herein Divinely adapted to test men's character and hearts. And besides, our own nature vindicates Christianity in this respect. The morbid excitability of one part of our frame is best relieved by the increased activity of another. An irritable faith is a symptom of defective action elsewhere, and is often best cured by attention to acknowledged duty. Doubts, which no arguments can remove will often melt away amidst the warmth and vigour of active love. Practise what you already believe—do His will as far as you hold it. Whereto you have attained, walk by the rule you admit, and in due time all else will be made plain! This arrangement is itself a reasonable law; and becomes in turn a fresh evidence in support of our faith.

I end as I began. I depreciate no evidence, historical, prophetic, miraculous, literary. God gives all, and we need all. But the evidence which is at once the strongest to convince and the easiest to understand, provided only we are morally disposed to receive it, is the evidence which appeals to our hearts and to our experience. "Christianity," says Coleridge, "finds me in the lowest depth of my being, as no other system can. It meets there my direst needs." Herein is proof of its Divine origin, and of the love of Him that gives it! Yes, we are every one of us God's witnesses. If we believe, we can set our seal to it, that this Gospel is true. " He that believeth on the Son of God hath the witness in himself." " We know that the Son of God is come, and hath given us an understanding, that we may know Him that is true ; and we are in Him that is true, even in His Son Jesus Christ. This is the true God, and eternal life." *

* 1 John v. 10, 20.

THE END.

www.ingramcontent.com/pod-product-compliance
Lightning Source LLC
Chambersburg PA
CBHW051846300426
44117CB00006B/275